War in Roman
Myth and Legend

By the Same Author

Women in Ancient Rome (2013)
Roman Women – The Women who Influenced Roman History (2015)
In Bed with the Romans (2015)
Wars & Battles of the Roman Republic (2015)
Roman Military Disasters (2015)
When in Rome: Social Life in Ancient Rome (2017)
Women at War in Ancient Greece & Rome (2017)
How to be a Roman (2017)
Roman Record Keeping & Communications (2018)
Republic into Empire: The Civil Wars of the First Century BCE (2019)
The Romans in the North of England (2019)
Reportage from Ancient Greece & Rome (2019)
War in Greek Myth (2020)
Roman York in the Roman Empire (in press)

War in Roman
Myth and Legend

Paul Chrystal

Pen & Sword
MILITARY

First published in Great Britain in 2020 by
Pen & Sword Military
An imprint of
Pen & Sword Books Ltd
Yorkshire – Philadelphia

ISBN 978 1 52676 612 0

A CIP catalogue record for this book is
available from the British Library.

Typeset by Mac Style
Printed and bound in the UK by TJ Books Ltd,
Padstow, Cornwall.

Pen & Sword Books Limited incorporates the imprints of Atlas,
Archaeology, Aviation, Discovery, Family History, Fiction, History,
Maritime, Military, Military Classics, Politics, Select, Transport,
True Crime, Air World, Frontline Publishing, Leo Cooper, Remember
When, Seaforth Publishing, The Praetorian Press, Wharncliffe
Local History, Wharncliffe Transport, Wharncliffe True Crime
and White Owl.

For a complete list of Pen & Sword titles please contact

PEN & SWORD BOOKS LIMITED
47 Church Street, Barnsley, South Yorkshire, S70 2AS, England
E-mail: enquiries@pen-and-sword.co.uk
Website: www.pen-and-sword.co.uk

Or

PEN AND SWORD BOOKS
1950 Lawrence Rd, Havertown, PA 19083, USA
E-mail: Uspen-and-sword@casematepublishers.com
Website: www.penandswordbooks.com

Contents

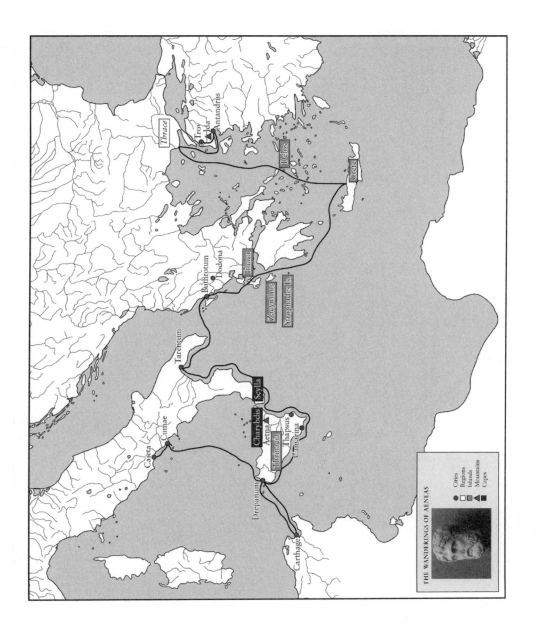

THE WANDERINGS OF AENEAS

Cities ●
Regions ☐
Islands ☐
Mountains ◢
Capes ■

Thrace

Troy
Ida
Antandrus

Delos

Crete

Buthrotum
Dodona
Epirus

Zacynthos
Strophades Is.

Tarentum

Caieta
Cumae

Scylla
Charybdis
Aetna
Thrinacia
Thapsus
Camarina

Drepanum

Carthage

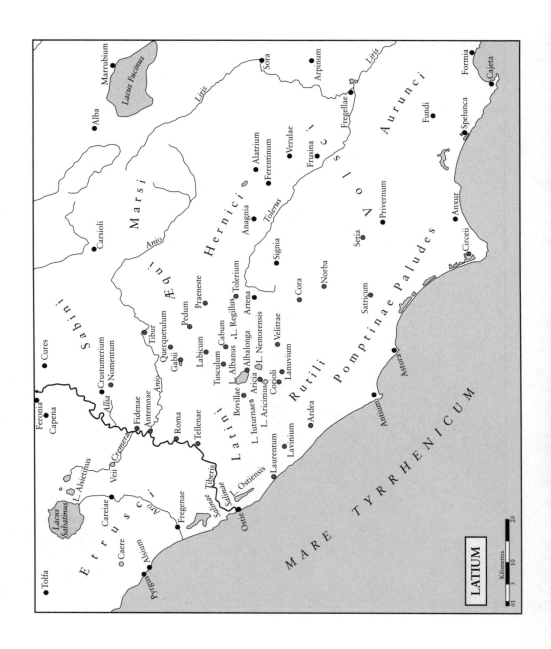

LATIUM

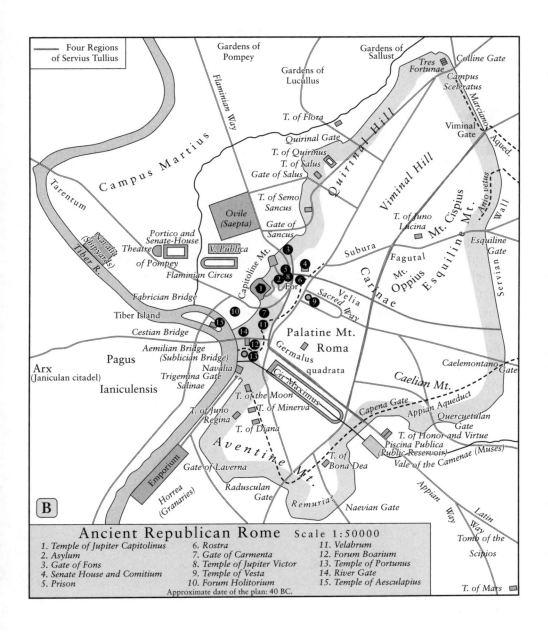

Four Regions
of Servius Tullius

Gardens of
Pompey

Gardens of
Lucullus

Gardens of
Sallust

Tres
Fortunae

Colline Gate

Campus
Sceleratus

Flaminian Way

T. of Flora

Quirinal Gate

T. of Quirinus

T. of Salus

Gate of Salus

C a m p u s M a r t i u s

Tarentum

*Navalia
(Shipyards)*
Tiber R.

Portico and
Senate-House

Theatre
of Pompey

*Ovile
(Saepta)*

V. Publica

T. of Semo
Sancus

Gate of
Sancus

Capitoline Mt.

3

5
8 6
2 4
1
For.

Flaminian Circus

Fabrician Bridge

Tiber Island

Cestian Bridge

Pagus

Arx
(Janiculan citadel)

Ianiculensis

Aemilian Bridge
(Sublician Bridge)

Trigemina Gate
Salinae

Navalia

Quirinal Hill

Viminal Hill

Viminal
Gate

Marcianio Aqued.

T. of Juno
Lucina

Mt. Cispius

*Mt.
Oppius*

*Esquiline
Mt.*

Esquiline
Gate

Servian Wall

Anio vetus

Subura

Carinae

Fagutal

Velia
Sacred Way

9

7
11
15
10
14
12
13

Germalus

Palatine Mt.
Roma

quadrata

Caelemontano
Gate

C a e l i a n Mt.

Cir. Maximus

T. of the Moon

T. of Juno
Regina

T. of Minerva

T. of Diana

A v e n t i n e Mt.

T. of
Bona Dea

Capena Gate

Appian Aqueduct

Quercuetulan
Gate

T. of Honor and Virtue

Piscina Publica
(Public Reservoir)

Vale of the Camenae (Muses)

Emporium

Gate of Laverna

Horrea
(Granaries)

Radusculan
Gate

Remuria?

Naevian Gate

Appian Way

*Latin
Way*

Tomb of the
Scipios

T. of Mars

B

Ancient Republican Rome Scale 1:50000

1. Temple of Jupiter Capitolinus
2. Asylum
3. Gate of Fons
4. Senate House and Comitium
5. Prison
6. Rostra
7. Gate of Carmenta
8. Temple of Jupiter Victor
9. Temple of Vesta
10. Forum Holitorium
11. Velabrum
12. Forum Boarium
13. Temple of Portunus
14. River Gate
15. Temple of Aesculapius

Approximate date of the plan: 40 BC.

About the Author

Paul Chrystal took classics degrees at the Universities of Hull and Southampton. He then went into medical publishing for over thirty years, but now spends his time writing features for national newspapers and history magazines such as *Minerva Magazine*, *BBC History Magazine*, *Ancient History Magazine*, *Omnibus* and *Ad Familiares*. He has appeared regularly on BBC local radio, on the BBC World Service and Radio 4's *PM* programme. He has been history advisor for a number of York tourist attractions and is the author of 100 or so books on a wide range of subjects, including many on ancient Greece and Rome, and specifically covering women, sexuality, war and conflict in those civilizations. He is a regular reviewer for and contributor to *Classics for All*, and a contributor to the Classics section of OUP's *Oxford Bibliographies Online*. He is History Editor of the *Yorkshire Archaeological Journal*. Paul is also guest speaker for the prestigious Vassar College New York's London Programme, in association with Goldsmith University. He lives near York and is married with three grown-up children.

York, October 2020

List of Plates

1. One of the two magnificent statues of war god Mars in the Yorkshire Museum in York. (*Courtesy of York Museums Trust*)
2. Bellona presenting the reins of his horses to Mars, by Louis Jean François Lagrenée (1766), in the Princeton University Art Museum. Possibly it refers to a passage from the Latin writer Claudian: 'Fer galleam Bellona mihi, nexusque rotarum tende Pavor.' (*Source: http://www.the-athenaeum.org/art/full.php?ID=140334*)
3. Bellona, the goddess of war – Waterloo Station. The Victory Arch, built of Portland Stone, commemorates the London and South Western Railway and the Southern Railway men who gave their lives in the First and Second World Wars. It features figures representing war and peace, beneath a statue of Britannia. The Victory or Memorial Arch was built from 1919–22. Bronze plaques under the arch bear the names of 585 LSWR employees who lost their lives in the First World War. The chief features are two sculptural groups: one dedicated to Bellona and dated 1914, and the other, dated 1918, to Peace, under the names of the greatest fields of battle, set around a glazed arch set with a clock in a sunburst, and surmounted on the roof by Britannia. The sculptor was the otherwise little-known Charles Whiffen. The special significance of the monument within the post-First World War genre is that the LSWR staff themselves were, uniquely, consulted on its design.
4. A colossal statue of the Roman goddess Juno Sospita (the Saviour). She wears a goatskin over her head and torso. It is probably from a temple in the Forum Olitorium, Rome, in the second century CE. (*Courtesy of Vatican Museums, Rome*)
5. The Witch Erichtho by John Hamilton Mortimer ARA (1740–1779). Detail from 'Sextus Pompeius consulting Erichtho before the Battle of Pharsalia'. (*Source/Photographer: Flickr: Playing Futures: Applied Nomadology, 2012-01-05*)
6. Mithras sacrificing the bull (100–200 CE), Borghése Collection, purchased by the Louvre in 1807 and on display in the Gallery du temps au Louvre-Lens. (*Author: Serge Ottaviani*)

7. An eighteenth-century depiction of the sacking of Troy by Johann Georg Trautmann (1713–1769). From the collections of the granddukes of Baden, Karlsruhe. (*Source/Photographer: http://www.zeller.de/*)
8. Sinon as a prisoner before the walls of Troy, in the Vergilius Romanus, fifth century CE.
9. Laocoön and his sons, also known as the Laocoön Group. Marble copy after an Hellenistic original from c. 200 BCE. Found in the Baths of Trajan, Rome, 1506. The figures are near life-size and the group is a little over 2m (6ft 7in) in height, showing the Trojan priest Laocoön and his sons, Antiphantes and Thymbraeus, being attacked by sea serpents. The group has been called 'the prototypical icon of human agony' in Western art. The statue, standing some 8ft in height, is made from seven interlocking pieces of white marble. (*Courtesy of Early First Century BCE Collection, Vatican Museums, Museo Pio-Clementino, Octagon, Laocoön Hall. Source/Photographer: Marie-Lan Nguyen, 2009*)
10. Aeneas tells Dido about the fall of Troy by Pierre-Narcisse Guérin (c. 1815); Georgia Regents University.
11. The death of Dido (1631) by Guercino (1591–1666). (*http://www.galleriaborghese.it/spada/it/didone.htm*)
12. Aeneas's flight from Troy (1598), by Federico Barocci (1535–1612); Galleria Borghese, Rome. Based on Aeneid 2.671–729: in the sack of Troy, Aeneas flees the burning city with his young son, Ascanius, at his side and carries on his shoulders his father, Anchises, who clutches the family's household gods.
13. Aeneas and his family fleeing burning Troy (1654) by Henry Gibbs (1631–1713); Tate Gallery, London. Aeneas' wife, Creusa, who in Virgil merely falls behind and is lost, is here shown being captured by a Greek soldier. This last detail is rare, if not unique, in representations of this scene.
14. Landscape with Aeneas at Delos (1672), by Claude Lorrain (1600–1682); National Gallery, London. In the last ten years of his life, Claude painted six stories of Aeneas. Claude had often illustrated Ovid's Metamorphoses, and it may be that this was why his interest in Aeneas' adventures was first aroused. In Book 13, Ovid relates the hero's flight from burning Troy; Claude's painting is based more closely on this passage than on Virgil's description in Book 3 of the Aeneid. Ovid tells how – taking with him sacred images of the gods, his father Anchises (the bearded man in blue) and his son Ascanius (the child on the right), Aeneas (in short red cloak):

'set sail … and … reached with his friends the city of Apollo [Delos]. Anius [in white on the left], who ruled over men as king and served the sun god as his priest, received him in the temple and his home. He showed his city, the new-erected shrines and the two sacred trees [olive and palm] to which Latona had once clung when she gave birth to her children [Diana and Apollo].'

'This is one of the most evocative pictures ever painted. The figures, elongated perhaps in the belief that the ancients were taller than we, are dwarfed by the sacred trees and the majestic buildings. Apollo's round temple recreates the original appearance of the Pantheon, reminding us of the Delian oracle's prophecy of Rome's future splendour. A dual longing, for both the Trojan past and Aeneas' future as founder of Rome, is embedded in the perspectival construction.' (*https://www.wga.hu/html_m/c/claude/3/07delos.html*)

38. Horatius Cocles defending the bridge (c. 1642/43), by Charles Le Brun (1619–1690). (*Dulwich Picture Gallery*)

39. Jean Bardin: Tullia drives over the corpse of her father (1765); Landesmuseum Mainz. (*Source/Photographer: http://galatea.univ-tlse2. fr/pictura/UtpicturaServeur/GenerateurNotice.php?numnotice=A5287*)

40. The Battle of Actium, 2 September 31 BC (1672), by Lorenzo A. Castro (fl. 1664–1700). (*National Maritime Museum, London*)

41. Virgil reading the Aeneid to Augustus and Octavia (1787), by Jean-Joseph Taillasson (1745–1809); National Gallery, London. (*Source/ Photographer: National Gallery, London. Uploaded to Wikipedia by Neddyseagoon, 24 November 2006*)

    Octavia's son, Marcellus, was prominent in Augustus' plans for the succession, but Marcellus died prematurely in 23 BCE. Octavia went on to celebrate her late son's life, living on to enjoy the opening ceremony of the Library of Marcellus and Augustus' completion of the Theatre of Marcellus in 13 BCE. When Virgil recited Books 2, 4 and 6 of his near-complete Aeneid before Augustus and Octavia, Octavia is said to have fainted upon hearing the lines by Anchises to Aeneas: 'Poor boy, if somehow you can burst free of your harsh destiny, you too shall be Marcellus!' ('heu, miserande puer, si qua fata aspera rumpas ! tu Marcellus eris'). When Octavia revived, she granted 10,000 sesterces to Virgil for each of the lines.

42. The meeting of Erasmus and St Maurice (between c. 1520 and c. 1524), by Mathias Grünewald (c. 1475/80–1528); Alte Pinakothek, Munich.

43. The Battle of the Milvian Bridge (between 1520 and 1524), by Giulio Romano (1499–1546); Vatican City, Apostolic Palace.

Introduction

This is the second of two books on war in Greek and Roman mythology and legend. As I said in the preface to the first volume, 'even though war, and conflict generally, are a seminal part of Greek mythology and Roman legend, relatively little has been written specifically on the subject either in books or in scholarly articles. This is surprising because wars and battles in the mythologies and legends of both civilizations are freighted with symbolism and were laden with meaning for the ancient Greeks and for the Romans. The gods of war are prominent members of the pantheons of both Greece and Rome.' In short, the conflict-flavoured myths and legends had enormous symbolic importance to the history, politics, social norms and cultural values of both civilizations and societies. For Rome, mythology is used as an eloquent vehicle to explain the very origins of Rome and some of its most enduring religious, political and social practices.

The foundation myths – amongst the most famous, celebrated and important of Roman myths – are the founding of Alba Longa (the future site of Rome) by the descendants of Aeneas and the building of Rome by Romulus and Remus, with a number of derivative stories which are of national relevance and consequence. With both being inextricably associated with war, they are war as well as foundation myths. Both were contrived centuries later, largely at the end of the first century BCE, to reflect and promote an aura of social, political and moral regeneration as part of a well-oiled state propaganda machine. And both were designed to leave a Roman in no doubt as to what values and ethics a good Roman needed to embrace, which were later embodied in a ideal called 'Romanitas'.

We can sketch out a rough timeline relating to Rome's bellicose foundation myths. In the last quarter of the fourth century BC, Romulus and Remus were beginning to feature in Greek versions, thanks largely to the Sicilian Callias and Alcimus, while the Latin origin of Rome was starting to predominate. By 300 BCE, the twins were integral to the foundation myth, as evidenced by the 296 BCE Capitoline Wolf sculpture and the finding of a coin from 269 depicting the twins. By the time of Fabius Pictor (254–201 BCE), the awkward time difference between Aeneas' arrival in Italy and the Varronian date for the foundation of Rome (753 BCE) had been corrected by the invention of the mythical Alban dynasty. Roman history writing emerged around this time, and may have been accelerated by Cato the Elder's *Origines*, which was begun about 170 BCE.

Just as significantly, the time gap between the supposed semi-mythical/semi-historical events from vaguely remembered pre-historical times and their promulagation in the new age of historicity allowed the eclectic writer (Livy, Dionysius *et. al.*) to mix and match, to choose what to adopt and adapt, to rationalize and modify so as to chime with the political requirements of the day, in this case the nationalist demands of the new emperor of the new empire, Augustus. And that is exactly what we have got; a mixture of entertaining and edifying stories ultimately designed to connect the emperor with the Trojans, allowing him, in the end, to claim divine descent.

As Kenneth Scott says in his *Emperor Worship in Ovid*:

'Beyond question the worship of the emperor and the imperial house played an important part in the establishment of the Roman empire. The great court poets of the imperial age Virgil, Horace, Propertius and Ovid sang the divinity of the ruler and helped to establish the worship of the Roman emperor.'[1]

The first chapter of this book, *Interpretatio Romana*, addresses the question of Roman syncretism in its mythology. Were the Romans just being lazy, pragmatic and opportunistic by adopting Greek myths and legends and appropriating them as their own? Not at all: the Romans did adopt much Greek mythology, but they also *adapted* it to define many things specifically Roman, so that a modified Greek myth became the vehicle for an essentially Roman concept or significant event. One of the things which made Rome great was its facility to recognize, re-fashion and repurpose the better things they found in their allies and enemies – making foreign things Roman, explaining essentially Roman things through transcultural modification to suit their own specific aims, policies and agenda. Conflict in mythology and legend is a good example of this in practice.

So, one of the aims of the book is to challenge the notion that the Romans had no mythology to speak of, and to show how, on the contrary, the Romans used their myths and legends to elucidate fundamental interpretations relating to the founding of Rome, and how they adapted Greek mythology for the same ends (*Interpretatio Romana*). They Latinized and Romanized the Greek names, shifting their emphasis to reflect what they, the Romans, considered to be vital, associating them with important historical events and individuals, politicizing them by focusing them on the preservation and development of the state of Rome, and reinterpreting them to reflect Roman ideas and values. During the Augustan Age, Roman writers were eager, as indeed was Augustus, to forge a connection between the wondrous legendary tales of Rome's birth and its present supremacy, and to show that it was the city's divine origins which had ensured its global success.

Aeneas' battles in Italy led to the foundation of Rome. Crucially, this established the lineage of the early Empire Julio-Claudians, reaching way back to the heroic Trojans and their post-Troy diaspora. Myths and legends (as expounded in Livy, Dio and others) formed the bedrock for the establishment of Rome and its core values – conflict that was integral to those myths and legends contributed profoundly to the expansion of Rome, to the pivotal move towards a republic and away from a monarchy, to a somewhat fairer political and social representation of the Roman people, and to the relative appreciation of women and female qualities. Conflict in mythology helped shape Roman religion, philosophy and morality. It populates Roman poetry, drama, philosophy and historiography.

All of this is covered here in a book which shows how war in mythology and legend resonated loudly as an essential, existentialist even, symbol in Roman history and culture; how it was a key ingredient of 'Romanitas'; and how it is represented in classical literature, philosophy, religion, feminism, art, statuary, ceramics, architecture, numismatics, etymology, astronomy and even vulcanology.

Rome as a political entity was all that mattered, the *sine qua non* to the educated and influential Roman with his *pietas* (dutifulness and loyalty to family, gods and state) and patriotism. Rome's military and political sway over the region was paramount: Roman myths were fashioned to illustrate and promulgate this very clearly. We can add *gravitas* to *pietas* as another, closely related ideal celebrated in the myths: this was a focused and serious sense of purpose in championing Rome. *Frugalitas* – a life led simply, modestly and frugally, with restraint – was another paradigm of the Roman way, a *modus vivendi* variously championed by, amongst others, the two Catos, Horace and, ultimately, Augustus in his programme for change in an increasingly decadent, self-interested, over emotional and venal early Empire.

The synthesis of myth and history is clearly seen in the *Aeneid* when Virgil makes Romulus the ancestor of Julius Caesar and ultimately of Augustus – Virgil's patron. By the simple expedient of adding a vowel to Ilus, Aeneas' son, he becomes Iulus, and so the progenitor of the *gens* Julia and hence

Julius Caesar. This melding of myth and history can still be seen on the reliefs snaking round Trajan's Column in Rome. Its primary purpose when built around 110 CE was to celebrate and illustrate Trajan's victory over the Dacians – and it achieves this most graphically. But wait: the river god of the Danube, Jupiter and Victory are in there too, thus freighting the historical facts with an aura of the divine and supernatural, and the mythological with a veneer of reality.

There were, though, problems. With no Roman historiography to speak of recorded until the third century BCE, a dependence on Greek mythology was inculcated which, up until that point, discouraged the dissemination of native Roman myth in Latin. Moreover, Greek colonization imbued southern Italian and Sicilian towns with Greek culture and mythology, crowding out, in effect, native legend and myth. A facility with Greek myth was the sign of an educated man and carried with it considerable kudos; it was a badge of elite culture and something to be acquired.

If you did not know your Greek myths, you would not understand most of the allusions in the poets, playwrights and orators. You would flounder at the many recitals, and nor would you be able to identify and expatiate on the scenes depicted on the mosaic floors and wall paintings decorating your cultivated friends' houses, or on the silverware on their tables. If you confused your Castor with your Pollux, or did not know your Chyrseis from your Briseis, how embarrassing would that be at the next dinner party?

Mythology now had to be learned formally in school, as shown by the prodigious, encyclopaedic amount of elementary mythological information in the many surviving ancient commentaries on the classics, notably Servius, who offers a myth for almost every person, place, and even plant Virgil mentions.

Mythographers wrote myth handbooks by the score, providing everything you needed to know about Homer, Hesiod, Euripides and the rest. From before about 200 CE, they proliferated with *The Library* of Apollodorus, the *Metamorphoses* of Antonius Liberalis and the works of Ptolemy the Quail, to name but three. All of these factors served as a drag on the publishing and acceptance of Roman mythology until the first century BCE, when the works of Dionysius of Halicarnassus (born before 53 BCE), Livy and Virgil, Horace, Propertius and Ovid, then Cassius Dio (155–235 CE), gave Roman myth a platform which allowed it to become a vehicle for the aetiological explanation of the origins and development of the Roman state, its constitution, its very 'Romanitas'.

What is this 'Romanitas'? We can identify certain qualities which are commonly and consistently attributable to Romans, wherever and whenever they were. Those qualities fall conveniently under the term 'Romanitas', a word that was never actually used by the Romans themselves until the third-century CE Roman writer, Tertullian. Tertullian's use is pejorative, used to describe his fellow Carthaginians who aped Roman ways. Juvenal (b. 50 CE) had said much the same, vilifying his fellow Romans who were slaves to the ways of Greeks and to all things Greek. To Juvenal, Greece was polluting and diluting 'Romanitas' (Juvenal 6, 184–191). Martial (b. *c.* 40 CE) agreed (Martial 10, 68). The concept of 'Romanitas' took on an air of respectability and nobility in tune with the 'grandeur that was Rome'. It came to mean quintessential 'Roman-ness' – what it means to be a Roman and how the Romans regarded themselves. It defined a true Roman and encapsulated the Roman ideal. Despite the best efforts of foreign influences to adulterate 'Romanitas', there was always an element of conservatism and traditionalism running through the marrow of the Roman people. This evolved over time into a national character which had its roots in the early humble, agricultural days and was characterized as demonstrating hard work and honesty, exuding *gravitas* (dignified, serious or solemn conduct) and being diligent in every way. Moreover, the true Roman lived by and respected the *mos maiorum*, the way the ancestors had gone about things. He, or she, was expected to be dutiful, to exhibit *pietas*, in every sphere of life: towards family, friends, country, fellow citizens, comrades in arms and gods. 'Romanitas', *gravitas* and *pietas* did indeed define the Roman.

War was a fact of life at Rome, a constant in the Roman journey towards regional domination, so it is no surprise that the salient myths and legends, not least the foundation myths, are myths of war. What follows is the story of war in Roman myth and legend.

Chapter 1

Interpretatio Romana – 'Translating' the Greek and the Beginnings of Roman History

Roman mythology has had a bad press down the years. For example, 1902 saw Georg Wissowa bemoan the Roman gods' affinity to 'places and things', devoid of 'personal qualities and individual characteristics' and lacking interpersonal skills. Where were the divine marriages and babies, where was the intermarriage with mortals, he demanded? To Kurt Latte in 1926, the Romans were an 'unspeculative and unimaginative people' with no mythology to their credit. In 1928, H.J. Rose concluded his *Handbook of Greek Mythology* with a grudging chapter entitled 'Italian pseudo-myths', in which he dismissively declared 'this rubbish need not trouble us long'. He went on to assert that to understand early Roman history we have to rely on Greek writers, and that 'the mythologist ... must share the disgust of the historian when he realises that the overwhelming majority of [Roman myths] are not genuine popular native traditions at all but comparatively late, artificial tales, put together by Greeks or under Greek influence'.

Not much had changed by 2003, when the *Oxford Dictionary of Classical Myth and Religion* (pp.364–65) sniffily pronounced:

'Rome, on the other hand, was situated at the margin of the "civilized" world and was late to assimilate Greek myth. When the Roman élite started to write down its history at the end of the third century BC it had one fixed mythological concept at its disposal: the foundation of Rome by Romulus and Remus. A few names such as Janus and Picus hint at the sometime existence of other myths, but nothing suggests an original rich mythology, and the absence of a *Götteraparat* has even led some scholars to the suggestion that the Romans lacked a mythology altogether.'

The travesty was repeated verbatim in the 2012 *Oxford Classical Dictionary* (p.992) and in the 2014 *Oxford Dictionary of Classical Civilisation*, in which, also, the index gives entries for 'mythology, Greek' – but none for 'mythology, Roman'.

The Oxford authors go on to say that the influx of neighbouring elites into Rome discouraged the survival of Italic myths, and that the founding of Praeneste by Caeculus is all that is left. Moreover, the important thing to the Romans was the foundation of the city rather than the creation of man and gods.

The Romantics and nineteenth-century classical scholarship had not helped matters, but it is clear that Rome was never on the margins of the civilized world and that there are stories a-plenty to regale, inform and please us. The painters of Europe from the fifteenth to the eighteenth centuries, Dante and Shakespeare all seem to have thought so too. Indeed, it could be argued that the lessons Roman myths teach us regarding tyranny, virtue, conviction, social justice, patriotism, liberty, dutifulness and honour are essentially more edifying than the story of the rape of Leda by a god disguised as a swan...

A number of scholars have dismissed Roman myth and legend as simply a derivative of Greek myth, whereby all that the Romans did mythographically was translate a Greek deity, or the actions of a Greek deity, over to an apparent direct Roman equivalent. This is what is known as *Interpretatio Romana*. The *Oxford Classical Dictionary* defines *Interpretatio Romana* thus:

> '*Interpretatio Romana*, lit. "Latin translation" (Tac. Germ. 43.3); a phrase used to describe the Roman habit of replacing the name of a foreign deity with that of a Roman deity considered somehow comparable. At times this process involved extensive identification of the actual deities, while in other cases, the deities, though sharing a name, continued to be sharply distinguished. Different Latin names could sometimes be substituted for the same foreign name, depending on which characteristic of the god was chosen as the basis for comparison. The earliest of these "translations" were from Greek: thus "Zeus" was translated as "Iuppiter". The process continued as the Romans came into contact with other cultures, so that the German "Wodan" was called "Mercurius" by Roman writers.'

In the *Germania* (43), Tacitus describes two German gods worshipped as brothers and twins (the Alci) as being the equivalent to Castor and Pollux. He also mentions worship of Hercules and Mars.

Cicero explains this polytheistic babel, this multiplicity of acceptable versions (*Natura Deorum*, 1, 83–84):

'Tell me, do we also reckon the gods to have the same names as those by which they are known to us? In the first place the gods have as many names as mankind has languages. You are Velleius wherever you travel, but Vulcan has a different name in Italy, in Africa and in Spain.'

In doing so, Cicero tells us how foreign religions were thereby rendered explicable and meaningful to the educated Roman elite, while Caesar spells it out (*De Bello Gallica*, 6, 17–18) when he describes the gods of the Gauls:

'Among the gods, they mostly worship Mercury. There are many images of him; they say he is the inventor of all arts, the guide for every road and journey, and they believe him to have the greatest influence for all commerce and traffic. After him they have Apollo, Mars, Jupiter, and Minerva. Of all these deities they have almost the same idea as all other nations: Apollo expels diseases, Minerva supplies the basics of arts and crafts, Jupiter holds heaven, Mars runs wars. ... The Gauls say that they are all descended from a common father, Dis, and say that this is the tradition of the Druids [too].'

As far as Gallic counterparts are concerned, at least thirty-five gods are identified with Roman Mars, including Mars Alator, Mars Albioris, Mars Barrex, Mars Nodens, Mars Segomo, Mars Smertrios and Mars Teutates. Which epithet was applied depended on time, place and action. To complicate things further, the *Berne scholia* – a collection of glosses on Lucan's *Pharsalia* originally written in the fourth century CE, but only surviving in a single medieval manuscript – identifies Teutates with either Mercury or Mars, and Esus with either Mars or Mercury. There is only inscriptional evidence to support the identification of Teutates with Mars.

From the earliest times, the Roman pantheon was identified with the much older Greek pantheon: Minerva was identified with Athena, Diana with Artemis, Mars with Ares, Saturn with Cronos – even though they were not always an exact match. This was especially true in the case of Mars, whose counterpart was the much-mocked, despised and belligerent maniac of an Olympian Ares. Mars, while a god of war, was also described as a more rational warrior and god of agriculture and husbandry. His role was progenitor of the Romans (as father of Romulus and Remus) and guarantor-protector of the Roman people's livelihood, whether as a warrior or god of agriculture. The apparent dichotomy here may be accounted for by the movement over time of the rural Italic tribes into larger settlements and towns, which had been fought for in war under a foreign policy built on expansionism. Mars eventually became much more than just a god of war.

For the Romans, the translation from Greek to Roman allowed the Roman deity the inherent prestige and intellectual kudos implicit in the Greek version. Looking, Janus-like, the other way, *Interpretatio Germanica,* for example, permitted the Germanic tribes to assume a Roman appearance, which was valuable in obtaining the status and benefits of a Roman citizen should they be desired. *Interpretatio Romana* was, therefore, part of the process of Romanization, a step on the way to *Romanitas.* Rome was generally quite relaxed when it came to tolerance of religious practices of defeated populations: one way of allowing foreigners access to the Roman gods was through *Interpretatio Romana*, which associated Roman deities with local gods and goddesses, and permitted the grafting-on of local divinities.

Indeed, when Ovid came to compose his *Metamorphoses* around 5 CE, he, perhaps unwittingly, demonstrated an example of *Interpretatio Romana* in his opening lines when he sets out his aims and scope. The poet asserts '*In nova fert animus mutatas dicere formas / corpora*' ('I mean to speak of forms changed into new bodies'). These 'new bodies' describe not just the metamorphoses he intends to describe but an appropriation and adaptation of the Greek myths which are his primary source; these 'forms' are Greek forms changed into the Roman – the linguistic connection between 'metamorphoses' and *mutatas formas*, when the '*m*' and '*f*' in *formas* are transposed, speaks volumes for Ovid, who has cleverly subjected the word for 'form' to a metamorphosis all of its own.

Roman mythology was essentially different from Greek mythology. Greek mythology was anthropomorphic: the Greeks contrived legends and embellished their gods and goddesses with fabulous and thrilling tales, allowing them to exhibit human qualities such as love, hate and jealousy. As a consequence, Romans and Greeks – but especially the Greeks – could recognize themselves in these universal tales, and through them comprehend social realities and their relationship to the rest of the world, as well as their relationship with the gods. Roman mythology tended to be more cult-based, pragmatic and nowhere near so dependent on anthropomorphism and human emotional characteristics. It did not lend itself to storytelling in the way that its Greek equivalents did so well. There was no place for Titanomachy or Gigantomachy here, no rapacious swans or hobbling cuckolded blacksmith gods.

Roman mythology was based on the ancient religions of pre-Roman Italic tribes such as the Sabines and Etruscans. The Romans had a highly developed system of rituals and priestly colleges, and a fertile, but limited, set of historical myths about the foundation and rise of their city involving human actors, with occasional divine interventions. This made 'borrowing' Greek myths and applying *Interpretatio Romana* to Romanize them an attractive and exciting option with which to enrich their own literature. As Morford points out in his chapter on Roman mythology, 'it requires more imagination than the Romans possessed to create a legend, for example, about Robigo, the goddess who prevents blight.'[1]

This, from McGill University, is as good a summary of the distinction between Greek and Roman myth as any:

> 'The Roman model involved a very different way of defining and thinking about gods than that of Greek gods. For example, if one were to ask a Greek about Demeter, he might reply with the well-known story of her grief at the rape of Persephone by Hades.
>
> 'An archaic Roman, by contrast, would tell you that Ceres had an official priest called a flamen, who was junior to the flamens of Jupiter, Mars, and Quirinus, but senior to the flamens of Flora and Pomona. He might tell you that she was grouped in a triad with two other agricultural gods, Liber and Libera. And he might even be able to rattle off all of the minor gods with specialized functions who attended her: Sarritor (weeding), Messor (harvesting), Convector (carting), Conditor (storing), Insitor (sowing), and dozens more.
>
> 'Thus the archaic Roman "mythology", at least concerning the gods, was made up not of narratives, but rather of interlocking and complex interrelations between and among gods and humans.'[2]

Furthermore, Roman and Italic history is a lot older than Roman historiography: by the time the early historians such as Quintus Fabius Pictor (fl. about 200 BCE) started writing, much water had flowed under the bridge – some of it contrived myth and legend which eventually elided into the historical. Archaeology tells us that sixth-century BCE Latins, for example, knew about Greek myth and how they appropriated it into their cults. The terracotta group of Hercules and Minerva found in 1938 in the *Forum Bovarium* in Rome, and the discovery twenty years later of the bronze dedication plaque to the Dioskouroi unearthed at Lavinium ('to Castor and Podloukes', the *kouroi*), are visible and incontrovertible evidence.

Then, if more is needed, five Greek characters (EYOIN or EYΛIN) were found scratched on a grave marker pot six inches tall from Iron Age Gabii (tomb 482). This is assigned to *cultura Laziale* IIB, the dates for which are 830–770 BCE, possibly up to 100 years earlier if dendrochronological evidence is accepted. It is currently the earliest Greek graffito found anywhere.

Pictor's history (in Greek, and surviving only in fragmentary form) opens with the arrival of Aeneas in Latium – he dated the founding of Rome to the 'first year of the eighth Olympiad', or 747 BCE – and ended with the Second Punic War (218–201 BCE). Pictor was succeeded by Gnaeus Gellius (*c.* 140 BCE), who wrote his history from Aeneas down to 146 BCE; Lucius Calpurnius Piso Frugi (*c.* 133 BCE), who was preoccupied with why Roman civilization had begun to decline, describing Rome from the foundation until 154 BCE, at which point he believed that society was at its lowest ebb; and Publius Mucius Scaevola (*c.* 133 BCE), who edited a history from the foundation of the city in eighty books.

Then there was the *Tabula Pontificum* or *Annales Maximi* – a dense record of important public events and the names of the magistrates, a year book, compiled by the Pontifex Maximus in successive years and published by him in digest form on a whiteboard (*tabula dealbata*) outside the Regia, the office of the Pontifex Maximus on the Sacra Via. Information relating to, for example, eclipses and food prices was communicated to the Roman public by this means. It became an important source for historians and lawyers; early social media indeed. Cicero declared:

'History began as a mere compilation of annals, on which account, and in order to preserve the general traditions, from the earliest period of the city down to the pontificate of Publius Mucius, each High Priest used to commit to writing all the events of his year of office, and record them on a white surface, and post up the tablet at his house, that all men might have liberty to acquaint themselves therewith, and to this day those records are known as the Pontifical Chronicles.'[3]

Cato the Elder (234–149 BCE), or Cato the Censor, was a staunch conservative. As a champion of the *mos maiorum*, and contemptuous of anything Greek, he had spoken angrily against what he saw as a time of moral decline and an erosion of the robust principles on which Rome was built.[4] The defeat of Hannibal at Zama in 202 BCE, the victory over the Macedonians at Pydna in 168 BCE and the final extinguishing of the Carthaginian threat in 146 BCE all allowed Rome to relax more, leading to an unprecedented influx of Greek and eastern influences and luxuries into an increasingly receptive Rome.[5] Cato was irritated by what he saw as the trivial content of the *Tabula*, the superstition and what he judged to be the pedalling (or tweeting!) of bad news and fake news, famines and the like.[6] Its earliest records were mythological events, hence Cato's criticism, but Cicero argued that reliable records went as far back as 400 BCE. Publication of the *Tabula* had ceased by 130 BCE, by which time it filled eighty books and was published by Pontifex Maximus Publius Mucius Scaevola (130–115 BCE).

Cato responded with the *Origines*. Despite his alleged criticism of the mythological, Cato could not resist the legends surrounding early Rome. Cornelius Nepos tells us that Cato's *Origines* consisted of seven books.[7] Book I covered the foundation of Rome and its kings. Books II and III described the origins of major Italian cities and gave the work its title. The last four books dealt with the Roman Republic, its wars and its rising power up to 149 BCE.

Lucius Cincius Alimentus (fl. *c.* 200 BCE) was author of the *Annals* – lost, and known only from fragments – another version of the annals of the pontifex maximus and other Roman sources to present a year-by-year prose Greek narrative of Roman history. Alimentus would have included myths and legends relating to the foundation of Rome, and is an altogether less triumphalist account of the early relations between the Romans and the early Latins. What we might call 'real' extant history arrived with Diodorus Siculus, a Greek historian, author of the monumental universal history *Bibliotheca Historica* between 60 and 30 BCE, much of which survives. The first part covers mythic history up to the destruction of Troy, arranged geographically, describing regions around the world from Egypt, India and Arabia to Europe. The second covers the Trojan War to the death of Alexander the Great. The third covers the period to about 36 BCE, when it records how Octavian expelled a group of citizens for supporting Sextus Pompey; they went on to found a colony at Tauromenion. Next came Julius Caesar and Sallust, and then, of course, Livy.

Roughly contemporary with Livy was the polymath Gnaeus Pompeius Trogus, a Gallo-Roman historian from the Celtic Vocontii tribe in Narbonese Gaul whose father served Julius Caesar as his secretary and interpreter. His main work was his forty-four-volume *Historiae Philippicae et Totius Mundi Origines et Terrae Situs*, which had as its principal theme the Macedonian empire founded by Philip II but functioned as a general history of all the parts of the world which fell under the sway of Alexander the Great and his successors, with extensive ethnographical and geographical digressions. Trogus began with Ninus, legendary founder of Nineveh, and ended at about the same point as Livy (9 CE). The development of the East, from the Assyrians to the Parthians, is given extensive coverage, while early Roman history and the history of the Iberian Peninsula is in the last two books. He was very much with those Romans who deplored the enervating influences on Roman society and culture flowing in from Greece and from all points east (18, 2, 7–10; 31, 8, 8–9). Trogus glorified instead the ancient traditions of Rome: to Trogus, the conquest of Greece had corrupted Rome (36, 4, 12). The original text is lost and survives to us in excerpts by other authors (including Vopiscus, Jerome and Augustine) and in an epitome by the historian Justin. Justin was highly selective and only preserved the parts he felt most important or interesting, with the last recorded event being the recovery of Roman standards from the Parthians in 20 BCE.

Nicolaus of Damascus, born around 64 BCE, was a Hellenized Jewish historian and philosopher who lived during the reign of Augustus. His prodigious output is nearly all lost, but his chief work was a universal history in 144 books. He also wrote a life of Augustus, a life of Herod, some philosophical and scientific works and some tragedies and comedies. Of the *Life of Augustus* (Bios Kaisaros), completed after the death of the emperor in 14 CE, two long fragments survive, the first covering Octavius' youth and the second the assassination of Julius Caesar.

But the writings were by no means all prose. Gnaeus Naevius (*c.* 270–201 BCE) was a Roman epic poet and dramatist who covered the early myths surrounding the birth of Rome. Clearly influenced by Greek epic and New Comedy, he adapted Greek tragedies and comedies to the Roman stage, as these titles show: *Romulus*, or *Alimonium Romuli et Remi* ('The Nourishing of Romulus and Remus', a *fabula praetexta*, national drama); *Triphallus* ('The Man With Three Penises', a comedy); *Equus Troianus* ('The Trojan Horse', a tragedy); and *Hector Proficiscens* ('Hector Setting Forth', another tragedy) – altogether an interesting blend of the Greek and Roman.

Quintus Ennius (*c.* 239–169 BCE) is most famous for his *Annales* – an epic poem in eighteen books, covering Roman history from the fall of Troy in 1184 BCE down to the censorship of Cato the Elder in 184 BCE. Much of it was military history; not surprising, given Rome's military-soaked past. The *Annales* was adopted as a school text for Roman schoolchildren until publication of Virgil's *Aeneid* replaced it on the reading list. About 600 lines survive; including lines which suggest that Ennius opened his epic with a recollection of a dream in which Homer told him that his spirit had been reborn into him. Ennius also wrote a *Sabine Women* and a panegyric of Scipio Africanus. In similar vein was an epic by the poet Aulus Licinius Archias (fl. 121–61 BCE, famously defended by Cicero) in the first century BCE on the army career of Lucullus in the Mithridatic Wars.

Lucius Accius (170–86 BCE) was a prolific tragic poet, his oeuvre comprising mainly imitations or translations of the Greek, especially Aeschylus. He also wrote on matters Roman, one of which, the *Brutus*, takes as its subject the tyranny of L. Tarquinius Superbus and his expulsion by Lucius Junius Brutus.

Julius Caesar's military achievements were celebrated by Furius, while Varro of Atax focused on Caesar's Gallic campaigns in his *Bellum Sequanicum* of 58 BCE. To bring us right up to date, there is the *Panegyricus Augusti* of Varius, friend of Horace and Virgil, and the lost work of Cornelius Severus on the Sicilian War of 38–6 BCE. Even Virgil could not resist some historical excursions, giving us a description of the prehistory of Carthage (1, 12ff) and an anthropological passage on Italy and its Golden Age (8, 314ff). The significant difference between Virgil and what seems to have gone before is that his predecessors celebrated military success stories by generals bathed in glory, living out established Roman military ideals, while Virgil's hero was on the losing side and forced into exile, a leader with no great love of the atrocities of war.

In any event, the Romans had a lot of catching up to do and would have leant heavily on Greek writers writing in a number of genres – epic, choral lyric and tragedy, for example. This dependence entailed using much Greek mythology from a canon of literature that had been established since the days of Homer, Hesiod and the Homeric Cycle, a canon the Romans simply did not have to call upon from their own literary hinterland. In the early days of Roman literature, the early Roman myths and legend were bound to have been crowded out to a large extent. Things were not helped by the destructive fire of 386 BCE during the Gallic invasion, in which many irreplaceable records of earlier times were torched.

Nevertheless, by the end of the millennium, things were about to change and Roman myths shared the stage with their Greek counterparts through the writings of Dionysius of Halicarnassus, Livy, Virgil, Horace, Propertius and Ovid, all of whom introduced Roman myth in their works. No one can accuse the Romans of not taking their myths seriously: as we have noted, and as we shall see in greater detail, they used them to embroider and explain serious matters of state and religion and issues of the highest consequence. In commissioning Virgil to compose the *Aeneid*, and maybe even dictating the brief, Augustus was forging a link between his family and the heroes of Troy; he was fashioning a propaganda campaign, based on a blend of Greek and Roman myth, which would cover his regime in glory, all with impeccable mythological-historical credentials.

Greek colonization played its part too. From the eighth century BCE, Greek settlers started arriving in southern Italy and Sicily, establishing numerous Greek colonies from Capua to Syracuse, from Tarentum to Selinunte – a huge area which became known as Magna Graecia. Naturally, they brought with them their Greek culture, which percolated into native Italic culture in respect of languages, the alphabet and eventually storytelling and literature, a literature which will have been increasingly freighted with the Greek myths and legends which the Romans would find only too easy to adopt and adapt.

As I wrote in the introduction to my *War in Greek Myth*:

'Greek myths were essential and fundamental. They became an indispensable and inextricable fact of everyday Greek life on every level, insinuating themselves into all aspects of culture and civilisation, in politics, education, philosophy, religion and ritual. They answered the need for an answer to why things were as they were. The mythology of the Greeks explained for the Greeks the meaning of Greek life. A deep and extensive knowledge of Homer, for example, was considered by the Greeks to be the basis of their culture. Homer was the "education of Greece" (Ἑλλάδος παίδευσις), and his poetry "the Book".'[8]

Still, there is no getting away from the fact that much of Roman legend and myth 'are not really Roman but Greek stories reclothed in Roman dress ... there is practically no extensive story from early Roman history which cannot be proved to be Greek in origin'.[9] For example, the myth of the survival of Romulus and Remus, with its shepherd and *lupa*, derives from a Near Eastern myth and can be identified in the Greek myth of Neleus and Pelias. Furthermore, the fateful leap of Remus over the walls of Romulus reminds us of the legends of Oeneus and Toxeus, or of Poimander and Leucippus.

But for all that, Greek myths and their Romanized versions in Roman mythology were nevertheless essential and fundamental to the Romans too, except that they used them pragmatically, not so much to adumbrate the meaning of life but more to define and describe aetiologically political, religious and social systems that were fundamental to the rise of the Roman state.

Chapter 2

The Gods of War

The Romans, it seems, had a god, or goddess – or *numen* (spirit) – for every aspect of Roman life – and death. As a general illustration, the following is how the Romans covered conception, childbirth and neonatal development:

Women who sacrificed to Rumina, responsible for breastfeeding as the she-wolf which suckled Romulus, did so with milk and not wine because Rumina knew that alcohol is harmful to babies. Rumina was by no means on her own: the Roman delivery room was as crowded as any bridal suite. Alemona presided over the foetus; Nona and Decima were responsible for the ninth and tenth months of gestation; Parca or Partula watched over the delivery – at the birth, Parca established the extent of the baby's life in her guise as a goddess of death called Morta. The *profatio Parcae*, or 'prophecy of Parca', indicated that the child was a mortal being. Egeria delivered the baby. Postverta and Prosa averted breech birth, which was considered unlucky, while Lucina was the goddess of the birth. Diespiter (Jupiter) introduced the infant to the daylight; Vagitamus opened the baby's mouth to emit the first cry; and Levana lifted the baby from the ground, symbolizing contact with Mother Earth. Cunina looked after the baby in the cradle, protecting it from malevolent forces and magic; Statina gave the baby energy; and Candelifera was the nursery light, which was kept burning to deter the spirits of darkness that would threaten the infant in the crucial first week of birth, and to banish the bogey-women – child-snatching demons such as Gello. On the *dies lustricus*, the *Fata Scribunda* were invoked – the 'Written Fates', which was a ceremonial inscription of the child's new name. The giving of a name was as important as the birth itself: receiving a *praenomen* established the child as an individual with its own fate. Potina allowed the child to drink, Edusa to eat; Ossipago built strong bones, Carna healthy muscles, defending the internal organs from witches. Cuba was there to ease the child's transition from cradle to bed; Paventia deflected fear from the child; and Peta attended to its first demands. Agenoria bestowed an active life; Adeona helped it learn to walk. Iterduca and Domiduca watched over it as it left the house for the first time and returned home again. Catius Pater made children clever; Farinus taught children to talk; Fabulinus gave the child its first words; Locutius helped it to form sentences; and Mens provided intelligence.Volumnus made the child want to do good; Numeria was there for counting, Camena for singing; the Muses bestowed an appreciation of the arts, literature and sciences – and so it went on, with a host of *indigitamenta* – spirits – or gods attending every single stage of life and death.

What follows is a list of the most prominent deities with a portfolio involving war to illustrate just how important and pervasive war was in the life and afterlife of the Roman man and woman.

The consequences of not fulfilling the correct observances before a battle could be dire, as an incident before the Battle of Drepana, near the modern Trapani, in 249 BCE during the First Punic War clearly shows.

The Romans, led by the consuls Publius Claudius Pulcher and Lucius Junius Pullus, laid siege to Lilybaeum – but to no avail. Leading a small flotilla, Hannibal (son of Hamilcar) broke the siege by day and replenished the garrison by night. Indeed, the only real consequence of the now-humiliated Roman efforts was to encourage the Carthaginians to rebuild their fleet. Claudius then attacked Drepana, the site of the Punic shipyards. Adherbal, the Carthaginian commander, headed out of the harbour, and when Claudius saw this he ordered his fleet to head for the open sea. The result was a Roman naval calamity of massive proportions, with multiple collisions and total confusion. The Romans were exposed along the shoreline; Adherbal captured ninety-three of Claudius' vessels and their crews. The remaining thirty Roman ships, under Junius Pullus, were attacked by the Carthaginian admiral Carthalo and driven onto rocks off Cape Passaro, where they were wrecked in a strengthening gale. However, not to be outdone, Pullus assailed lofty Eryx by land, taking the fortress and with it its strategic importance. Nevertheless, Lucius Iunius Pullus committed suicide rather than returning to Rome in disgrace. The war-weary Romans had, for the time being, gone as far as they could – militarily and financially.

In his *De Natura Deorum*, Cicero tells us that the defeat was due to Claudius' disrespect for the pre-battle auspices. The sacred chickens refused to eat the grain – a terrible omen which indicated that the gods were clearly not in favour of a battle. In a foolish bid to calm his frightened crew, Claudius unceremoniously threw the chickens overboard, pronouncing: '*bibant, quoniam esse nolunt*' ('Let them drink, since they won't eat'). Claudius survived the battle, but not the aftermath; he returned to Rome in disgrace and was charged with treason; not for his ineptitude, but for his sacrilege in the chicken incident. He was exiled.

Aius Locutius

Aius Locutius, or Aius Loquens, was a Roman deity, or *numen*, very specifically associated with the Gallic invasions of Rome during the early fourth century BCE. The legend reveals that a Roman plebeian named M. Caedicius heard a supernatural-sounding voice one night coming from Vesta's sacred grove, at the foot of the Palatine Hill. This voice warned him of an imminent Gaulish attack, recommended that the walls of Rome be fortified and instructed him to pass these messages on to the tribune of the plebs. This crucial divine intelligence fell on deaf ears, though, because of the messenger's humble station. Consequently, the Gauls stormed and burned the city (*c.* 391 BCE). The Gauls pressed on to Rome. The Romans now ignominiously barricaded themselves in the citadel on the Capitol, under the command of Marcus Manlius Capitolinus. The rest of the city was wide open and undefended, as it was fortified only with a ditch and a wall made from turf. The Gauls, astonished at the absence of security or viable defence and fearing a trap, were eventually able to sack and plunder at will. Livy paints a picture of abject misery among the older non-combatant men, and lamentations from the women, who were denied a place on the Capitol. Excavations have revealed contemporary scorch marks in the Forum and on the Palatine, which indicate extensive burning in Rome around this time. Groups of poorer citizens left the city for the surrounding countryside, rather like the city-dwellers of British cities during the Blitz: the so-called 'trekkers', who each left their homes and took refuge in the country in the late afternoon to avoid that night's German incendiaries and high-explosive bombs.

When the Gauls retreated, an embarrased Senate built a temple and altar known as Ara Aius Locutius, or Ara Saepta, to propitiate the unknown deity they had indirectly snubbed.

Bellona

Bellona, the goddess of war, is often recognizable by her helmet, along with other accoutrements of conflict: sword, spear or shield. She is frequently brandishing a bloody torch or whip as she hurtles into battle in a four-horse war chariot.[1] The main reason for worshipping Bellona was to inculcate a warlike spirit and war frenzy, which no enemy could resist. It was for this reason, in 296 BCE during the war against the Samnites, that Appius Claudius dedicated the first temple of Bellona, which was erected in the Campus

Martius close to the Circus Flaminius. Her annual festival was celebrated on 3 June.[2]

Varro tells us that she was originally named Duellona in various Italic languages,[3] a cult figure deriving from an ancient Sabine goddess of war and linked with Nerio, the sister or wife of the war god Mars – and later with her Greek equivalent Enyo. We can gauge how odious and savage Bellona was by glimpsing at Enyo: Enyo was the goddess of war and calamitous destruction, partner of the war god Ares. She is also his sister Eris, and a daughter of Zeus and Hera.[4] She is the mother of the war god Enyalius, god of soldiers and warriors, by Ares.[5] The wholesale destruction of cities was Enyo's speciality; she is 'supreme in war'[6] and a frequent fighter alongside Ares.[7] Quintus Smyrnaeus describes her in his *The Fall of Troy* (8, 286ff):

'Deadly Enyo talked through the midst [of the battle] her shoulders and her hands blood-splashed, while fearful sweat streamed from her limbs. Revelling in equal fight, she aided none, lest Thetis' or Ares' wrath be stirred.'

Bellona's priests, known as Bellonarii, ritually self-harmed, wounding their own arms or legs, and either offered up the blood or drank it themselves in order to become inspired with a belligerent zeal. Traditionally, this ritual took place on 24 March – the day of blood (*dies sanguinis*), called so after the ceremony.

Bellona enjoyed significant importance in Roman diplomacy and in the protocol regarding the declaration of war. When diplomacy failed and war was the only remaining option, the chief *Fetial* priest was then empowered to declare war within thirty-three days; after ratification by the Senate and the people, the two adversaries would officially be at war, as sanctioned by the gods. A sacred spear was then ceremoniously hurled into the enemy's territory to delimit their power (*indictio belli*). In 270 BCE, a special location, near the Temple of Bellona in the Campus Martius, was reserved for the spear hurling. The Campus Martius was outside the city's gates near the Circus Flaminius and the temple of Apollo: envoys from foreign states, who were not allowed to enter the city proper, stayed here. The area around the Temple of Bellona symbolized foreign soil, enemy territory, and there the Senate met with ambassadors and received victorious generals before their triumphs. It was here, too, that Roman Senate meetings relating to foreign war were held. The war column (*columna bellica*), which represented the frontier of Rome, was adjacent to the temple. To declare war on a foreign state, a javelin was hurled over the column by one of the *Fetiales*, from Roman territory toward the direction of the enemy land, and this symbolic attack was considered the beginning of war.[8]

Aptly, the Temple of Bellona was near where Sulla, as dictator, carried out the massacre of 6,000 or so Roman citizens who had surrendered after the Battle of the Colline Gate in 82 BCE: 'just a few senators who I have ordered to be dealt with' is how Sulla glibly described his atrocity. Although Sulla suffered an unexpected heavy reverse on his left flank, he won the day in a narrow victory when the Samnites and the Marian army both collapsed: more than 50,000 troops died that day. Sulla systematically murdered what was left of the opposition and emerged as the undisputed master of Rome.[9]

Three thousand Marian troops were taken prisoner, while another 3,000 surrendered; all were imprisoned on the Campus Martius until executed. Their corpses were thrown into the Tiber, which became clogged with bodies – an estimated 10,000 men perished in this way. After the revolutionary actions of Marius and Sulla, the Republic was in constitutional tatters.

In Roman poetry, the name 'Bellona' is usually a synonym for war, although in Statius' *Thebaid* she is fleshed out as a character, representing the destructive and belligerent aspect of war, and, as we have seen, brandishing a spear and flaming torch or riding in a chariot and waving a blood-stained sword. In Gaius Valerius Flaccus' *Argonautica*, she is described as 'Bellona with bare flank, her brazen weapons clanging as she moved' (3, 60). Louis Jean François Lagrenée's 'Bellona Presenting the Reins of his Horses to Mars' (1766) illustrates a speech from Claudian's *In Rufinum* where Mars requests, 'Let Bellona bring my helmet and Terror guide the reins' (*'Fer galleam Bellona mihi, nexusque rotarum tende pavor'*).

While never an actual character in Shakespeare's plays, Bellona is mentioned several times: in *Henry IV, Part I*, Hotspur describes her as 'the fire-eyed maid of smoky war' (IV.i.119); in *The Two Noble Kinsmen*, Hippolyta's sister will solicit her divine aid for Theseus against Thebes (I.iii.13). In *Macbeth*, Macbeth is introduced as a violent and brave warrior when the Thane of Ross calls him 'Bellona's bridegroom' (I.ii.54), that is, the equivalent of Mars.

Bellona features in much more art, sculpture and architecture, particularly in war memorials. The Bellona on the First World War victory archway at Waterloo station is especially poignant, depicting as it does not the dead, but the forgotten living victims of war cowering and grieving beneath the demonic sword-brandishing wraith with her gorgon necklace.

Castor and Pollux

After an eventful, dashing and daring career in Greek mythology – which took in the hunting down of the Calydonian Boar, signing up to the crew of Jason's ship, the *Argo*, rescuing their sister Helen from the clutches of Theseus and thus indirectly causing the Trojan War, and some light cattle raiding – the Spartan Dioscuri moved seamlessly into Roman mythology from about the fifth century BCE.

The Battle of Lake Regillus (296 BCE) was a decisive encounter between Rome and cities of the Latin League who had come together under Tarquinius Superbus to form an alliance against Rome; it also marked the last of Tarquinius' futile attempts to restore his monarchy. The lake was close to what is now Pontano Secco, near Frascati. The Latins were led by Tarquinius' son-in-law, Octavius Mamilius of Tusculum, and by the nonagenarian Tarquinius, who had turned to the League now that the Etruscans had been defeated. The Romans were led by Aulus Postumius Albus Regillensis, who had been appointed dictator to quell the Latin threat; his *magister equitum* was Titus Aebutius Elva. By dispatching his personal cavalry force to cut the deserters down, Postumius rallied the Roman forces which were fleeing the battle. The Romans turned and attacked the Latins with the help of the cavalry, who dismounted and assisted their comrades on foot. Postumius then set an important tactical precedent when he hurled a Roman standard into the midst of the enemy, where it was to be retrieved by a fervid and frenzied horde of Romans. The Latins fled, with the loss of 30,000 men.[10]

Ending the threat of a return to monarchism once and for all as it did, the Battle of Lake Regillus lived long in the memories of the Romans, so much so that it was imbued with divinity. Legend has it that the Dioscuri, Castor and Pollux, rode to the aid of the Romans during the battle; afterwards they called in at Rome and paused to water their horses at the Fountain of Juturna (in Virgil, Juturna is the sister of Turnus) in the Forum, and announced the victory to the anxious Romans congregating there for news. A temple was built on the spot and dedicated in 484 BCE.

In 168 BCE, the boys were back to perform another epiphany: Cicero (*Natura Deorum* 3, 5, 11–12) and Valerius Maximus (1, 8, 1) tell how Publius Vatinius, a farmer, was on his way to Rome late one night when he bumped into the Dioscuri. They asked him to convey to the Senate the news of the victory by commander Lucius Aemilius Paullus over Persius, king of Macedon, at the Battle of Pydna. Vatinius did so, but all he got for his troubles was imprisonment for disrespecting the Senate with his alleged gossip (*fabellae*), which was strongly suspected to be fake news. However, when the victory was confirmed by Aemilius Paullus, Vatinius was released and rewarded with land. The twins were also said to have watered their horses at the very same fountain in the Forum as they had after Lake Regillus.

When the original 484 BCE temple burnt down, a new temple was built on the site in the first century BCE. The temple was a huge structure measuring 32 × 50 metres and reaching a height of almost 19 metres. The facades had eight Corinthian columns, whilst the sides each had eleven. The temple served as the office of weights and measures, and as a bank. Three of its tall columns still stand in all their splendour today. At the same time, Augustus salvaged what had become a lapsing cult and made the cult of Castor and Pollux officially imperial, associating his heirs with the twins and initiating a new feast day for the pair on 27 January.[11] Tables of food were set out in these temples (*theoxenia*) and in private homes, and offered to guests and travellers in an attempt to gain favour from the twins. There was also a temple dedicated to the Dioscuri in Rome's Circus Flaminius, and there were temples at Assisi, Cori, Naples and Tusculum. There were springs of Juturnum at Lavinium and a temple of the Dioscuru at Ardea close by. Today, the twins proudly stand sentinel either side of the steps leading up to the Capitoline Museums in Rome. Each stands by his horse, and although much restored in the sixteenth century, they incorporate fragments found at the site of the Temple of Castor and Pollux in the Forum.

The contribution the Dioscuri made to the victory was celebrated every year, with the Romans making the most of the twins' symbolic connection with the Roman equites and cavalry. Each year on 15 July, the feast day of the Dioskouroi, 5,000 or so young men would be led by two impersonators of the heroes through the streets of Rome in a great military spectacle in which each rider wore full military dress complete with any decorations won. This was the *Transvectio equitum* (review of the cavalry). Dionysius of Halicarnassus (6, 13) states that the procession began at the Temple of Mars situated along the Via Appia, some 2km outside the Porta Capena. The procession paused at the Temple of Castor and Pollux in the Forum Romanum before continuing on to the Temple of Iuppiter Optimus Maximus on the Capitoline Hill.

Honos

Honos, the god of chivalry, honour, military justice and virtue, was closely linked with Virtus, the goddess of manliness and bravery; the two are often seen together. Honos is typically shown wearing a chaplet of bay leaves, while Virtus is identified by her helmet.

In 234 BCE, Quintus Fabius Maximus Verrucosus (later the Cunctator – scourge of Hannibal) dedicated a temple to Honos just outside the Porta Capena, one of Rome's main gates, after his victory over the Ligures. In 246, after Marcus Claudius Marcellus defeated and slew the Gallic king, Viridomarus, at the Battle of Clastidium to win the *spolia opima*, he vowed a temple to Honos and Virtus. The 'spoils of honour' were the arms taken by a general who killed an enemy chief in single combat; this was the third and last time this happened in Roman history.

Another temple to Honos and Virtus was built by Gaius Marius during his fifth consulship in 101 BCE, using the booty he had captured from the Cimbri and the Teutones. The shrine was probably built on the Velia, near Marius' house on the Via Sacra.

Juno

She qualifies as a goddess of war through her dogged and persistent harrying of Aeneas on his journey from the wreckage of Troy. Juno is unequivocally martial in the role she plays in the attempted derailing of Aeneas and his mission to found Rome. She is the patron goddess of Rome, the mother of war deities Mars and Bellona; Queen of the gods, she also looks after women and is goddess of love and marriage, so in this capacity Hera is her Greek equivalent.

In the *Aeneid*, Juno bears Aeneas and the Trojans a monumental grudge, which manifests itself throughout the poem as she tries ceaselessly to thwart Aeneas. Juno had remained implacable after the insult meted out to her when Paris overlooked her in the divine beauty contest in favour of Aphrodite. Juno vehemently favoured Carthage and Dido, both slighted and prophetically doomed to destruction by Aeneas and his historical descendants. Virgil wrote:

'This town, they say, was Juno's favourite dwelling, preferred to all lands … here were her weapons, her chariot … she cherished the aim that this should be, if fate allowed, the mother city of all nations.'

By Juno's way of thinking, if you stopped Aeneas then the city of Rome would never be established – Carthage would achieve its destiny and control the Mediterranean. She also supported Turnus and the Rutulians in the fighting against Aeneas in Italy. She is, then, a prime, cruel and avid mover of war, a major dynamic force in stoking the *arma* (arms) and confounding the *vir* (man) that are, of course, the themes underpinning Virgil's poem.

Right from the start of his odyssey, Aeneas' progress is compromised by this persistent and antagonistic Juno. She makes a dramatic entrance into the action when she persuades Aeolus to raise a storm to blow Aeneas, literally and figuratively, off course (1, 50ff). She conspires to have lovesick Dido detain him in Carthage (Book 4) and arranges for the scuttling of the Trojan fleet (5, 680ff) to try to get a marooned Aeneas to found his homeland in Sicily, not Italy. Luckily, Jupiter and rain save the day. By Book 7, Juno has accepted Fate and restates her determination to at least delay Aeneas (313–16). She possesses Amata through Alecto and turns her against Aeneas and his desire to marry Lavinia; and she inspires Juturna to save the life of Turnus, her brother and Aeneas' enemy.

Juno exhibits a number of other associations with war. She was celebrated on 1 March each year, as this was the birthday of Romulus and also the date of the peaceful alliance of Romans and Sabine peoples through treaty and marriage after their war, a conflict which, as we shall see, was ended by the intervention of women.

As Juno Caprotina, Juno was centre stage in the festival of the Nonae Caprotinae, which took place on 7 July and was exclusively celebrated by and for women, particularly female slaves. They ran about punching each other and hitting themselves with rods. Obscene language was much in evidence, and finally a male goat was sacrificed to Juno Caprotina under a wild fig tree. One derivation has it that, after the damaging siege by the Gauls in the fourth century BCE, the dictator of the Latins, Livius Postumius from Fidenae, demanded from the Roman Senate that the *matronae* and daughters of the most prominent families be surrendered to the Latins as hostages on threat of destroying the vulnerable and weakened city. An inspired slave-woman, Tutela, along with other slave-women dressed as *matronae*, approached the enemy forces and, pretending to be out on a hen night and to be the wives and daughters of Roman families, got the Latins drunk. When the soldiers were sleeping it off, the slave-girls relieved them of their weapons and Tutela climbed a fig tree (*caproficus*) – a symbol of fertility – to wave a brand, signalling the Romans to attack. The women were rewarded with their freedom and a dowry at public expense.

Martianus Minneus Felix Capella, a Latin prose writer (fl. *c.* 410–420 CE), believes that as Juno Curitis, Juno must be invoked by those who are involved in war: *Curitim debent memorare bellantes*. Juno Curitis had a temple, fittingly, on the Campus Martius.[12]

We can recognize more martial characteristics in Juno as Juno Moneta, the Warner. Her temple on the Capitol was dedicated in 348 BCE by the dictator L. Furius Camillus during a war against the Aurunci, although the origins of the cult and of the temple were much more ancient. The sacred geese of the Capitol lived in her temple: they are recorded in the episode of the ultimately successful Gallic siege (*c.* 396–390 BCE) by Livy, so the temple would have existed before Furius' dedication.[13] The Gauls blockaded Rome for seven months, finally gaining victory when the Romans surrendered in the face of impending starvation. Luckily for Rome, the Gauls were more interested in revenge and financial gain than the domination of Italy, slaying or enslaving the population. They were accordingly paid off in gold, and promptly returned to their lands in the north.

This episode, embarrassing and shameful to the Romans, was soon embellished and larded with fictional anecdotes to mitigate the reality of the disaster and rebuild Roman pride with *exempla pietas*, such as in the story of the Vestal Virgins and the handcart. This, and the tale of the gold-selling, hair-cutting Roman women, were no doubt invented to highlight the patriotism and *pietas* of the average Roman citizen in times of extreme danger.

To these we can add more propagandist stories. In the first, the Gauls came across Rome's venerable senators defiantly sitting in their ivory chairs. In what amounts to a kind of *devotio*, they stoically awaited their inevitable doom in full regalia, resplendent with their military decorations and former badges of office. The Gauls were initially impressed, but later slew them all. In the second – and this is where Juno's sacred geese come in – the Roman defenders would have been caught off-guard by the Gauls (before the city fell) had it not been for an alert and vociferous flock of geese whose warning enabled Manlius to repel the attackers.[14]

As Sospita, Juno is portrayed as an armed deity. She was invoked all over Latium, and particularly at Lanuvium, originally as a saviour of women and as the protector of those in confinement – pregnant women awaiting the impending birth of their child – but this eventually extended to saviour of the state. At the beginning of the battle against the Insubrians in 197 BCE, the consul Gaius Cornelius Cethegus vowed a temple to Juno the Saviour, or Juno Matuta, in the Forum Holitorium if the enemy should be routed. The soldiers shouted out that they would make his prayer come true.[15] This forum was a marketplace (*macellum*) for vegetables, herbs and oil. It was outside the Porta Carmentalis in the Campus Martius, between the Forum Boarium (Cattle Market) and buildings located in the Circus Flaminius. A temple had been dedicated to Matuta at Rome by King Servius Tullius, destroyed in 506 BCE and rebuilt by Marcus Furius Camillus in 396. Livy makes frequent references to a temple of Matuta at Satricum.[16]

Julius Obsequens tells us that in 90 BCE:

> 'Metella Caecilia said that she learned in a dream that Juno the Saviour had fled from her temple because it had been polluted by filth, and that only with the greatest difficulty was the goddess persuaded by Metella's prayers to return: women had desecrated Juno's temple with an obscene and sordid business [prostitution], and a dog gave birth to a litter of pups and had even made her home at the base of Juno's statue. Metella restored the temple to its original splendour after it was purified with prayers of adoration.'[17].

Jupiter Dolichenus and the Hand of God

In 2018 archaeologists discovered a hand-shaped Roman artifact described as the 'hand of God' near Hadrian's Wall in the north of England. It is made of solid bronze weighing 2.3 kilos and is believed to be related to Severus's campaign as a tribute to a god of war as the Romans launched a brutal invasion of Scotland in AD 209–210. The bronze hand was probably buried in a boggy area close to a Roman fort at Vindolanda shortly after the end of the conflict. Archaeologists say that the child-sized hand was probably buried as part of a religious ritual to mark the completion of a temple dedicated to the god close by. The hand is associated with a Roman god of Middle Eastern origin called Jupiter Dolichenus – a mystery cult popular with the Roman military. Such hands were often mounted on the top of a pole – and used to bless worshippers during religious rituals. The 4-inch hand originally had an attachment, now missing, that was inserted into the palm. The earliest datable evidence for the Roman cult is an inscription (CIL VIII, 2680) from Lambaesis in Numidia where the commander of Roman troops and de facto governor dedicated an altar in AD 125. Jupiter Dolichenus was typically depicted holding a thunderbolt in his hand with upraised arm signifying his destructive power. The open hand also symbolizes protection and well-being.

'The discovery of Jupiter Dolichenus' bronze hand, deposited as a thanksgiving offering, demonstrates just how serious the conflict was and how relieved the Roman soldiers were that it had ended,' says Andrew Birley, director of the Vindolanda excavations. 'It is further evidence illustrating how deeply religious they were and how seriously they took their relationship with their god.'

Of the nineteen temples dedicated to Dolichenus discovered so far, significantly, only the two in Rome are not sited at frontier settlements like Vindolanda; they include Syria, Ukraine, Germany, Austria, Hungary and Slovakia. Of the 260 devotees named in votive inscriptions, 97 are for soldiers. In CIL XIV, 110 from Ostia Antica, an inscription from around AD 186, an entire naval unit – a detachment of the fleet at Misenum – is named as dedicator. Several votive tablets include depictions of military standards and war trophies.

Lua

Lua was the goddess to whom soldiers gave up captured weapons. She sometimes goes by the name of 'Lua Mater' or 'Lua Saturni', the latter of which may make her a consort of Saturn. She also has connections with sowing, plague (on plants and on man) and burning, as in battle. Lua was also a protector of the city of Rome, but this function always went unspoken as it was prohibited to mention Lua's name: Lua was the ineffable goddess.

Mars

The Roman god of war, and an equivalent of sorts to Ares. We have noted how Mars began life as a god of agriculture, and that this elided into a martial role as the Romans became more belligerent and expansionist – their agricultural endeavours being replaced, to some extent, by service in the army.

We have seen, too, how the Greek god Ares was something of a buffoon, much despised and mocked by his Olympian colleagues and prone to uncontrolled atrocity on the battlefield. Mars, on the other hand, was much more measured in his conduct. Second only to Jupiter, Mars was the 'go-to god' for soldiers in the field; he was most in demand in March, the month named for him (*Martius*), and in October, which marked the end of the military campaigning season, and the beginning of the farming season. The first festival was actually on 27 February, with the first *Equirria*; then there was the *feriae Marti* festival, held on 1 March (the old New Year's Day), the second *Equirria* on the 14th, the *agonium Martiale* on the 17th, the *Quinquatrus* on the 19th and the *Tubilustrium* on 23 March and again on 23 May. The *Armilustrium* came on 19 October, which saw the purification of arms before they were stowed for the winter, and the Equus October on the 15th, which entailed a horse race: the prize for the unlucky winning horse was immediate sacrifice and decapitation – the head being vied for by the residents of the Saburra and the via Sacra. The Salii priesthood resumed their dancing (*arma ancilia movent*), *ancilia* being ancient shields fashioned in the figure-eight.

These festivals were clearly related to war and the instruments of warfare. The *Tubilustrium* in the Atrium Sutorium involved a series of rites to cleanse trumpets, whilst the *Equirria* was to ensure the wellbeing of the horses when on campaign. Another important ritual was performed by the commander of the army about to depart, who shook the sacred spears of Mars which were kept in the Regia. The general shouted '*Mars vigilia*' and requested a swift and easy victory.

As might be expected, Mars' altar was in the Campus Martius (named after the god); it was dedicated by Numa, the pacifist-leaning semi-legendary second king of Rome. It was, then, originally located outside the sacred boundary of Rome (the *pomerium*), but Augustus made the god centre stage when he established the Temple of Mars Ultor in his new Forum Augustum in 2 BCE. The previous altar in the Campus Martius was built to fulfil a vow made by Titus Quinctius in 388 BCE during the Gallic siege of Rome.[18]

When Augustus built his new temple for Mars Ultor, the 'Avenger', it was revenge for the murder of Julius Caesar, his great uncle, as won by the defeat of the assassins of Caesar at Philippi in 42 BCE, and for the military disaster at Carrhae in 53 BCE, when the Parthians captured precious Roman standards. When some of these standards were recovered, they were housed in the new temple. The date of the temple's dedication, 12 May, was aligned with the heliacal setting of the constellation Scorpio, the sign of war. The god is shown wearing a cuirass and helmet, and standing in a martial pose, leaning on a lance he holds in his right hand. He holds a shield (*ancile*) in his left hand. The *ancile* was his sacred shield. Legend says that this shield fell from heaven during the rule of Pompilius, and that while the shield remained in the city, Rome would be safe and the mistress of the world. The Salii were commissioned to protect the shield, and eleven exact copies were made on the advice of the nymph Egeria, reportedly to fox potential thieves.

Mars rode a chariot drawn by appropriately named fire-breathing horses. The names were Aithon (red fire), Phlogios (flame), Konabos (the din of battle) and Phobos (fear). The goddess Ultio, a divine personification of vengeance, had an altar and golden statue in his temple. The new temple became the departure point for magistrates as they left for military campaigns abroad. Augustus also had the Senate convene at the temple when deliberating questions of war and peace.

Mars is at the very epicentre of Roman foundation mythology: as we know, he was the father of Romulus and Remus by Rhea Silvia, and he was amorously involved with Venus, who was the divine mother of Aeneas, the

Trojan refugee who 'founded' Rome several generations before Romulus built the city walls.

The synergy between the twin roles in agriculture and war can be seen when the priesthood of the Arval Brothers called on Mars to repel 'rust' (*lues*), which can mean both wheat fungus and the red oxides that affect metal; a threat, therefore, to both iron farm implements and to weaponry. To the Arval Brothers (in the surviving text of their hymn), Mars is described as as *ferus*, 'savage' or 'feral' like a wild animal. The Arval Brothers (*Fratres Arvales*, 'Brothers of the Fields') were a body of priests who offered annual sacrifices to the Lares and gods to guarantee good harvests.

Two of the three animals associated with Mars are connected to the foundation myth and sustained Romulus and Remus, sons of Mars: the woodpecker (*picus*) brought food for the twins when they were exposed, and the she–wolf (*lupa*) suckled them. The woodpecker was revered by the Latin peoples, who would not eat its flesh; it was one of the most important birds in Roman and Italic augury. The wolf appears in a statue group on the Appian Way with Mars, and at the Battle of Sentinum in 295 BCE, the appearance of the wolf of Mars (*Martius lupus*) was a sign that Roman victory was in the offing.[19] The third animal of significance to Mars is the bear.

A temple to Mars was built around 133 BCE in the Circus Flaminius, paid for by Decimus Junius Brutus Callaicus from war booty. It housed a huge statue of the god and a nude Venus.[20] A large statue of Mars was part of the short–lived Arch of Nero, which was built in 62 CE but dismantled after Nero's suicide and disgrace as part of his *damnatio memoriae*.

Just as Jupiter wields the lightning bolt, Neptune the trident and Saturn the scythe or sickles, so the defining emblem of Mars is the spear. A relic called 'the spear of Mars' was kept in a *sacrarium* at the Regia, the former residence of the kings of Rome. It was said to tremble or vibrate at impending war or any other danger to the state, for example before the assassination of Julius Caesar.[21] When Mars is pictured as a peace-bringer, his spear is wreathed with laurel or other vegetation, as on the Ara Pacis or a coin of Aemilianus.

The high priest of Mars was the Flamen Martialis, one of the three major priests in the fifteen-member college of *flamens*. Mars was also served by the Salii, a twelve-member priesthood of patrician youths who dressed as Bronze Age warriors and danced a kind of war dance around the city on 1, 9 and 23 March.

Mars Gradivus was popular with soldiers wishing to swear an oath to be brave, sure-footed and victorious in battle.[22] His temple outside the Porta Capena was a muster point for armies. The archaic priesthood of Mars

Gradivus was the Salii, the 'leaping priests' who danced ritually in armour as a prelude to war.

Statius calls Mars Gradivus 'the most implacable of the gods',[23] while Valerius Maximus ends his history by invoking Mars Gradivus as 'author and support of the name "Roman"':[24] Gradivus is asked – along with Capitoline Jupiter and Vesta, as the keeper of Rome's perpetual flame – to 'guard, preserve, and protect' the state of Rome, the peace and the *princeps* (the emperor Tiberius at the time) .

Mars Quirinus was the guardian of the *Quirites* ('citizens' or 'civilians'), as divided into *curiae* (citizen assemblies), whose oaths were required to make a treaty. As a guarantor of treaties, Mars Quirinus is thus a god of peace: 'When he rampages, Mars is called Gradivus, but when he's at peace Quirinus.'[25] The deified Romulus was identified with Mars Quirinus.

Mars Pater is one of the gods invoked in a *devotio*, by means of which a general sacrificed himself to secure a Roman victory, as Decius Mus, for example.

Minerva

While primarily goddess of wisdom, medicine, music, arts and crafts, Minerva did have a responsibility for strategic warfare, although this was a fairly low-key duty for the Romans. She was, however, associated with the Quinquatrus festival of 19 March, which, as noted, celebrated the opening of the army's new campaigning season.[26] Ovid alludes to her martial aspect at *Fasti* 3, 5–8, 175–76 and 675–96.

Mithras

Mithraism was a mystery religion centred on the god Mithras that was practised in the Roman Empire from the first to the fourth century CE. The religion was inspired by Persian Zoroastrianism worship of the god Mithra. Mithras was eternally at war with the forces of evil. According to legend, he captured a bull – symbolic of primeval force and vitality – and slew it in a cave, to release its concentrated power for the good of mankind. Mithraism offered an escape from darkness into light, but required in return a lifelong commitment, hence its popularity with the military, whose commitment to the army or navy was often lifelong. Also, Mithraism was based on mutual interest, friendship and intimacy; the standard temple, the Mithraeum, accommodated only small groups, in semi-clandestine conditions. These characteristics would appeal to soldiers as they provided close camaraderie and a degree of safety when death was always just round the corner.

Mithraism offered an escape from darkness into light but required in return a lifelong commitment; it offered fraternity and was a clubbish benefit society with inspirational ideals which embraced duty, *pietas*, endurance and self-discipline – hence its popularity with the military; soldiers were, of course, predisposed to aspire to similar qualities.

Mithraic temples were typically small, gloomy, semi-subterranean structures, intended to evoke the legendary cave where Mithras killed the bull. Inside, secret ceremonies would be followed by ritual feasts, the devotees reclining on benches (*podia*) running along the side walls. In York (Eboracum), the cult of Mithras features on a sculpture showing Mithras characteristically slaying a bull and in a dedication to Arimanius, the god of evil in the Mithraism tradition. The Mithraic relief found in 1747 near St Martin-cum-Gregory Church in Micklegate, York, could suggest the existence of a temple to Mithras in the centre of the *colonia*.

The substantial inscriptional evidence for Mithraism comes to us largely from soldiers, of all ranks, imperial officials, slaves and freedmen – just the sort of people who would be looking to improve their chances of survival in the field or at the imperial court, or who may have invoked the god in the hope of quick promotion.

Nerio

Nerio, warrior goddess and personification of valour, was the consort of Mars. She represents the vital force (*vis*), power (*potentia*) and majesty (*maiestas*) of Mars. Her name is Sabine in origin and is equivalent to the Latin *virtus*, 'manly virtue' (from *vir*, 'man').

Quirinus

Quirinus was an early Roman god of some importance whose name may come from the Sabine word *quiris*, 'spear thrower', probably making him a Sabine god of war. By the end of the first century BCE, Quirinus was synonymous with Romulus and before that with Mars. He also has associations with the Greek Enyalios, an epithet of Ares.

According to Suetonius, Julius Caesar made contemptuous use of the term *Quirites* (*Life of Caesar*, 70) to berate soldiers who had revolted; Roman citizens who were drafted into the army, *cives* who had become *milites*, remained *Quirites*. The ancient formula used to mobilize the army quoted by Varro (*De lingua Latina* 6, 88) refers to *Quirites pedites armatos*, or 'Quirites footsoldiers', and thus retained a link to Quirinus.

Victoria

The personification of victory, Victoria was equivalent to the Greek goddess Nike. She owes her origins to the Sabine agricultural goddess Vacuna, and had a temple on the Palatine Hill. The goddess Vica Pota (deriving from *vincendi atque potiundi*, 'conquering and gaining mastery') was also identified with Victoria.[27]

Victoria played a major part in Roman society and religion, with a plethora of temples erected in her honour. When Gratianus removed her statue in 382 CE, it caused much anger in Rome.[28] Victoria was routinely worshipped by triumphant generals returning from war.

Victoria also had an existential role: she was a symbol of victory over death and determined who would be successful during war. Winged Victory figures, usually in pairs, were common in Roman iconography, typically hovering high and filling spaces in spandrels or other gaps in architecture, especially triumphal arches. They continued to appear after the Christianization of the Empire, and slowly mutated into Christian angels.

Augustus had an altar to the goddess Victoria installed in the Senate building, the Curia Julia, with a statue of the winged Victoria, a victoriola, symbolically standing with one foot on a globe. A victoriola was awarded to a victorious general; it symbolized a gift of victory, and was highly prized and prestigious.

Vica Pota

Vica Pota was probably an earlier Roman or Italic form of victory goddess who predated Victoria and was the influence of the Greek Nike. Vica Pota was thus the older equivalent of Victoria.

Virtus

The god of manliness, bravery and military strength, Virtus was the equivalent of the Greek Arete. He was often identified with the Roman god Honos (honour) and was frequently honoured together with him, for example in the Temple of Virtus and Honos at the Porta Capena in Rome itself.

Virtus was essential: men were obliged to demonstrate *virtus*, while women had to display *pudicitia*, sexual propriety and chastity – between the two, the Romans had the glue which bound the family unit together and the wherewithal to produce children, continue the line and stock the army and the labour force and satisfy the demands of 'Romanitas'. *Virtus* was part of that ideal. Virtus the god was a vital player in Roman religion, society and war.

Chapter 3

Wall-to-Wall War & the Fetiales

W hy was it that so many of the major Roman myths involve war
and battles? The answer is that wars and their battles were an
inextricable and constant part of the Roman way of life, from the
traditional foundation in 753 BCE to the fall of the Roman Empire some 1,200
years later. This endless warring is reflected in the number of key myths
which are characterized by war. To fully understand the national importance
and symbolism of these myths, we need to look briefly at Rome's association
with war.

The belligerent Roman state machinery was always integral to and
inseparable from Roman political life; Rome's bellicosity shaped its economy
and defined its society. Josephus, writing in the first century CE, had it that
the Roman people emerged from the womb carrying weapons. Centuries
later, F.E. Adcock echoed these words when he wrote, 'A Roman was half a
soldier from the start, and he would endure a discipline which soon produced
the other half.'[1]

Rome's preoccupation with war, an obsession almost, endured over the
1,200 years of its history and saw Roman armies fighting in and garrisoning
the full extent of its territiories: from Parthia in the east (modern-day Iran)
to Africa (Tunisia) and Aegyptus in the south and as far Britannia in the cold
north-west. The constitution and equipment of the Roman war machine
evolved throughout its long history, from its early days as a citizen militia to
its later status as a professional army. During the Republic, few years passed
by in which there was no conflict: each summer, when the campaigning
season began, an army was raised, consuls – or occasionally dictators – took
command, battles were fought and the army was disbanded at the close of
the fighting year. The myths – and the glory and success they celebrated –
helped explain this, particularly in the new regime under Augustus at a time
when he was striving to herald a new, less warlike dawn.

Warfare, of course, was nothing new in ancient societies. Territorial defence
or expansion, mineral deposits, naked aggression, trade protectionism and
despotism all played their part, long before the Romans, in fuelling wars,
conflict and confrontation. Ovid, in his *Metamorphoses*, writing at the dawn

of Empire, would have us believe that, once upon a time, men were ever true to their word, and that they inhabited a righteous, peaceful world in which laws, punishment, armies and fortifications were superfluous.[2] This golden age, this *aurea aetas*, never existed, of course: violence, wars, and the battles that constitute them, have been as constant and ubiquitous as taxes and death.

Warfare was a fact of life, *the* Roman way of life for most Roman men in the monarchy and early Republic: they would have seen active service at one time or another unless they were of the lowest orders, freedmen or slaves. Back home, women – wives and daughters – would have assumed responsibility for running the farmstead and the household during their husbands' and older sons' increasingly frequent absences at the 'front'. Indeed, the doors of the Temple of Janus in Rome, traditionally closed only during times of peace, remained firmly shut on two occasions only between the reign of Numa Pompilius (Rome's second king after Romulus, 715–673 BCE) and that of Augustus some 600 years later. Livy tells us that the first occasion was soon after the First Punic War during the consulship of Titus Manlius Torquatus in 235 BCE, and the second after Augustus' victory at the Battle of Actium. The rest of the time, the doors gaped resolutely open, announcing that Rome was fighting a war somewhere or other with someone or other. The temple was a visible, eloquent sign of Rome's pugnacious character, ironic in that its construction was one of Numa's first acts when he re-established his city on peaceful religious and forensic grounds, in direct contrast to its warlike origins. Uniquely almost, Numa himself was able to keep the doors closed for the duration of his reign. He clearly saw the civilizing benefits of protracted peace: his successors, though, throughout monarchy, the Republic and Empire, were to civilize more often than not through force of arms.

Roman warfare, then, was inextricably linked with Roman politics, society and economics: land and the Conflict of the Orders were, in the earlier years of the Republic, constant soundtracks to the prosecution of wars. Returns on his land gave the soldier the economic wherewithal to qualify for service and to pay for his armour and weapons. The Conflict of the Orders ran from 494–287 BCE, a 200-year struggle by the plebeians to win political equality. The *secessio plebis* was a powerful bargaining tool with which the plebeians effectively closed Rome down and let the patricians get on with it: the Roman equivalent to a general strike. The first *secessio* in 494 BCE saw the lower orders withdrawing military support during the wars with the Aequi, Sabines and Volsci.

Servius Tullius, Rome's sixth king (578–535 BCE), fought successful campaigns against the Veii and the Etruscans. He is often thought to have taken the first steps in militarizing Rome when he divided the citizenship into wealth groups – their status in the army being determined by what weapons and armour they could afford to buy, with the richest serving in the cavalry. While this is unlikely to be the case, Servius was responsible for a far-reaching shift in the organization of the Roman army: he moved the emphasis from cavalry to infantry, and with it came the inevitable change in battlefield tactics which was to serve Rome well for years to come. Servius is also credited with the organization of the army into centuries and the concomitant formation of the political assemblies, highlighting the inextricable link between Roman politics and the Roman military; his ground-breaking census presumably had the purpose of establishing who was fit, physically and economically, to serve in the Roman Army.[3] It is no accident that the census was held at the Campus Martius – home of military training and the meeting place of the centuriate assembly. Eligibility extended from age 17 to 46 (*iuniores*) and 47 to 60 (*seniores*) – the latter usually forming a kind of home guard. By the second half of the second century BCE, there was anything between 380,000 and 480,000 men under arms – three-quarters of whom were *iuniores*. The Second Punic War saw the army at its greatest strength, with twenty-two legions on hand, each comprising on average 4,200 infantry and 200 cavalry.

Military service demonstrated patriotism, *pietas* and responsibility. It was also prestigious, offering the soldier's *gens* and the family palpable opportunities for glory that were visible in decorations, citations, prizes and – the pinnacle of them all – a triumph processing through the celebrating streets of Rome. Moreover, military service allowed the proud and patriotic Roman to demonstrate his *virtus*, his bravery and virtue. Glory and kudos were boosted by the complex system of decorations, *dona militaria*, and rewards that was established to reflect military success. Discipline and loyalty were also strengthened by a tangible and noticeable array of benefits, which included elevation to the rank of centurion, where, after Marius, the pay was double that of the common soldier and the booty share sizeably bigger. Gratuities, pay rises, better rations, settlement land for veterans and promotion all contributed, as did social mobility for the common soldier and political success for the elite. Make no mistake, though, the average pay for the average soldier or sailor was niggardly. He could earn three times more doing manual labour, at twelve asses per day; it took until the time of Julius Caesar for a soldier's remuneration to be raised to ten asses per day in 49 BCE. Pay was probably introduced around 406 BCE after the wars with the

Veii, but it was never meant to provide a living wage – rather, it was more of a contribution to the cost of food, equipment and clothing. Increasingly, booty provided the financial answer.

The Roman war machine, of course, needed to be constantly fuelled with new recruits, a fact which in itself created something of a vicious circle. By the end of the third century BCE, approximately one-third of Italians south of Rome had been subdued and were Roman citizens. Consequently, they were eligible for military service, and these were supported by troops supplied by allies, often as auxiliary forces. However, the casualties sustained in war after bloody war often meant that Rome had to keep on conquering if it was to maintain that steady supply of recruits to keep its forces up to strength. Also, it was commonly felt amongst more conservative Romans that a cessation of conflict encouraged laxity and moral decay amongst the menfolk of Rome.

Religion, morals and ethics played an influential part in the prosecution of Roman war. Cicero provides the first surviving attempt by a Roman to give moral justification to and rules for conduct in a just war, *iura belli*, in his *De Officiis*. Livy also details various criteria: these include keeping one's word of honour, *fides*, with allies; retaliatory action when that *fides* is not reciprocated; and maintaining security, *salus*, when boundaries and territory are threatened by hostile forces. A three-stage procedure had to be performed before a war could be deemed just: the war had to be declared (*denuntio*); a formal warning had to delivered (*indictio*); and reparations had to be sought (*rerum repetitio*) by a delegation of four *Fetiales*, or *Oratores*. Declarations of war were the responsibility of the *Fetiales*, whose involvement introduced a religious element to the business of war. These twenty priests were responsible for establishing the *fas*, the rightness of any conflict, and for acting as ambassadors and diplomats before any hostilities began. The *Fetiales* were devoted to the religious administration of international affairs of state and to applying the fetial law *(ius fetiale)*, checking rigorously that *fides*, treaties (*foedera*) and oaths had been properly observed. Iuppiter Lapis was their god, whom the chief *Fetial* invoked in the rite surrounding a treaty, *foedus*. Three *Fetiales* and the chief *Fetial* (*pater patratus*) were dispatched as envoys to the enemy, or to the perpetrator of the crime committed against Rome, which might be anything from cattle stealing to full-scale incursion. Their task was to secure restitution (*ad res repetundas*); failure by the 'enemy' to comply after thirty days would lead to action (*denuntiatio*, or *rerum repetitio*). If after thirty days there was no response, the *Fetiales* returned and called the gods to witness that the Romans' case was right and legitimate (*fas*), the *testatio deorum*. Jupiter and Quirinus would be invoked as witnesses to any potential violation of the *ius*. The chief *Fetial* was then empowered to declare war within thirty-three days: after ratification by the Senate and the *concilium plebis* (People's Assembly), the two adversaries would then officially be at war, as sanctioned by the gods. A sacred spear was then ceremoniously hurled into the enemy's territory to delimit their power (*indictio belli*). Over time, as Rome's reach extended further from the city, it became increasingly difficult and impractical to adhere to all of these traditions: the *Fetiales* often needed longer than thirty days, and it was not always possible to find a suitable place to hurl the spear. Consequently, in 270 BCE, a location near the Temple of Bellona was reserved for the spear hurling. By the start of the Second Punic War, the whole procedure was secularized and the *Fetiales* were replaced with senatorial *legati*, envoys, with the traditional three journeys telescoped into one without recourse to Rome.

In the *De Officiis*, Cicero asserts that:

'The only excuse, therefore, for going to war is that we may live in peace unharmed; and when the victory is won, we should spare those who have not been blood-thirsty and barbarous in their warfare. For instance, our forefathers actually admitted to full rights of citizenship the Tusculans, Acquians, Volscians, Sabines, and Hernicians, but they razed Carthage and Numantia to the ground ... the rights of war must be strictly observed. For since there are two ways of settling a dispute: first, by discussion; second, by physical force [*unum per disceptationem alterum per vim*], and since the former is characteristic of man, the latter of the brute, we must resort to force only in case we may not avail ourselves of discussion [*illud proprium sit hominis, hoc beluarum*]. We should always strive to secure a peace that shall not admit of guile ... Not only must we show consideration for those whom we have conquered by force of arms but we must also ensure protection to those who lay down their arms and throw themselves upon the mercy of our generals, even though the battering-ram has hammered at their walls.'[4]

Cicero could point to the magnanimity of the Romans when they defeated the Tuscans and other Italian cities. He deplored the brutal sacking of Corinth, but saw this as a necessity if a future threat to Roman hegemony in the Mediterranean was to be avoided and deterred. Cicero's noble sentiments are echoed by Virgil a few decades later when the ghost of Anchises prescribes to Aeneas the Roman way of civilizing in what is regarded as the classic expression of the imperial ideal, a cornerstone of which is sparing the conquered and crushing the proud – *parcere subiectis et deballare superbos*. Horace took up the theme in the *Carmen Saeculare*, with specific reference to Augustus. Before them all, the Greek historian Polybius has Titus Quinctius Flamininus say the following at the Congress of Nicaea, after he defeated the Macedonian Philip V at the Battle of Cynoscephalae in Thessaly in 197 BCE:

> 'For brave men, when actually at war, should be terrible and full of fire; when beaten, undaunted and courageous; when victorious, on the other hand, moderate, placable, and humane.'[5]

Cicero and Polybius, then, were at pains to separate the men from the brutes. Plunder and booty were legitimate reasons for going to war, but fair play was important too.

As we have described, the opening and closing of the Roman campaigning season were both marked by important rituals. The Roman religious calendar was replete with sacred preparations for warfare: in February and March, the Salii performed their sacred dances, striking their holy shields, purifying the ordnance and horses in races at the feast of *Equirria*; trumpets were sanctified on the day of the *tubilustrium*, and weapons on the *armilustrium* in the autumn, and the October horse (the one on the right in the winning team in the Field of Mars chariot race) was slain. Before an army left for war, it was lustrated, or purified; the commander shook the Salian shields and held up the lance of Mars. The doors of the Temple of Janus were also opened (if they were ever shut). During a campaign, omens were sought at every critical juncture, sacrifices were made and auspices taken.

Waging war was, of course, indicative of 'Romanitas' – 'Roman-ness' – that is, the essential qualities of a Roman and of how a Roman conducted himself in the world. He did so with virtue and bravery, both qualities being embodied in the same word, *virtus*, which has its root in *vir*, 'man'. Although it was possible for a woman to exhibit *virtus*, it was essentially a badge and expression of masculinity. Indeed, *virtus* was often associated specifically with courage in war: Caesar, Sallust and Horace all use it in this context.[6] Conversely, Rome's enemies were often portrayed as weak, lazy and effeminate, devoid of *virtus*; both Greeks and Carthaginians felt the lash of the xenophobic Roman tongue.[7] Carthaginians were said to have no control over their sexual urges, they were cowards and they ate dogs. Greeks, according to Tacitus, were all cowards, while Lucan, through Julius Caesar, would have us believe that they were soft, lazy and startled by their own shouting.[8] On the other hand, we are led to believe that Romans excelled at war while its enemies did not: Rome's multiple victories proved that. Indeed, the sickening-to-some influx of things Greek in the late Republic, in a tide of Hellenization, was seen as a dangerous threat to the security of the Roman state. As we have seen, that champion of the good old days and Greek-hater, Cato the Elder, spoke for many when he vilified all things Greek.

The early Romans were an agricultural, pastoral society made up of people who built their houses on hilltops and grazed their sheep in the pastures on the plains below around the River Tiber. Propertius describes it well in 4.1. They had arrived in Italy in the second millennium BCE, a branch of the Italian peoples, one of the Indo-European tribes who settled in Italy. The early Romans were, however, heavily influenced by the Etruscans, who had come in two waves of immigration in the tenth and eight centuries BCE from Asia Minor; they brought with them expertise in city building, skills in metalworking and ideas tinged with Phoenician and early Greek influences. The result was a series of Etruscan cities extending from the Po valley to Rome. These urban dwellers traded enthusiastically with the Greek cities of Italy; they commanded important trade routes close to Rome, with crossings over the Tiber at Fidenae and Lucus Feroniae. Metalwork and pottery in particular were exported to and imported from Egypt, Phoenicia and Greece. Rome was the last point at which the Tiber could be crossed before the sea, and the mouth of the Tiber was a vital source of salt, much coveted by Romans and Etruscans alike. From about 625 BCE, the relatively cosmopolitan Etruscans swamped pastoral Rome, infusing new ideas in architecture, town planning, commerce, science and medicine, and art. The Romans can thank the Etruscans for the Latin alphabet, the *fasces* – symbols of magisterial power and jurisdiction – temple design, elements of their religion and many aspects of their heritage.[9]

Rome was gradually transformed over 200 years or so to the end of the monarchy in 509 BCE, from a society living in hilltop huts to an increasingly sophisticated, thriving conurbation complete with a religion and mythical history. Rome was now one of the biggest cities in Italy. It would eventually boast a past with myths and legends – Aeneas, Romulus and Remus, Lucretia, Verginia and others – a socio-political system, a burgeoning culture and a citizen army. These myths and legends are dealt with in detail in the next chapters.

The monarchy, traditionally dating from 753 BCE, was unusual in that it was elective rather than hereditary. When the hill dwellers came down from the highlands and populated the valleys, they built a central market there, the forum, and business boomed. The earliest evidence of the Sacra Via, the main street of ancient Rome, dates from around 575 BCE, suggesting that Rome was already a *polis* by then. The king had *imperium*, absolute power, and the ability to consult the gods, *auspicium*. Very little was done without the sanction of the gods, including, as we have just seen, declarations of war and all manner of military action.

The Etruscans were in conflict with the early Romans over land disputes in central Italy for two hundred years or so between 700 and 500 BCE. Initially, though, Rome was just one of many settlements in Latium vying to defend and preserve their lands from un-neighbourly attacks; they just happened to be the largest. The early hostilities are shrouded in the mists of legend, as described by Livy in the opening books of his *Ab Urbe Condita* and by Virgil in the *Aeneid* – both some 700 years after the alleged events. In the beginning, the Etruscans, under King Mezentius, formed an alliance with King Turnus of the Rutuli and attacked the Latins and Trojans, led by Latinus and Aeneas. The Latins and Trojans were victorious, but Aeneas died in the battle.[10] Peace came with the agreement that the River Tiber would form the frontier between Latins and Etruscans.

During the reign of Romulus (mid to late eighth century BCE), the Etruscan Fidenates saw Rome as a threat and duly attacked. Romulus retaliated by marching on Fidenae, where he ambushed the Fidenate army and took the town. This unsettled the neighbouring Veientes, Etruscan allies of the Fidenates, who then invaded Roman territory, only to be defeated by Romulus outside Veii. Romulus did not have the resources to besiege the city, so he devastated the lands of the Veientes instead. The Veientes sued for peace, and a treaty was signed which required the Veientes to cede parts of their territory to Rome.[11]

Before all that, though, Romulus had an existential problem he needed to resolve if his incipient Rome was to survive and thrive. His new city was populated by a motley mix of hopeful colonists, fugitives seeking asylum and displaced soldiers of fortune, most of whom were young, unmarried men; and single men greatly outnumbered women. With no prospect of intermarriage between Rome and its neighbours, the new city would surely fail. Romulus sent envoys to neighbouring towns, appealing for them to allow intermarriage with Roman citizens, but his overtures were in vain. Romulus then resorted to guile and formulated a plan to acquire women from other settlements. This was the legendary Rape of the Sabine Women.

The Fidenates and Veientes would not lie down. During the reign of Rome's third king, the bellicose Tullus Hostilius (r. 673–642 BCE), the Fidenates and Veientes were secretly incited to war by Mettius Fufetius, the dictator of Alba Longa. Mettius was still smarting from an earlier defeat by the Romans and his ignominious new status as a vassal of Rome.[12] Tullus called on the Albans for aid, and together the two armies marched on Fidenae, crossing the Anio and camping at the confluence of the Anio and the Tiber. The Fidenates and Veientes lined up against the Romans. Mettius and the Alban army toyed with the idea of deserting and retreated to a hilltop, where they waited to see who would be victorious before committing themselves. But Tullus saw this and craftily encouraged his troops, telling them that the Alban army had moved exactly according to his plans. Crucially, the Fidenates believed that the Albans were about to attack from the rear, and thus fled. The Romans then routed the Veientes. Tullus ordered Alba Longa to be destroyed and forced the Albans to Rome, where they became Roman citizens.[13] Tullus' neat, decidedly unforensic assessment of the battle was that, since Mettius had been torn between two cities, so would his body. Accordingly, his arms were tied to two chariots, which were driven off at speed in different directions – a graphic, gruesome warning to anyone who dared betray Rome.[14] Livy was disgusted by the atrocity, pointing out that it was, apparently, never repeated to his day.

Here is a humorous rendition of the tale:

'METTIUS FUFETIUS. In which it turns out to be a bad idea to disappoint a Roman king.
'Mettius Fufetius didn't have a clue.
'Mettius Fufetius couldn't follow through.
'They started out with one of him
'And ended up with two
'And neither one of him knows what the other's gonna do.

'Mettius Fufetius had a fickle will.
'Mettius Fufetius ran up on the hill.
'Mettius Fufetius was torn apart and killed
'By some horses and some chariots, and all his guts were spilled.

'So if you ever find yourself the king of Alba Longa,
'Here's a little tip to stop the gig from going wrong:
'It's dangerous, derangerous — oh what could be so silly as
'To fail to match the mettle of one King Tullus Hostilius?

'Mettius Fufetius died in awful pain.
'Mettius Fufetius was strewn across the plain.
'His head is bound for Sicily. His bottom is in Spain.
'Now don't you think the punishment was rather inhumane?'
(© 2014, Jeremy J. Boor, http://jboor.net/?page_id=1168)

Despite his impressive victory, however, Tullus was not quite as prudent or circumspect as he might have been. He routinely snubbed his gods and underestimated the importance of keeping them onside. Towards the end of his reign, Rome was beset by bad omens: a shower of stones fell on the Alban Mount; a voice boomed out complaining that the Albans had failed to show due devotion; and a plague struck Rome. Tullus fell ill, obsessed with superstition. Sacrifices, as recommended by Numa Pompilius to Jupiter Elicius, were ineffective because Tullus failed to perform them correctly. Jupiter was enraged and dispatched a thunderbolt, which struck Tullus and his house, reducing both to ashes. It was another warning, this time to successful commanders and kings, who were well advised to show *pietas* to the gods at all times.[15] Hubris got you nowhere.

Upon the expiry of an earlier truce, the sixth king of Rome, Servius Tullius (r. 578–535 BCE) declared war on the Veientes and the Etruscans: his subsequent victory consolidated his tenuous position in Rome. According to the *Fasti Triumphales*, Servius celebrated three triumphs over the Etruscans, the first two of which were in 571 and 567 BCE.[16]

In 509 BCE, the monarchy, under Lucius Tarquinius Superbus, was deposed and replaced by a republic. The evil deception and rape of Lucretia by Sextus Tarquinius, a son of the king, were major catalysts in this political upheaval. In an attempt to regain his throne, Tarquinius enlisted the support of the similarly disaffected cities of Veii and Tarquinii, but they were defeated by the Romans at the Battle of Silva Arsia. The victorious consul, Publius Valerius Poplicola, returned to Rome laden with Etruscan booty to celebrate a triumph, in which he rode in a four-horse chariot; this set a template for subsequent triumphs.[17] The other consul, Lucius Junius Brutus, fought a duel with Arruns, another son of Tarquin, in which both combatants died. Brutus was awarded a lavish funeral; the women of Rome mourned him for a year – a fitting tribute to the revenge he took on Sextus Tarquinius after he had raped Lucretia, one of Rome's foremost *matronae* and a paragon of feminine virtue.

The following year, Poplicola did battle with Lars Porsena, king of the powerful Etruscan city of Clusium, who was in league with Tarquinius

Superbus. The war with Clusium and Lars Porsena spawned three famous legends. When Porsena approached the Pons Sublicius, one of the Tiber bridges leading into Rome, Publius Horatius Cocles commandeered the bridge to hold off the enemy, allowing the Romans, by then a quaking rabble (*trepidam turbam*), time to destroy it.[18]

The second legend involved a Roman boy, Gaius Mucius Scaevola, who was detailed to infiltrate the Etruscan camp and assassinate Porsena. Unfortunately, Mucius could not distinguish the king from his secretary, and murdered the secretary in error.

The third legend involved Cloelia, a young woman who was part of a group of hostages – ten young noblemen and ten maidens – given by Rome to Porsena to secure a peace treaty. Cloelia led the girls in an escape, swimming across the Tiber, despite a hail of enemy spears. However, as the peace deal was more important than the security of his daughter, Cloelia's father returned all the hostages until the treaty was finalized. Upon her return, Porsena admired Cloelia's bravery and granted her freedom along with half of the other hostages. She chose to free the young noblemen as they would be able to fight in the future against Rome's enemies.

The stories of Publius Horatius Cocles, Gaius Mucius, and Cloelia are, of course, mythical and legendary, all set in a landscape of war, conquest and occupation. Their purpose is not to pose as reliable history, but to demonstrate to Romans of Livy's day the virtues of good old-fashioned values at a time when Augustus was struggling to introduce a programme of moral reform. The three heroes here – one, notably, a woman – exemplify conspicuous bravery in the face of death, quick-wittedness in extreme situations and unquestioned, unselfish loyalty to Rome, *pietas*. Furthermore, they clearly show that the Roman state was only too ready to reward publicly and financially such virtues and valour, and that enemies could be persuaded to act humanely and honourably, with *fides*, when faced with such deeds.

The female of the species, of course, features prominently in the Greek and Roman pantheons and in mythical representations of war: Andromache, Athena and the Amazons, for example. She is present in epic poetry as Helen of Troy or Briseis, and in drama in the shape of the vengeful or victimized women of the tragedies, or as the 'revolting' women in the *Lysistrata*. In the real world, or what was imagined to be the real world, she populates the strange foreign countries described with some incredulity by, for example, Herodotus – take Queen Tomyris, Artemisia and Pheretima, for example, and she emerges even as a poet warrior in Telesilla.

As we shall see, women played a pivotal part in the myths of Rome, with leading roles in landmark, groundbreaking events such as the early establishment of the city, the expulsion of the monarchy and the Conflict of the Orders. Rape, suicide, banishment and filicide are their sad and tragic lot, but their participation in and contribution to Roman mythology and legend is enormous in the annals of Rome.

Chapter 4

The Aeneas Foundation Myth: From Troy to Italy

rom the day the mighty Greek armies finally arrived at Troy to win back Helen from Paris to the day when Aeneas succeeded in defeating Turnus to secure the foundation of Rome and the settlement of the surviving Trojans in Italy, Aeneas was at war. Virgil is unequivocal from the very first line of the *Aeneid* about his subject and his subject matter: *arma virumque*, 'arms and the man', and that man is Aeneas. The message is resoundingly reprised in Book 7, where we are reminded of Virgil's – and Aeneas' – mission (*Aeneid*, 7.37–44; adapted from the translation by T.C. Williams):

'Hail, Erato! while I reveal ancient kings and thrones and all their back story! How Latium's honour stood, when foreign ships brought war to Italy, and from what cause the primal conflict sprang, O goddess, breathe upon your poet in song. Dread wars I tell, battle ranks, and high-hearted kings thrust forward to die, when Etruria's host and all Hesperia gathered to the fray. Greater events impel my song, and a loftier task I try.'

While there is no doubt at all about the ubiquity of Aeneas in the poem, the *arma* content is somewhat less pervasive, taking up only about 20 per cent of the content. As noted already, the urbane and educated Virgil may not have been a great advocate of war and conflict – factors which may have manifested in the framework of his epic and hero. His main concern, it seems, was to get Aeneas to Italy so that Rome might be established, culminating in the rule of Augustus, without the tedium of over-descriptive and serial battling.

Virgil's brief, and Aeneas' mission in fleeing from Troy and fighting the campaigns in Italy, was to forge a link between himself and Augustus in turn-of-the-millennium Rome via Julius Caesar, his great uncle. Julius Caesar was the progenitor of the *gens Julia*, as headed in Virgil's day by Imperator Caesar Divi filius Augustus (23 September 63 BCE–19 August 14 CE). Emperor Augustus was to be seen as a direct descendant of Aeneas and the

Trojans. The post-Troy wanderings of Aeneas and his companions are of course most famously described in Virgil's *Aeneid*, but when Virgil came to write his national epic, he had a rich tradition on which to draw.[1]

The *gens Julia* was one of the most ancient and prestigious patrician families in Rome. Members of the *gens* reached the highest offices of state in the earliest days of the Republic, the first of the family to obtain the consulship being Gaius Julius Iulus in 489 BCE.

The Julii were Albans in origin and one of the foremost Alban houses, which Tullus Hostilius moved to Rome when Alba Longa was destroyed. The Julii also existed at Bovillae, as evidenced by an ancient inscription on an altar in the theatre there which reveals their offering sacrifices according to the *lege Albana*, or Alban rites.

Julius Caesar was never shy of referring to the divine origin of his *gens*, as, for instance, in the funeral oration which he gave for his aunt Julia, and speeches to his troops at the battles of Pharsalus and Munda. Julius Caesar is said to have visited Mount Alba to preside over the Feriae Latinae, Latin rites originally celebrated by the kings of Alba Longa. While it seems likely that the Julii first came to Rome during the reign of Tullus Hostilius, the name occurs in Roman legend as early as the time of Romulus. It was Proculus Julius who informed the mourning Roman people, after the apotheosis of Romulus, that their king had descended from heaven and appeared to him, bidding him tell the people to honour him in future as a god, by the name of Quirinus (Livy, 1.16).

Augustus reciprocated this prodigious honour and propaganda coup by building his Forum Augustum, as described already in the 'Mars' section in the Gods of War chapter above. The unfinished forum and its temple dedicated to Mars Ultor were inaugurated in 2 BCE, some forty years after they were first vowed. As already mentioned, an important use that Augustus made of the temple was to store the standards taken by the Parthians from Crassus, after Augustus retrieved them through diplomacy in 20 BCE, as depicted by the Augustus of Prima Porta. Three *Aquilae* were also lost in 9 CE in the disastrous Battle of the Teutoburg Forest between modern Gütersloh and Paderborn in north Germany: the standards of the Legio XVII, Legio XVIII and Legio XIX. All three were recovered – one in 14 CE from the Marsi, another in 15 CE from the Bructeri and the third in 41 CE from the Chauci – and placed in the Temple of Mars the Avenger. It is hard for us to comprehend the trauma and shock that the loss of a legionary standard evoked in ancient Rome; their recovery and safe storage would have been met with equal jubilation and relief, and would have resonated loud and clear to the benefit of Augustus' reputation.

Augustus was careful to reinforce his divine descent by populating the Forum with a judicious selection of statuary. Prominent were the statues of Augustus himself in full military uniform in the centre of the Forum, and of Mars and Venus in the Temple. In total, there were 108 portrait statues, with inscriptions (*elogia*) of each individual's achievements, providing us with an invaluable idea of how Augustus viewed his place in Roman history and the august company he liked to be seen keeping. As well as bronze or marble statues of all the Roman *triumphatores*, placed along the left side of the Forum and in the left exedrae, the entire right side and right exedrae were filled with statues of men in the Julian-Claudian family, including M. Claudius Marcellus, C. Julius Caesar Strabo and Julius Caesar. They trace Augustus' lineage back through the fourteen Alban kings to the founding ancestors, Aeneas and Romulus, thus reinforcing the importance both of Roman lineage and the prestigious lineage that Augustus himself was now confirmed to have held. By advertising this lineage, he reinforced his power and authority as a leader. Also, by situating himself amongst Rome's great figures and heroes, he left no one in any doubt about his own importance. It was propaganda at its most pronounced.

But the mythology surrounding Aeneas' circuitous journey to Latium goes back much further. Athenian black figure vases found in Etruria, dating from the sixth century BCE, depict Aeneas' flight from Troy. The Etruscan town of Veii has yielded votive statuettes and jewellery with the same motif. Hellanicus, the fifth-century BCE Greek historian, is the first to mention Aeneas when he writes that Aeneas founded Rome, naming it after Rhomê (the Greek for strength), one of the Trojan women who was with him who got fed up with all that Mediterranean cruising and burned the Trojan boats. Damastes of Sigeum (*c.* 400 BCE) says much the same, as does Aristotle, who calls Rome 'Latinion'. Other Greeks, though, ascribe the foundation to a son of Odysseus and Circe; others still make Aeneas the father or grandfather of the founder of Rome.

Romulus and Remus were also nominated as founders of Rome by some, but the timings were all wrong. Eratosthenes of Cyrene (275–194 BCE) demonstrated in his universal chronology, *Chronographia*, that the fall of Troy should be dated to 1184 BCE; so what do we make of the gap between that and the accepted date of Rome's founding, 753 BCE? We have Cato the Elder (234–149 BCE) to thank for solving the problem: he simply interpolated a line of kings, starting from Iulus' son or brother, Silvius, until he had filled enough generations to arrive at the birth of Romulus and Remus.

The gods, of course, were inextricably involved. Aeneas started his wanderings at Delos, where Apollo revealed that 'the land which bore your first ancestors shall welcome you into its fertile bosom when you return. Seek out your ancient mother [Italy].' Ascanius recalled that Teucer was an ancestor of the kings of Troy and came from Crete, so the Trojans sailed to Crete, where they stayed for a year, thinking this to be their new home, but were forced to leave by pestilence and a vision of the Penates. They then reached the Strophades, where they made the mistake of slaughtering some cattle and preparing a meal. This attracted the monstrous bird women, the Harpies, who fouled the food. One of them, Calaeno, uttered a mysterious prophecy: 'You will go to Italy and will be allowed to enter harbour but you will not be given a city and build its walls until, because of the wrong you have done to us, extreme hunger makes you gnaw and devour your tables.'

They came across Helenus, Priam's son, in Epirus. He was ruling over a city with Andromache that was a facsimile of Troy. Helenus prophesied (Virgil, *Aeneid* 8.42ff; adapted from the translation by T.C. Williams):

'Fear not the looming war. The wrath of Heaven has stilled its swollen wave. A sign I tell: In case you should think this prophecy a vain, deluding dream, you will soon find among the oak trees on my green margins, a huge sow, with her newly-littered brood of thirty young; on the ground she lies, snow-white, with her white young all around her udders. That is where your city will stand, and there your hard work shall find untroubled rest. After thirty continuous years, Ascanius will found a city there of noble name, White-City, Alba; this is not a dream!'

The sow and her litter represented the Latins, and the thirty piglets, according to Fabius Pictor, were the Latin League, which the Romans finally defeated in 338 BCE. When the Trojans arrived at the Tiber estuary via Sicily, Dido's Carthage and the underworld, they rested for a meal and ate, not just their food, but the flatbreads they were using as plates; these were the 'tables' they were destined to eat. The prophecy was fulfilled and the Trojans approached King Latinus. The sow and the litter were spotted by Aeneas as he and some companions set off to find Evander to win more support.

Virgil and Augustus

Virgil presumably began writing the *Aeneid* when commissioned by Augustus Caesar. Caesar assumed power around 31 BCE with the birth of what we now call the Roman Empire after decades of catastrophic, internecine civil war (*c*. 49–31 BCE) had reduced the Roman Republic to ashes. Everyone, it seems, was personally affected: just to reference the Augustan poets, Virgil had his family estates confiscated to pay off army veterans, Horace disastrously fought agains Augustus (when he was Octavian) at Philippi and had to rebuild his life, while Propertius lost relatives in the fighting in central Italy and became something of a pacifist.

The unconventional, un-Roman way of life (*otium*) pursued by some outré poets might have been expected to encourage not only outrage amongst patriotic conservatives, but also a pacifist, anti-war attitude amongst its adherents. And to some extent it did: Propertius (50–15 BCE) indignantly demanded to know (2.7.13f) 'why should I breed sons for Rome's triumphs? No blood of mine will ever produce a soldier.' However, Catullus (*c*. 84–54 BCE), thirty-five years or so earlier, as unconventional as any of the new poets (*neoteroi*, νεώτεροι), had, surprisingly perhaps, taken the establishment line that marriage and procreation was very much a civil duty: in his wedding hymn (61.71–73), he urges the happy couple to 'produce sentries for the borders'. It was the duty of the young and fertile to produce legitimate children to maintain the birth rate, to ensure the survival of a particular family, and to supply the Roman Army and bureaucracy, the land and the law with a source of recruits. In Catullus' case here, the exigencies of genre seem to have overruled any pacifistic sentiments he may have held.

Although this new period under Augustus came to be optimistically known as the Golden Age, or *pax Romana*, no one could have had the remotest idea of how long it, or indeed Augustus, would last. Indeed, the *princeps*, or First Citizen, fell dangerously ill in 23 BCE and nearly died aged 39. This naturally made an edgy administration even more edgy as it agonized over the succession. Given the atrocious events of the last few decades, the odds must have been on a short interlude before the resumption of civil hostilities on an even more destructive scale. Values and virtues such as chastity (as exemplified by the best of idealized Roman *matronae* such as Lucretia and Cornelia), humility, fidelity (as opposed to adultery and divorce), morality, social sobriety, selflessness and piety (to country, state, family and the like) were all targets for Augustus. Augustus himself reels off the laws which he implemented in his *Res Gestae* (8.5).

It may, however, have been this tenuous political situation, this uncertainty, which prompted Augustus to cast around for a viable and credible propaganda campaign to support his fledgeling regime, underscore his credentials for the leadership and inject new-found patriotism and optimism into a populace still reeling from those civil wars and half-expecting more carnage to come.

Epic was part of the answer. What better way to energize his subjects, to remind them of their glorious rather than the calamitous past, to inject patriotism and old-style Roman values? What better way than to hire the best poet of the day and have him link him, Augustus, directly with heroic Aeneas and warlike Romulus, and show the world how he would deliver a new Golden Age built on protracted peace, high culture, civilization and 'Romanitas'? The *mos maiorum* was coming back.

Augustus used the past, the Rome of the *mos maiorum*, as a vehicle for his political programme to restore the moral well-being of the Roman state and society. The *Aeneid* was, in turn, an excellent vehicle with which to convey this, extolling as it did the heroic past and his connection with it through Aeneas, Romulus and Julius Caesar. His political agenda was particularly focused on restoring the moral fibre of Roman society, on promoting modesty in one's lifestyle and rejecting extravagance, on strengthening the family and restoring traditional religion to something like what all things had purportedly been in the early days of Rome.

Moral and social reform was, therefore, high on Augustus' legislative agenda. He tried to inculcate the belief that his own domestic arrangements and *familia* provided the blueprint for the best Roman way of life. In the earlier days of the Republic, Lucretia had demonstrated how spinning and weaving (*lanam fecit*) and looking after the household were crucial skills in Roman houses at all levels of society, and they became the badge of the good mother and wife. Augustus himself supposedly wore home-spun clothes and promoted the traditional skill of weaving, boasting that all the women in the Augustus household could spin and work the wool. His wife, Livia, exemplified this; she dressed modestly, without ostentation, while her domestic staff comprised five patchers, two supervisors, six women in charge of clothing, one cloak-maker, one tailor and two fullers.

Augustus' sartorial simplicity was but one item in a programme of domestic frugality. He was at pains to show the Imperial household and domestic lifestyle as being typically Roman, modest and conservative. At his home, dinner parties were sociable and entertaining enough while not being crassly sumptuous. The Imperial home was comfortable but not palatial, marble-free and mosaic-free; the furniture, according to Suetonius, was plain, and Augustus' bed was rudimentary. The family's holidays were what we would now call 'budget' and 'staycation', relatively local, and Augustus' diet was frugal and simple.

Livia's fidelity to Augustus, her comparative 'univira-ness' (one-man womanness), likewise gave some much-needed credibility and substance to

Augustus' attempts at social reform. It was a bid to reverse the decline in marriages, the increasing levels of adultery and the falling birth rate. Livia's probity (*pudicitia*) was above question. Even the critical Tacitus, writing later in the century, never suggests *stuprum* (fornication) on Livia's part; indeed, her morality was consistent with the moral rectitude of the old days (*priscum ad morem*).

As far as Augustus was concerned, Romans needed to be reminded what marriage was for. In his eyes, it was indubitably there for producing children; the marriage that ended in the death of one of the partners, rather than in divorce, had seemingly become something of a rarity. Virgil reflects the casual, contemporary *mores* in the behaviour of Aeneas: he loses Creusa, his first wife, at Troy, deserts Dido in Carthage – although they were not of course married – and marries Lavinia, daughter of an Italian king. The 'Lex Julia de Maritandis Ordinibus' of 18 BCE prohibited get-out marriages such as those between senators and their near relatives or freedwomen. It banned marriage to convicted adulteresses, those in a dubious profession, and fallen and stigmatised women – the *probosae* (actors, dancers, prostitutes and convicted women). It rewarded fertile women with favourable inheritance rights and relaxed the requirement for a woman to be saddled with a guardian, also remunerating fertile men with fast-track political advancement.

Under the 'Lex Iulia de Adulteriis Coercendis', passed in the same year, adultery was criminalized, with banishment as punishment. A new court (the *quaestio perpetua de adulteriis*) was set up to try adultery cases in public, an initiative which abolished the privacy hitherto afforded by the family courts in which the woman was tried by her relatives. If found guilty, the man and woman were dispatched to different islands (*dummodo in diversas insulas relegentur*), and some of their property was seized. A woman lost half of her dowry and a third of her property, and the man lost half of his property. Other penalties increased the offender's infamy, such as the ending of the adulterer's right to act as a witness in court. Women were prohibited from marrying freeborn Romans; they gained a reputation (*probosae*) and were barred from wearing the *stola*, the dress of the *matrona*. They were then stigmatized by being made to wear the toga, as worn by men and prostitutes. The *stola* was almost sacrosanct, metaphorically and actually untouchable, whereas the toga was certainly not. Seduction also became a criminal offence, defined as when a man seduces a virgin or a respectable widow without the use of force.

Here is the full programme of Augustus' moral legislation:

- Lex Iulia de Ambitu (18 BCE): penalizing bribery when acquiring political offices.
- Lex Iulia de Maritandis Ordinibus (18 BCE): limiting marriage across social class boundaries, prohibiting marriage between senators and their near relatives and freedwomen, or marriage to convicted adulteresses or those in a dubious profession (actors, dancers, prostitutes); banning marriage for serving soldiers below a certain rank (although many soldiers did marry local women) until the reign of Septimius Severus when the ban was relaxed in 197 CE. Provincial officials were prohibited from marrying women from the province, while guardians could not marry their wards.
- Lex Iulia de Adulteriis Coercendis (17 BCE): this law punished adultery with banishment. The two guilty parties were sent to different islands ('*dummodo in diversas insulas relegentur*'), and part of their property was confiscated. Fathers were permitted to kill daughters and their partners in adultery. Husbands could kill the partners under certain circumstances, and were required to divorce adulterous wives. Augustus himself was obliged to invoke the law against his own daughter, Julia (relegated to the island of Pandateria), and against her eldest daughter (Julia the Younger). Tacitus asserts that Augustus was stricter for his own relatives than the law actually required (*Annals* 3.24); this imposed a 5 per cent tax on inheritances, exempting close relatives.

Not surprisingly, Augustus' laws were generally unpopular – they amounted to what today we would term the workings of a 'nanny state'. Consequently, they were diluted somewhat by the lex Papia Poppaea (9 CE), named after the consuls of that year and intended to encourage and strengthen marriage and promote offspring (within lawful marriage), thus also discriminating against celibacy.

Aulus Gellius[2] probably summed up the public, or rather male public, mood when he quotes Augustus' speech in the Senate in 17 BCE:

'If we could survive without a wife, citizens of Rome, all of us would do without that nuisance, but since nature has decreed that we neither manage comfortably without them, nor live in any way without them, we must plan for our lasting preservation rather than for our temporary pleasure.'

The same audible sigh of resignation comes from Varro:

'A husband must either put a stop to his wife's faults or else he must put up with them. In the first case he makes his wife a more attractive woman, in the second he makes himself a better man.'[3]

Various creative efforts were made to circumvent the legislation. Suetonius says that attempts by men to delay marriage and the birth of children by engagements to young, prepubescent girls were met with stricter legislation relating to subsequent divorces and the length of engagements. Fiancés had been exempt from the penalties paid by bachelors (*caelibes*); now Augustus voided betrothals unless the marriage took place within two years. Earlier in his life, Augustus himself (when Octavian) had betrothed his daughter, Julia, to 15-year-old L. Junius Silanus, one of Mark Antony's sons, when she was only 2 years old. Tacitus confirms that the *lex Julia* was unsuccessful: the benefits of childlessness were too great.[4] The attractions of the mistress – a woman of a young man's choosing, not his father's – or of a courtesan, off-limits in the marriage stakes, or of an independent woman from a lower class, were all to obvious.

Iconographic visual promotion for the moral programme came in 9 BCE, when the Ara Pacis was completed. It was erected in thanks for Augustus' campaigns in Gaul and Spain, and it depicts the emperor and Livia with various children – symbolizing their role-model status as a good family. Augustus is made to resemble Aeneas, while Livia is reminiscent of a goddess; she is depicted on the east face, with her hair unusually worn in a much looser style than the characteristic *nodus*.

The Senate awarded him a golden shield displayed in the meeting hall of the Curia Julia, bearing the inscription '*virtus, pietas, clementia, iustitia*' – 'valour, piety, clemency and justice'. Augustus was later to record in his *Res Gestae Divi Augusti*, written just before his death in 14 CE:

'In my sixth and seventh consulships [28–27 BCE], after I had ended the civil wars and had achieved power over everything by universal consensus, I returned the state from my control to the guidance of the senate and Roman people. For this, the senate decreed that I would be named Augustus: the door posts of my house were decorated with laurel; a public crown was put up over my doorway, and a golden shield was dedicated in the Curia Julia, whose inscription declared that the senate and people of Rome gave it to me to recognize my virtue,

clemency, justice and piety [*et clupeus aureus in curia Iulia positus,
quem mihi senatum populumque Romanum dare virtutis clementiaeque et
iustitiae et pietatis*]. After that moment, I stood apart from all other
men in authority, but I had no more power than those who were my
associates in any magistracy.'

Augustus also made it his business to restore the increasingly moribund
religious fabric of Rome, as manifested in his refurbishment or rebuilding of
eighty-two shrines and temples. The traditional gods were relaunched in the
face of exotic, and erotic, arrivals from the East in the shape of Isis, Cybele
and others. Livia was similarly occupied, restoring the shrines of Plebeian
and Patrician Chastity, centres of moral rectitude which were exclusively
female. She followed this by financing work on the temples of Fortuna
Muliebris and Bona Dea Subsaxena – again, both very closely associated
with women. Ovid celebrates Livia's good works in state religion in his
Fasti. Here, as in her projection of a public persona redolent of the virtues
of a good *matrona*, she reflects and personifies aspects of Augustan domestic
policy relating to the restoration of the ailing state religion.

But Virgil may have not been totally on message, just trotting out
random and unsubstantiated imperial propaganda. When Aeneas is in the
underworld learning the future, his father, Anchises, tells him how Augustus
will 'restore our wounded state ... to pacify, to impose the rule of law, to
spare the conquered' (*Aeneid* 6.1143–54). This vision of peace, restoring
order and law, dispensing clemency (never the Romans' strong point during
the centuries of the Republic), is at odds with what happens in Aeneas'
campaigns and bloody battles to help establish a site for the future Rome. It is
also inconsistent with the hero's exit from the underworld via the ivory gate
of false dreams (6.1214–15) – was the *katabasis* (descent) all a dream? There
is more warmongering, with defeated nations quaking in fear (6.1073–76):
'At that man's coming even now the realms ... tremble, warned by oracles,
and the seven mouths of the Nile go dark with fear'. Aeneas also goes berserk
in his fight with Turnus at the end of the epic. Would Augustus have been
disappointed by this apparent contradiction in the national epic he had
commissioned? Probably not: epic was a medium in which war and warriors
were routinely celebrated. The Homeric epics certainly championed its
warring heroes, as did the extant epics which followed the *Aeneid*, as written
by Lucan, Statius, Valerius Flaccus and Silius Italicus.

Roman legend taught that Rome's prehistory and early history were born
of violence: the destruction of Troy, the fratricide committed by Romulus

and the abduction of the Sabine women. But in the end, as we shall see, it all comes good. There would be no Rome, no Romans and no Augustus without these dreadful opening events. Violence, destruction and death were necessary for the establishment of peace, stability and a new world.

Just as Aeneas had to fight against the Latins in order to deliver his divine mission, so Augustus had to fight the civil wars, initially against Caesar's assassins and then against Mark Antony, in order to create the Principate. Both Aeneas and Augustus brought political security and cultural order out of toxic disorder.

Augustus is mentioned explicitly three times in the *Aeneid*: in Jupiter's prophecy (1.286–96), in Anchises' underworld revelation of Rome's future (6.791–805) and in the description of Aeneas' shield (8.671–728). In the first, Jupiter proclaims Aeneas' future victories in battle and his foundation of Lavinium, Ascanius' establishment of and reign in Alba Longa, the birth of Romulus and foundation of Rome, and the Roman rule of the world, which would be unlimited in space and time. Finally, Jupiter prophesies that Augustus will enjoy limitless glory, be deified, end all wars and establish peace, with *Furor impius* (unholy rage) exterminated. Virgil's Augustus stands at the end point, the culmination, the *telos* of Roman history. In that role, he is the fourth in line of the great Roman city builders: Aeneas founded Lavinium; Ascanius, Alba Longa; Romulus, Rome; and Augustus re-founded Rome. Peace will come after war, and the toga – that badge of civil life and civilization – will prevail. All the hallmarks of Roman integrity, 'Romanitas', will come into play: *mores*, as in *mos maiorum*, *Fides* (good faith), Vesta (the guardian flame) and *iura* (justice).

Ovid, in his *Metamorphoses* (1.89–100), would have us believe that once upon a time, men were ever true to their word, and that they inhabited a righteous, peaceful world in which laws, punishment, armies and fortifications were superfluous. We have noted how this Ovidian golden age of course never existed; Augustus, like everyone else, would be only too aware that violence, wars and battles were as ubiquitous as taxes and death. Their appearance in his *Aeneid* would have been expected.

Nevertheless, in the underworld, Anchises tells Aeneas that Augustus is the son of a god, namely the deified Caesar, and is also a second Saturnus who will re-establish the Golden Age. Augustus will subjugate many peoples in the East, Anchises says. The emperor is not only equal to other gods, Augustus exceeds them. For Augustus' empire will comprise more countries than Hercules and Dionysus – inveterate travellers both – had ever seen. The Greeks could keep their arts and sciences – the Romans would rule and 'crown peace with civilisation' – and they will spare the subjugated.

Hitherto, Aeneas had been retrospective, living in the past he was so nostalgic for; after meeting Anchises, he is motivated into the future – his father had helped put his hesitation, along with the past, behind him. He was now much better equipped for his foray into Italy and the founding of Rome by his successors (6.889).

Virgil shows on the shield Augustus celebrating triumphs over many defeated peoples: in the South, the Nomads and Africans; in the East, the Leleges, Geloni, Parthians and Dahae; in the West, the Gauls; and in the North, the Germans (8.724–28).

When Augustus has completed all civil and foreign wars, he will be at liberty to close the doors of the Temple of Janus, that powerful symbol of total peace. However, it had been, at the same time, the symbol of total war. The temple was always really a visible sign of Rome's belligerence.

In Virgil's pageant of heroes, Augustus is a *theios aner*, a divine man, who, like Hercules and Romulus, will achieve divinity through his deeds. In the description of Aeneas' divinely crafted shield, Virgil focuses on the Battle of Actium and his success in overcoming Mark Antony and the luxurious, effeminate eastern influences as represented by the god Anubis and Cleopatra, Horace's *fatale monstrum* ('doom monster').

As well as these explicit references to Virgil's emperor and patron, Augustus figures elsewhere, implicitly but not far beneath the surface of the narrative. He is, appropriately, there right at the beginning of the epic in Book 1 when Juno and Aeolus conspire to brew up a storm which Neptune then calms. Virgil compares Neptune's mollifying action with a statesman's conduct in a civil riot (1.148–56) when he appeases the raging masses with his authority (*'pietate gravem ac meritis ... virum'*, 1.151–52). His authority is founded on his piety, worth and eloquence – the statesman in the simile is clearly Augustus, the man who dealt with the civil wars. A cameo from the late 30s BCE supports this; it shows Octavian as Neptune holding the trident (*tridenti*) mentioned by Virgil (1.145) and steers his *quadriga* drawn by horses (1.156) over an enemy who drowns in the waves – Sextus Pompeius or Mark Antony? It has also been interpreted as a metaphor for the contrast between the atrocity and chaos of the recent civil wars and the rule of law and order embodied by the upright-standing charioteer. According to Feeney, the simile in the first book of the *Aeneid* expresses one of the main themes of the epic, the 'correlation of divine power in the cosmos and human power in history'.

We can also see Augustus in Hercules. Hercules, like Aeneas, created order out of chaos. Aeneas had fled from the carnage of Troy to Italy, and had to fight against Mezentius and Turnus before he could found Lavinium and a new civilization by unifying the Trojans with the Latins. Hercules, meanwhile, saved the world from terrifying monsters and thereby brought culture and civilization to humankind. After the killing of Cacus, the locals set up an altar for Hercules and celebrated their salvation with hymns honouring and praising their saviour (*Aeneid* 8.184–305), and established a religious cult. Augustus, Aeneas' descendant, was a similar civilizing influence, restoring stability after the chaos and toxicity of the civil wars.

Aeneas

If warfare can ever be graded on a scale of good and bad, Aeneas did not have a particularly good Trojan War. Comparatively speaking, Aeneas – son of Anchises and Aphrodite, and cousin of Hector – though an important leader, assumes a rather low profile. But there again he has much bigger fish to fry, since he is to be called on to found the Roman state as a direct ancestor, no less, of Romulus and Remus.

Aeneas was, however, right there in the thick of it from the start: the abduction of Helen by Paris.

This had its genesis at the sumptuous wedding of Thetis and Peleus, attended by all the gods. Eros – Strife incarnate – was there to spoil the party when she mischievously rolled an apple inscribed 'to the most beautiful' amongst the guests. This had the desired effect of enraging Aphrodite, Hera and Athena, and causing an almighty row as each considered herself to be the fairest of them all. Hermes was delegated to lead the three to Mount Ida in Troy, where they would be judged in a divine beauty contest by Paris. Paris was persuaded by Aphrodite, who promised him the hand of the world's most beautiful woman – and daughter of Zeus – rejecting the regal power and military success offered by Hera and Athena.

Paris, of course, was blithely unaware of the curse under which he had lived since birth; Hecabe, his mother, was doomed to deliver a son who would be responsible for the fiery destruction of Troy. In a bid to avert this inevitability, the infant was exposed on Mount Ida, where he was raised by a she-bear and subsequently found by a shepherd. When the adult Paris returned to Priam's Troy to take part in games in his memory, his identity was confirmed by his sister, Cassandra, and he was welcomed back into the family fold.

Paris' somewhat whimsical, sex-driven decision at the divine beauty contest had the most serious consequences: Helen, of course, was already married, and her appropriation would involve relieving her husband – Menelaus, no less, King of Sparta and brother of Agamemnon, only the most powerful man in Greece – of his wife and exposing her complicity in a plan to abscond to Troy with Paris. Furthermore, the former suitors of Helen were all bound by the Treaty of Tyndareus, by which they were obliged to assist each other militarily should Menelaus ever find himself relieved of Helen. Paris, despite all these checks and balances, would still blithely run away with a willing Helen, and a cuckolded Menelaus would raise a huge Greek army to retrieve her. The stage was now nicely set for the Trojan War.

Aphrodite had instructed Paris to build ships to enable him to sail to Greece to abduct Helen – this he did, despite warnings of the dire consequences, not just from prophetic sister Cassandra but also from his own wife, for he too was already married, to the equally prophetic nymph, Oinone. Aeneas, our hero, was delegated by Aphrodite to accompany Paris on his quest for Helen. The two arrived in Sparta and were warmly welcomed by Helen and Menelaus. Menelaus, however, conveniently had to leave after nine days to attend the funeral in Crete of the former Spartan king, Katreus. Paris saw his chance, successfully wooed an increasingly besotted Helen and eloped with her – but not before he had loaded much of the Spartan royal treasure onto his ships. The affair was consummated, and despite some infelicitous inclement storms brewed up by Hera in her role as protector of the institution of marriage, the happy couple finally arrived in Troy, via Sidon in Phoenicia. These events were covered in the lost epic *Cypria*, the first poem in the Epic Cycle and a prequel to the *Iliad*.

We learn the details of Aeneas's birth from the *Homeric Hymn to Aphrodite*. Aphrodite made Zeus fall in love with mortal women, so, to get his own back, Zeus fills the goddess with passion for Anchises, who is minding his own business one day tending his cattle on the hills near Mount Ida. When Aphrodite sees Anchises, she is truly smitten, dresses up as for a wedding and shows herself off to him. He too is smitten, supposing her a goddess, although Aphrodite is pretending to be a Phrygian princess. They make love and Aphrodite reveals her true identity to Anchises, at which he becomes anxious that there may be consequences to his sexual relationship with a goddess. Aphrodite assures him that he will be protected, and reveals that she will bear him a son who will be called Aeneas. However, she cautions that he must never tell anyone that he has slept with a goddess. When Aeneas is born, Aphrodite takes him to the nymphs of Mount Ida, whom she instructs to raise until the age of 5, then take him to Anchises. Some have it that Anchises boasted about his liaison with Aphrodite, and as a result was struck in the foot by a thunderbolt courtesy of Zeus. This makes him lame, which is why Aeneas has to carry him from the flames of Troy.

In the *Iliad*, Aeneas is forever needing to be rescued, and as such, fulfils the role of a hero awaiting a greater destiny. A sometimes reluctant warrior at Troy, he was angry with Priam because he believed that, despite his bravery, he was being denied his due share of honour. Nevertheless, he did lead an attack against Idomeneus to recover the body of his brother-in-law Alcathous at the urging of Deiphobus. Aphrodite and Apollo rescued Aeneas from combat with Diomedes of Argos, who badly wounded and almost killed him, and carried him away to Pergamos to recuperate. Aphrodite herself was wounded by Diomedes, but then Apollo took over the protection of Aeneas, removing him from the battle to the citadel at Pergamos, where his temple was. In the sanctuary, Leto and Artemis healed Aeneas and made him even stronger. Apollo fashioned a phantom of Aeneas, so that Achaeans and Trojans killed each other around it in a bid to capture or retrieve the body, until the real Aeneas, having recovered, returned to the field.

Even Poseidon, who is usually pro-Greek, had occasion to come to Aeneas' rescue. After Apollo urged Aeneas to challenge Achilles to single combat, Aeneas was almost killed, but Poseidon rescued him, explaining to the other gods (Homer, *Iliad* 20.300):

> 'Even Zeus might be angry if Achilles killed Aeneas, who after all is destined to survive and to save the House of Dardanus from extinction … Priam's line has fallen out of favour with Zeus, and now Aeneas shall be King of Troy and shall be followed by his children's children in the time to come.'

Despite his shortcomings on the field of battle, Aeneas was uniquely qualified to lead the survivors out of Troy and into Italy, and help establish the new homeland that would culminate in the reign of Augustus. As Rome expanded over Italy and the Mediterranean, so it absorbed more and more of what was regarded as superior Greek culture, an inescapable reality which some conservative Romans found repellent. To mitigate this cultural edge, Aeneas, as a Trojan and thus an enemy of the Greeks, was an ideal foil to establish Roman greatness in the *Aeneid*.

Nevertheless, in the inferno of Troy, Aeneas fought bravely to the last, and was commanded by a ghostly and war-torn Hector to escape and found a great city overseas (Virgil, *Aeneid* 2.278–97; adapted from the translation by H.R. Fairclough):

> "'Ah, flee, goddess-born,'" he cries, "and escape from these flames. The enemy holds our walls; Troy falls from her lofty height … Troy entrusts to you her holy things and household gods; take them to share your fortunes: seek for them the mighty city, which, when you have wandered over the deep, you will at last establish!" So he speaks and in his hands brings forth from the inner shrine the fillets, great Vesta, and the undying fire.'

Aeneas gathered his family and followers, and obediently took the sacred flame of Vesta and the household gods (*penates*) of Troy. However, in the fog of battle, he lost his wife, Creusa, who later appeared to him as a ghost and, reinforcing the orders of Hector, prophetically informed him that he was to head for a western land where the Tiber River flowed (*Aeneid* 2.788–91; trans. H.R. Fairclough):

> 'Long exile is your lot, a vast stretch of sea you must plough; and you will come to the land Hesperia, where amid the rich fields of husbandmen the Lydian Tiber flows with gentle sweep. There in store for you are happy days, kingship, and a royal wife.'

Some say that Aeneas was allowed by the Achaeans, on account of his piety, safe passage to leave the burning city, whence he took refuge on Mount Ida, according to the *Iliu Persis*, a lost epic of the sack of Troy. Aeneas also took his son Ascanius (later named Iulus), and some claim that he took the Palladium with him to Italy as well, which eventually reached Rome.

The Palladium, which was said to have fallen to earth from the sky, was an ancient cult image upon which the safety of Troy, and later Rome, depended. The wooden statue (*xoanon*) of Pallas Athena, that Odysseus and Diomedes stole from the citadel of Troy, was later taken to the future site of Rome by Aeneas, where it was in the care of the Vestal Virgins. The Palladium was made by Athena to commemorate the death of Pallas, as part of the city's founding myth. Diomedes and Odysseus accessed the citadel in Troy by a secret passage and carried off the Palladium; the Greeks were then able to enter Troy and lay it to waste with the help of the duplicitous Trojan Horse. Odysseus, according to the epitome of the *Little Iliad*, went into Troy at night disguised as a beggar. Helen recognized him and revealed the whereabouts of the Palladium, after which he and Diomedes re-entered the city and stole the Palladium.

Aeneas fled the burning city of Troy, lame father on his back, and reached Mount Ida, where he was joined by other refugees from the war. The hope was to return home when the enemy had sailed away, but the Achaeans were set on eliminating all refugees. The Trojans sent heralds to the Achaeans and an agreement was reached, which allowed Aeneas, as well as his people and property, to leave the Troad once he had surrendered all arms to the Achaeans. Aeneas and his followers built a fleet of twenty ships, sailing away in the early summer.

Apollodorus tells us that 'the Greeks let him alone on account of his piety', and it is piety that is his defining characteristic – *pius* Aeneas shows *pietas* in his attitude to gods, country and family, and that is what makes him an eminently suitable founder of Rome.

Cicero (*De Legibus* 2.7.15, *De Re Publica* 6.16.1) tells us that the '*homo pius*', such as Aeneas, is a man always exhibiting his '*pietas*', or dutifulness towards the gods and religion, his fatherland, parents and fellow men. In doing this, he preserves the *pax deorum*, or 'peace of the gods'. Aeneas, in his *pietas*, lays the foundation of a concept that in later years became the cornerstone of Roman belief and society. The Etruscan '*homo impius*', Mezentius, on the other hand, wilfully violates this peace and, consistent with his nature as '*contemptor divum*', not only scorns the gods but also shows contempt for both his fatherland and fellow men.

Hyginus (*c.* 64 BCE–17 CE), in his *Fabulae* (115), tells us that Aeneas killed twenty-eight enemies in the Trojan War. Aeneas also features in the Trojan narratives attributed to Dares Phrygius (*De excidio Troiae*), who interestingly describes him as 'auburn-haired, stocky, eloquent, courteous, prudent, pious, and charming', and to Dictys of Crete. In the sixth century CE, John Malalas' eighteen-book *Chronographia* declares Aeneas to be somewhat less than heroic – 'short, fat, with a good chest, powerful, with a ruddy complexion, a broad face, a good nose, fair skin, bald on the forehead, a good beard, grey eyes'.

Aeneas built his fleet in Antandrus. He sailed first to Thrace, where he met Polydorus' ghost. Then, after being received in Delos by King Anius, he attempted unsuccessfully to settle in Crete. Later, having stopped in the Strophades Islands and Zacynthos, and sailed past Ithaca, Aeneas came to Buthrotum in Epirus. From there he crossed to Italy, skirting the waters of Tarentum, Lacinium and the Sicilian coast. Upon first reaching Drepanum, Anchises died. From Drepanum, Aeneas sailed to Carthage, where he met

Dido. After his love affair with the queen, Aeneas returned to Drepanum, later crossing to Italy. In Cumae, he descended to the underworld in his famous *katabasis*, ending his journey soon after in the harbour of Caieta.

Helenus prophesied Aeneas' founding of Rome when he and his followers stopped at Buthrotum, as described by Virgil in *Aeneid* Book 3. In the underworld, a horribly mutilated Deiphobus recounts Helen's treachery: he tells a shocked Aeneas how, when the Trojan Horse was admitted into the city, Helen was at the head of a chorus of Trojan women feigning Bacchic rites, brandishing a torch from the citadel – the signal the Greeks were waiting for to launch their deadly and cataclysmic attack.

Paris had died later in the war, and Deiphobus, his younger brother, then married Helen, only to be slain by Menelaus during the sack of Troy when Helen, again acting treacherously as a fifth columnist, hid his sword and rendered him easy prey. Virgil's graphic description of Deiphobus' mutilation serves only to magnify the enormity of Helen's crime, both as wife to her husband and as belligerent traitor to her country:

> 'Priam's son, his body slashed to bits, can now be seen – his face mangled, his face and hands covered in blood, his head shockingly shorn of ears and nose. Aeneas could barely recognise this shivering shade as Deiphobus'; it struggled to hide its face and the scar of shame.'

Deiphobus is unequivocal about Helen's crime, in words heavy with and redolent of deceit and dishonour:

> 'This was my fate [*fata*], and that Spartan woman's murderous crime [*scelus exitiale*] to mire me in this mess [*his mersere malis*] – these are the souvenirs she has left me with. We spent that final night in false [*falsa*] joy … when the deadly [*fatalis*] horse leaped into impregnable [*ardua*] Pergamon, pregnant with infantry armed to the teeth; she led the Phrygian women in choral dance and false [*simulans*] Bacchanalean song.'

At its simplest, the *Aeneid* can be seen as a poem of two distinct parts. The first half focuses on the fall of Troy and its consequences, along with unsuccessful attempts to establish cities during Aeneas' wanderings; while the second half depicts victory in battle and the beginnings of a new Troy at Rome. This mirrored Rome's recent history, with the bloody demise of the Republic after years of civil war, and the subsequent establishment of peace and prosperity with the new Roman Empire. It also reflected the Augustan propaganda which Virgil was commissioned to promulagte in the *Aeneid*: forget the past and celebrate the new world order of the Roman Principate and Empire. What Aeneas eventually achieved from the wreckage of Troy, namely laying the foundations for the founding of Rome, Augustus – his descendant – was now replicating with the establishment of a new Rome out of the internecine carnage of the civil wars.

The Aeneid

> 'something greater than the Iliad is being born.'
>
> (Propertius, 2.34.65–66)

High praise indeed: the *Aeneid* was being lauded as a classic even before it was completed and published. Virgil sets out his stall at the opening of the *Aeneid* in one single sentence of seven lines and forty-eight words which encompasses the theme of the poem: its salient features, *arma* and *Roma*, neatly bookend this resounding prelude (*Aeneid* 1.1ff; trans. H.R. Fairclough):

> 'Arms and the man I sing, who first from the coasts of Troy, exiled by fate, came to Italy and Italian shores; much buffeted on sea and land by violence from above, through cruel Juno's unforgiving wrath, and much enduring in war also, till he should build a city and bring his gods to Latium; whence came the Latin race, the lords of Alba, and the walls of lofty Rome.'

So the poem, all 9,896 lines of it, is about arms – warfare – a man, Aeneas, and Rome. While the poem describes events a millennium away from Virgil's time, significantly, these events are frequently shown to be political and military antecedents to events in his own day in the reign of Augustus. The fall and exile from Troy and the wanderings of Aeneas form the back story of the Augustan age. The *genus Latinum*, 'Latin race', owes its origins to a man 'from the coasts of Troy, exiled by fate', a *profugus* ('refugee') who introduced Trojan gods to Latium; his descendants would build the *altae moenia Romae*, the 'walls of lofty Rome'. The poem is also about city walls, a number of which, false starts all, come and go in the poem before 'the lofty walls of Rome' go up. Virgil makes it abundantly clear from the very start that the *Aeneid* will show his audiences and readers precisely where

Rome came from, who played a major role in its founding and, 100 or so lines later, how Aeneas was the ancestor of their Emperor Augustus. Just as pointedly, the 'walls of lofty Rome' are echoed with some resonance at line 95; here, Aeneas demonstrates survivor guilt when he bemoans the fact that he did not perish 'under the lofty walls of Troy'. The subtle difference in the agreement with the adjective is important: Troy had walls that were physically huge, but Rome as a city is a sublime and exalted place. Later in the book, Aeneas suffers an attack of 'city envy', reducing him to tears; awestruck by the industry and impressiveness of the construction of Carthage, Aeneas must have realized immediately that this was the template for his own city, his Rome and the Rome of Augustus. All the elements were here for the biggest and best city in the known world, physically and politically, and the prodigious transformation from rural idyll to buzzing metropolis. Virgil writes (*Aeneid* 1.421–35, 438–40; trans. H.R. Fairclough):

> 'Aeneas marvels at the massive buildings, mere huts once; marvels at the gates, the din and paved high-roads. Eagerly the Tyrians press on, some to build walls, to rear the citadel, and roll up stones by hand; some to choose the site for a dwelling and enclose it with a furrow. Here some are digging harbours, here others lay the deep foundations of their theatre and hew out of the cliffs vast columns, fit adornments for the stage to be … "Happy they whose walls already rise!" cries Aeneas, lifting his eyes towards the city roofs. Veiled in a cloud, he enters – wondrous to tell – through their midst, and mingles with the people, seen by none.'

He can barely contain his frustration, and perhaps anxiety, at the task ahead: '*O fortunati, quorum iam moenia surgunt!*' ('Lucky them! Their walls are already going up').

The irony that Carthage was to run his city close for military prowess and regional hegemony is unmissable (*Aeneid* 1.444–45; trans. H.R. Fairclough): '*sic nam fore bello egregiam et facilem victu per saecula gentem*' ('thus was the race to be famous in war and rich in victory through the ages').

Book 2 finds Aeneas at the other extreme of the civil engineering scale, describing to Dido in some graphic and dramatic detail a devastated Troy, a city reduced to rubble – a relic of his past. This is thrown into relief by another pathetic cityscape described in Book 3, line 349 – the pretend (*simulata*) Troy town in Epirus of exiled Andromache and Helenus, son of slain Priam; their little town (*parvam*) is a shadow of the once mighty

Troy, and, by allusion, of the future Rome. The torrential River Xanthus is replaced by an impotent wadi (l. 350 *arentem … rivum*). Andromache and Helenus are trying to recreate the glorious past; Aeneas, however, has a glorious future to orchestrate.

But in the meantime, Aeneas is befuddled by the same lovesickness which has incapacitated Dido. This has caused her to neglect her role as project manager of the Carthage construction works, and the building has ground to a halt – a case of *opera interrupta* (4.88): war fortifications are no longer surging skywards and cranes are idle. Aeneas, for his part, makes a senseless decision when he, obviously in a state of besotted confusion, takes over from Dido and resumes the building work. Jupiter is outraged: Aeneas is clearly building the wrong city in the wrong country, so he orders Mercury to Africa to tell him in no uncertain terms to remember his own kingdom and his destiny. Aeneas is way off course – geographically and psychologically – and is in need of serious redirection and remotivation. But it is not just the distraction of love and passion for Dido that is diverting a nostalgic, backward-looking Aeneas. In his farewell speech to the queen, he admits to her that, given a free choice, he would go back to Troy, preserve '*Priami tecta alta*', 'Priam's lofty palace' (4.343), and rebuild Pergamum.

However, he soon pulls himself together, convincing himself that Italy is the place for him: '*hic amor, haec patria est*' (4.347), 'this is my love, this is my homeland'. The sentiment implicit in Cato's resounding '*Carthago delenda est*' – 'Carthage must be destroyed' – cannot have been far from the minds of Virgil's audience, and it would have been very much on their lips.

Aborted city-building became something of a habit for Aeneas in his challenging quest. First there was Thrace, where the walls go up ('*moenia prima loco*', 3.17), followed by the city they all longed for that was Pergamea in Crete (3.132–34), a city which he encourages the happy inhabitants to cherish, to love as hearth and home. Then (5.755ff) he establishes a homeland under Mount Eryx in Sicily for those who can go no further, unable to face an uncertain future; Acestes is to be king, and parts of the new city are nostalgically named Ilium and Troy. Troia in Italy comes next, where a ditch marks the walls (7.157–58). After the action of the poem has ended, he founds Lavinium, and, after thirty-three years, his son founds Alba Longa.

Aeneas, of course, never gets to found Rome – that is a privilege reserved for Romulus, as we shall see. What Aeneas is pursuing is the idea of a Rome, a notion that has developed by Virgil's time into Augustus' Rome, a city of unassuming brick which he left as a city of magnificent marble. Aeneas does all the hard work in delivering the Trojan refugees to Italy; once there, it is up to Iulus, his son, and ultimately Romulus to establish the site and start construction. The closest Aeneas gets to Rome *per se* is when he visits Evander's Pallanteum (8.306ff), whose city is but a precursor to Rome.

Cities and their walls (*moeniae*) are clearly, then, a powerful motif for Aeneas – they embody his ultimate goal, which is to point the way to the foundation of Rome and its walls. The first thing Romulus does, we shall see, is to mark out the boundaries of his new city and lay the foundations for his walls – for it is these that provide protection and security, permitting everyday life to go on unimpeded, engendering civilizing activities and keeping potential enemies out. If a stranger wanted to come in, then he came in through the gates, not over the wall – that was for enemies of whatever stripe, as Remus was to find out to his cost.

Just as wall-building was a powerful actuality for Aeneas and those who followed him, so it was to be for Augustus, Aeneas's descendent. We are left in no doubt about the scale and magnificence of Augustus' civil engineering feats from his own *Res Gestae*. Here is just an extract from his long list of building work (*Res Gestae Divi Augusti* 19; trans. Frederick W. Shipley; Loeb, *Velleius Paterculus and Res Gestae Divi Augusti*, 1924):

'I built the curia and the Chalcidicum adjoining it, the temple of Apollo on the Palatine with its porticoes, the temple of the deified Julius, the Lupercal, the portico at the Circus Flaminius which I allowed to be called Octavia after the name of him who had constructed an earlier one on the same site, the state box at the Circus Maximus, the temples on the capitol of Jupiter Feretrius and Jupiter Tonans, the temple of Quirinus, the temples of Minerva, of Juno the Queen, and of Jupiter Libertas, on the Aventine, the temple of the Lares at the highest point of the Sacra Via, the temple of the Di Penates on the Velia, the temple of Youth, and the temple of the Great Mother on the Palatine.'

And so the list goes on in chapters 19 and 20. Virgil is clearly showing Aeneas to have paved the way for Romulus to lay the foundations of a Rome eventually beautified by Augustus.

The poem is also about exile. Exile, and its stablemate relegation ('exile-lite'), were familiar punishments in the Roman world, in the higher echelons of Roman politics and society and for the many citizens of enemy states who were displaced from the land of their birth. Exile indicated loss of national identity, loss of place and loss of identity. The idea filled those sent into exile with dread, shame, unbearable loss and aching nostalgia for their homeland.

Ask Cicero – 'what am I now?' (*Ad Atticum* 3.15.2). Ask Ovid – 'My body is sick, but my mind sicker. I miss ...' (*Tristia* 4.6.43–46). Seneca, with forensic precision, defined exile as being disgraced, impoverished and subject to scorn (*Dialogues* 12.6.1). The finality of the exile inflicted on Aeneas by the destruction of his city and his homeland, *patria*, and the deep anxiety and challenging bouts of despair it inflicts on him serves to make his achievement in paving the way for the foundation of Rome all the more estimable – he got there in the end, despite the temptation of a life with Dido within her city walls and his survivor's guilt (1.94–101) which makes him wish he had died in Troy.

Virgil references Julius Caesar's (Augustus' great-uncle) claim to divine ancestry as a descendant of Venus and Anchises. This comes in a speech by Jupiter, who mentions 'Trojan Caesar' as a descendant of Ascanius (Iulus) and therefore of Venus; this is Aeneas' destiny and, at the same time, the script for the founding of Rome as initiated by Aeneas and completed by Romulus (*Aeneid* 1.259ff; trans. H.R. Fairclough):

'[Aeneas] shall wage a great war in Italy, shall crush proud nations, and for his people shall set up laws and city walls, till the third summer has seen him reigning in Latium and three winters have passed in camp since the Rutulians were laid low. But the boy Ascanius, now surnamed Iulus – Ilus he was, while the Ilian state stood firm in sovereignty – shall fulfil in empire thirty great circles of rolling months, shall ship his throne from Lavinium's seat, and, great in power, shall build the walls of Alba Longa. Here then for thrice a hundred years unbroken shall the kingdom endure under Hector's race, until Ilia, a royal priestess, shall bear to Mars her twin offspring. Then Romulus, proud in the tawny hide of the she-wolf, his nurse, shall take up the line, and found the walls of Mars and call the people Romans after his own name. For these I set no bounds in space or time; but have given empire without end. Spiteful Juno, who now in her fear troubles sea and earth and sky, shall change to better counsels and with me cherish the Romans, lords of the world, and the nation of the toga. Thus is it decreed ... From this noble line shall be born the Trojan Caesar, who shall extend his empire to the ocean, his glory to the stars, a Julius [Augustus], name descended from great Iulus! Him, in days to come, shall you, anxious no more, welcome to heaven, laden with Eastern spoils; he, too, shall be invoked in vows. Then wars shall cease and savage ages soften; hoary Faith and Vesta, Quirinus with his brother Remus, shall give laws. The gates of war, grim with iron and close-fitting bars, shall be closed; within, impious Rage, sitting on savage arms, his hands fast bound behind with a hundred brazen knots, shall roar in the ghastliness of blood-stained lips.'

'*Illic fas regna resurgere Troiae*' (I. 206) – 'There it is granted to Troy's realm to rise again'. To Virgil, the Julio-Claudian dynasty is '*revocato a sanguine Teucri*' (I. 235), 'from the restored blood of Teucer'. Caesar was avenging '*infandos Troiae ... labores*' (I. 597), 'Troy's unutterable woes', and fulfilling his own destiny (as Jupiter had promised) to '*populos ... feroces contundet*' (I. 263), 'crush proud nations'.

At the beginning of Book 3 we are reminded that these immigrants were the once-mighty Trojans – not the wife-stealing Trojans of Homer's *Iliad*, but '*res Asiae Priamique ... gentem immeritam*' – 'the power of Asia and Priam's guiltless race'.

In Book 6, when Aeneas is in Elysium, his father describes descendants who will one day inherit their name. He describes Aeneas' children, followed by Romulus, then fast-forwards to Augustus Caesar, making a direct connection between Caesar and Romulus.

But it is Book 8 which focuses the eye directly onto Augustus and sets him centre stage, immortalizing his achievements, his *res gestae*. Here Virgil describes Aeneas' newly fashioned shield, on which the victorious Octavian-Augustus is shown to smash the real-world historical opposition presented by Antony and Cleopatra at the decisive Battle of Actium in 31 BCE, and mythologically, the wars of attrition on the Italian mainland with the arduous fight to found Rome. Octavian's supreme achievement shines out from the boss of the divinely crafted shield, focusing the propaganda, and the eyes and minds of the audience or reader, on this victory over internecine civil war, the decadence of the East, corruption, ostentation and venality.

Virgil was working on the *Aeneid* throughout the 20s BCE, at a time when Augustus had begun to usher in a degree of political and social stability. Nevertheless, as noted, memories of the horrendous civil wars were still raw and fresh in the minds of all Romans, as was the precarious geopolitical position Rome still found herself in. Virgil cannot have been the only educated and intelligent Roman in town who welcomed Augustus' regime as a comparatively stable alternative to the decades of internecine toxic horrors that had come before. We have no way of knowing if the idea of a national epic was suggested and then commissioned by Augustus, but if he did, it would have been while Virgil was still working on the *Georgics*, which includes a trail for his next project: 'And soon I'll gird myself to tell the tales / Of Caesar's brilliant battles, and carry his name / In story across … many future years.' He began work on the *Aeneid* around 29 BCE, and had all but finished when, ten years later, he died unexpectedly while returning home from a trip to Greece.

The *Aeneid*, as we have it – unfinished and rough at the edges in parts – is redolent with references to contemporary events which associate Augustus with this growing socio-political *pax Romana*, with economic prosperity and a realignment of Rome's moral compass. Myth, prophecy and the supernatural all conspire to fashion a clear picture of what it meant to be a Roman, what in effect constituted 'Romanitas', all the while forging links between the past, as exemplified by the *mos maiorum*, and the present age of Augustus. The Italian campaign fought by Aeneas not only reflected the various wars and battles the Romans fought to secure the peninsula, culminating in the dominance of Rome under Augustus, but also symbolized the good Roman, how he should conduct himself in pursuit of his *cursus honorum* and the values he should hold.

The Italian campaigns of Aeneas, as discussed above, were also at odds with Anchises' promise to crush the proud and spare the defeated. Indeed, Aeneas' belligerence in Italy has been seen by some (Daniel Mendelsohn, '"Epic Fail?" Is the Aeneid a Celebration of Empire – or a Critique?', *New Yorker*, 8 October 2018) as a 'tale of nationalistic arrogance whose plot is an all too familiar handbook for repressive violence: once Aeneas and his fellow-Trojans arrive on the coast of Italy, they find that they must fight a series of wars with an indigenous population that, eventually, they brutally subjugate.'

Mendelsohn goes on to ask some valid questions we should all perhaps ponder:

'Who exactly is Aeneas, and why should we admire him? What is the epic's political stance? Can we ignore the parts we dislike and cherish the rest? Should great poetry serve an authoritarian regime – and just whose side was Virgil on? Two thousand years after its appearance, we still can't decide if his masterpiece is a regressive celebration of power as a means of political domination or a craftily coded critique of imperial ideology – a work that still has something useful to tell us.'

Chapter 5

The Aeneas Foundation Myth:
The Italian Wars

Books 7–12 of the *Aeneid* are often said to be Virgil's *Iliad*, or a least a reflection of the fighting which predominates in the *Iliad*. It is in these six books that we encounter the '*bella horrida bella*' ('wars, horrible wars') prophesied to him by the Sibyl in the underworld – '*Thybrim multo spumantem sanguine*', the 'Tiber foaming with much blood' (*Aeneid* 6.86–87) – that Aeneas must endure, if not exacerbate, to secure his new homeland. If there was any doubt about what was to come, the *horrida bella* are revoked at the beginning of Book 7. Virgil would know only too well that appropriation of foreign territory, invasion indeed, was inevitable for Aeneas if he was to succeed in his quest; after all, 700 years of violent incursions and atrocities had served the Romans well so far and brought them to where, led by Augustus, they were in the 20s BCE.

The horrific wars do not just look forward to future Roman conquest; they also anticipate the first-century BCE civil wars which destroyed the Republic and gave birth to an empire, and which, according to the propaganda, Augustus had consigned to history. We can see allusions to the stain of civil war on Roman history throughout the poem, not just in the preface to Book 7 and in the discourse of Anchises and his prognostications in the underworld. Throughout his long and circuitous journey from Troy to Latium, Aeneas' task is seen as a reconciliation of East with West – a reconciliation which will be effected through the marriage of Asian Aeneas and Italian Lavinia. Troy, in modern geopolitical terms, was Asian, while Italy was European. We hear the dichotomy between East and West vocalized loudly and clearly by Numanus from the thick of battle, where he contrasts, not without some ironic humour, the rugged and hardy native Italians, who 'dip their softest new-born babes in chilling rivers, till they bear well the current's bitter cold', with the twice-conquered Phrygians, who, by contrast, are effeminate, culture-loving 'girlies' (*Aeneid*, 9.598–620; adapted from the translation by Theodore C. Williams):

'Our unfailing joy is rapine, and to pile the plunder high. But you! your gowns are saffron needlework or Tyrian purple; ye love shameful ease, or dancing revelry. Your tunics flow long-sleeved, and ye have soft caps ribbon-bound. Yes, you are Phrygian girls, not Phrygian men! ... Leave arms to men, true men! and lay down the the sword!'

Reminiscent as it was of contemporary, conservative Rome's contempt for all things eastern – Greece, Egypt and the like – this conflict between East and West also mirrors the recent civil wars. Aeneas had to reconcile the East with the West, just as Augustus was purportedly banishing any further civil war and eradicating foreign war in contemporary Rome, reconciling Romans with one another and reconciling the nations of the Mediterranean world with Romans. We see the impending conflict in Book 12 (l. 503), where Jupiter's desire to bring Trojan and Latin headlong against each other is questioned, even though they are fated to enjoy endless peace. Moreover, Latinus was the leader of the Italic side and prospective father-in-law of the leader of the Asian side – another example of how the two were fated to come together, and disturbingly reminiscent of Julius Caesar's conflict with Pompey, his son-in-law. Juno, despite being reconciled reluctantly to Aeneas' ultimate victory, spitefully spells out how she will make the concord between *gener atque socer* (son-in-law and father-in-law) as bloody as possible anyway. We have heard *gener atque socer* before, in the underworld with reference to Pompey and Caesar (6.850–51).

We can summarize *Aeneid* 7–12 as follows, highlighting the military elements and underlining how ubiquitous and pivotal war is to this foundation myth.

Book 7

Having ascended from Hell, Aeneas' first port of call in Book 7 is Caieta's harbour, named after his childhood nurse. After honouring Caieta's memory, the fleet prudently sails past the island ruled over by Circe, a goddess whom we know from Odysseus has a habit of turning her visitors into pigs. Neptune takes pity on Aeneas' men and sends them a wind to propel them past this dangerous place. Aeneas later sees the Tiber estuary and knows that he has finally arrived in the land that he is destined to rule. He eventually reaches Laurentum, where he is initially welcomed by the local king Latinus, who tactlessly pledges him his only child and daughter Lavinia's hand in marriage to seal peace between Trojans and Latins. Not surprisingly, this does not go down well with everyone, not least Latinus' wife Amata and the Rutulian prince Turnus, whom she had championed as her son-in-law and who had already been promised Lavinia in marriage. So, just as in the *Iliad* the conflict is exacerbated by a woman being taken from a warrior who has a rightful claim to her, the same unhappy scenario recurs in the *Aeneid*.

The gods, meanwhile, are busy. King Latinus receives a series of omens of war. He also receives a prophecy that he should choose a husband for his daughter from among the foreigners who have just arrived, and that he should allow these strangers to intermarry with the Latins, for the offspring of such a union is destined to rule the world: 'their blood will raise our name above the stars' (7.124–25). This is good news for Latinus and Aeneas, but not so good for the locals. Inevitably, war soon erupts between the Trojans and the Italians, much to Aeneas' dismay, even though the Sibyl had told him to expect this (*bella horrida bella*). Trojan-hating Juno was the catalyst: she was incensed by the proposed match between Aeneas and Lavinia, so much so that she determines to delay things as long as possible: 'so be it, let Lavinia be his wife as fates have fixed. But I can still hold off that moment and delay these great events, can still strike down the nations of both kings' (7.415–18). To help her belligerence, she enlists the Fury Allecto to incite a war between the Trojans and the Latins.

Allecto (the 'implacable' or 'unceasing anger') is one of the Erinyes, or Furies. Her credentials for evil are impeccable: Hesiod says that she was the daughter of Gaea, fertilized by the blood spilled from Uranus when Cronus castrated him; she is the sister of similar undesirables Tisiphone (Vengeance) and Megaera (Jealousy). Her job is to punish crimes like anger, especially if they are against other people; as such, she functions like Nemesis, who castigates crimes against the gods. The Furies had snakes for hair, sported bats' wings and blood dripped from their eyes.

Virgil's Allecto does not disappoint. She is an expert in internecine warfare, arming like-minded brothers in battle and overturning homes in hatred (7.335–36). So odious a monster is she that even her father, Pluto, and her sisters from hell hate her (7.327–28). The stark reference to fratricidal conflict will not have been lost on Virgil's audience and readers – as we have seen, the civil wars were still very fresh in the Roman mind.

Allecto approaches Queen Amata to bewitch her so that she will do all that she can to wreck the peace between the Trojans and the Latins. Amata begs her husband not to marry their daughter to 'Trojan exiles' (7.475). Latinus refuses, causing Amata literally to go insane, inciting the Latin mothers to riot against the Trojans, raging throughout the city and lighting fires while singing the wedding song of Turnus and Lavinia. She even conceals Lavinia in the mountains.

The Fury disguises herself as Juno's priestess, Calybe, and comes to Turnus in a dream, persuading him to begin the war against the Trojans. Turnus ridicules her, saying war is man's work, echoing Hector in the *Iliad* (to Andromache) and Telemachus in the *Odyssey* (to Penelope). An angry Allecto reveals her true self to Turnus, whereupon a terrified Turnus is frightened into assent. She attacks Turnus with a flaming torch, causing his blood to 'boil with the passion for war'.

Finally, hideous Allecto calls on Ascanius while he is hunting on the coast. She implants the scent of a stag owned and prized by a Latin family into the noses of Ascanius' dogs, and then guides Ascanius' arrow so that it kills the beast. The local farmers are outraged and take up arms against the Trojans; Allecto herself sounds the trumpet calling them to war. The Latins attack the Trojans, and there are casualties. Allecto returns to Juno for a debriefing. 'See the discord I made ripe for you in bitter war,' she exults (7.718–19). Allecto, insatiable in her warmongering, asks Juno if she can provoke more strife by sucking bordering towns into the conflict. Juno replies archly that she will manage the rest of the war herself. Turnus and the Latins then storm the palace, demanding war, but King Latinus refuses.

Juno throws open the gates of Mars' temple to signal the beginning of a war, and warriors muster from all corners of the kingdom to fight against the Trojans, including the malevolent Mezentius and the brave Camilla. Virgil is at pains to show that the Trojans are in no way, at least at this point, typical rapacious invaders; far, from it – they are more like benign intruders. When he approaches King Latinus, Aeneas' reasonable and diplomatic companion Ilioneus asks only for 'some small settlement: safe shore to house our native gods and air and water free to all' (300–02). Aeneas and his men want to find a peaceable way to coexist with the Latins, but events are by now largely beyond their control – it is a disaffected Turnus, the repellent Allecto and the implacable, meddlesome Juno who start and stir the trouble.

Book 8

We find Latin warriors signing up to Turnus, which concerns Aeneas greatly, particularly as the dangerous Trojan veteran Diomedes has been asked to support the Latin troops, although Diomedes refuses. That night, the river god Tiberinus appears to Aeneas in a dream, warning him that he will see an omen of a white sow with thirty white suckling pigs – this will signify the location of Alba, the city that Ascanius (Iulus) is destined to found. Tiberinus also advises Aeneas to seek help from King Evander and to pray to Juno in order to ease her anger.

The next day, Aeneas comes across the white sow with her sucklings – incontrovertible proof that he and his companions are destined to build a great city in Latium. The sacrifices to Juno then begin.

Aeneas and his men head for Evander's city, where they find the townsfolk honouring Hercules, who saved them from the repulsive monster Cacus. Evander's son, Pallas, suspects Aeneas and his men are hostile invaders, taking up weapons to confront them, which Aeneas counters when he extends an olive branch. Evander thereupon pledges support for the Trojans.

Meanwhile, Venus is alarmed by the Latin revolt and asks her husband, Vulcan, to make Aeneas a set of weapons. Vulcan orders the Cyclops to drop what they are doing and get to work on this new commmission – *arma virumque* ('arms and the man'). The weapons include the famous shield described in the 106-line *ekphrasis* in which Virgil describes in detail its ornate and prescient decorations (626ff). As we have seen, these include a magnificent combination of the mythical and the historical, past and future, extending from Romulus and Remus being suckled by the *lupa* to a central panel depicting the Battle of Actium, with Augustus and Agrippa on one side, opposing Antony and *fatale monstrum* Cleopatra on the other. The first seven scenes take up forty-one lines (630–70), while the eighth alone has fifty-seven lines. It depicts Actium and the subsequent triumph, with Augustus peacocking through the capital while its temples resound with the joyful singing of *matronae*, and – that other by-product of *imperium* – a throng of conquered peoples paraded ignominiously through the streets: nomads, Africans, Germans and Scythians. The vanquished may have been spared, but the Romans are still exhibiting the characteristic arrogance they vowed to eradicate.

This is how the *ekphrasis* breaks down:

Suckling of Romulus and Remus by the she-wolf (630–34)
Abduction of the Sabine women and the ensuing treaty (635–41)
Punishment of Mettus Fufetius (642–45)
Porsena, Horatius Cocles and Cloelia (646–54)
The Gauls' attack on Rome; Manlius and the geese (655–62)
Dance of the Salii, Lupercalia (663–66)
Tartarus and Ilium, Cato and Catiline (666–70)

Evander advises Aeneas to approach the Etruscans for help. They suffered terribly under the lash of the cruel Mezentius, now one of Turnus' allies, so they would jump at any chance to rise up against their former oppressor and bring him to justice. Evander also entrusts his son Pallas to Aeneas; Pallas is a brave young man, on the threshold of life, and Aeneas feels a strong avuncular affection for him. Aeneas is initially wary of Evander's advice, but Venus sends crashing thunder and an image of weapons hanging in the sky as a sign that he is indeed to seek Etruscan aid. With Pallas by his side, Aeneas and the cream of his men meet with the Etruscans, led by King Tarchon. At their camp, Venus appears to him with Vulcan's weapons.

Book 9

This opens with Juno still fanning the flames of war. She sends Iris to tell Turnus and his Rutulians to attack the Trojan camp. The Rutulians surprise the Trojans, who, as ordered by Aeneas, dutifully retreat behind their ramparts despite the counter-intuitive nature of their actions as warriors. Aeneas is still away parleying with Evander in Pallanteum. Turnus makes an unsuccessful attempt to burn the Trojan fleet: Jupiter transforms the blazing ships into sea nymphs, who flee into the ocean and douse the flames.

Nisus and Euryalus bravely volunteer to carry word of the attack to Aeneas. Although Nisus tries to dissuade Euryalus from accompanying him, Euryalus is adamant he goes along. Ascanius, impressed by their courage, promises to reward them handsomely upon their return, but all that Euryalus asks is that his mother be provided for.

On the way, the intrepid Nisus and Euryalus slay a number of Rutulians. Finally, however, they are spotted, and the Rutulian horsemen give chase through the forest. Euryalus, laden with booty from his victims, falls behind and is captured by Volcens, a Rutulian warrior. Nisus retaliates by hurling spears at Euryalus' captors, but, in revenge for the earlier deaths, Volcens mercilessly slays Euryalus. Nisus, enraged, rushes at Volcens, thrusting his sword through Volcens' mouth, but is then slaughtered by the other Rutulians.

The Latins carry Volcens back to their camp, and then stick the heads of Nisus and Euryalus on pikes and parade them before the Trojans. Euryalus' mother hears rumours of his death. Angered by the killing of their comrades, the Trojans return the Latins' attack and the battle begins in earnest: a wall collapses, killing many Trojans, and Ascanius draws his first blood in battle. He slays Turnus' brother-in-law, Remulus, who made the mistake of taunting the Trojans. Apollo appears to Ascanius and tells him that while he has done well, he should never again engage in war, but instead must work to maintain peace.

The Latins tear down the gates to the Trojan camp, but Pandarus, with superhuman effort, slams the gates shut once again. Turnus runs amok, killing anyone in his way. The Trojans finally get the upper hand and begin to close in on Turnus, but Juno sends word to him that he must flee. He escapes by jumping into the Tiber and allowing the current to carry him back to the safety of the Latin camp.

Book 10

This opens with the gods in session: Jupiter ordains that the Olympian gods must stop meddling in the affairs of mortal men, saying (10.160) 'what each man does will shape his trial and fortune'. Mortal men (and women) are now on their own.

The fighting on earth goes on, with the Trojans holed up inside their battlements as the Latins storm the gates. Aeneas, Pallas and the other men arrive back; their return immediately gives the Trojans much-needed hope. Aeneas and his men are attacked by the Latins amid scenes of horrendous fighting, with numerous casualties. Pallas does battle with Lausus, son of Mezentius, but is slain by Turnus, who cynically slings Pallas' belt across his shoulders – a belt which will come back to haunt him. Aeneas is apoplectic at the sight of the body of the boy who was his ward.

Subsequently, a raging Aeneas cuts a wide, bloody swathe through the Rutulian army – like a 'torrent or black whirlwind' (829–30) – desperately seeking Turnus. Juno, fearing for Turnus' life, asks Jupiter to help her protect her favourite, and he consents to this one favour (despite his recent ruling regarding the assisting of mortals). Juno spirits up a mist in the shape of Aeneas, which Turnus glimpses boarding a ship. Turnus pursues the

wraith as the ship sets out to sea. An angry and tricked Turnus is seen to
have deserted his troops in battle and considers suicide, but instead elects
to try to swim back to shore. He vows to either return to the battlefield and
fight Aeneas, despite the ultimately hopeless outcome, or drown – what is
certain is that he will not be seen as a coward who abandoned his men and
his convictions. Three times he tries to jump into the water, but three times
Juno holds him back.

Meanwhile, Aeneas and Mezentius confront each other. Mezentius is
wounded, but escapes when his son, Lausus, comes between the two. Aeneas
warns the young boy to back off – 'Why are you rushing toward certain
death?' (1113) – but Lausus refuses to back down and Aeneas slays him. As
the boy dies, however, Aeneas thinks of his own father and feels remorse for
what he has done. Grief-stricken, Mezentius sets out determined to avenge
Lausus' death or to die himself. He battles with Aeneas and is thrown from
his beloved horse. As Aeneas holds his sword poised above Mezentius' body,
Mezentius bares his throat, his final words a plea to be buried alongside his
beloved son – more paternal *pietas*.

Virgil says that Mezentius, an Etruscan king of Caere, came to Latium
with something of a reputation. He had been exiled because of his cruelty
and moved to Latium, finding sanctuary with Turnus, whom he helped
against the Trojans. Bloodthirsty by nature, he was something of an animal
on the battlefield.[1] King Evander tells Aeneas how, founded long ago by
Lydian settlers, Caere was a flourishing Etruscan settlement until Mezentius
came onto the scene, subjecting the city and its people to a tyrannical rule
based on a ferocious use of violence. Mezentius perpetrated acts of bloody
cruelty, underpinned by insanity and evil. The pinnacle of his depravity
comes in Evander's account of how Mezentius emulated a perverted and
hideous practice popular among Etruscan pirates. Mezentius would bind
together ('*iungebat*', l. 485) live and dead people hand-to-hand and face-to-
face, leaving them to endure the utmost agony (485–88).[2] More significantly
for Virgil's audience, he was a '*contemptor divum*', a 'despiser of the gods' – a
quality which, like the torture described above, set him in direct contrast to
pius Aeneas.

Virgil's version of the myth of Mezentius differs somewhat from earlier,
traditional accounts. R.G. Austin comments: 'He has taken a traditional
story, of which we possess faint echoes, and has removed it from the museum
of myth into the living world.'[3] Cato the Elder, Varro, Livy, Dionysius of
Halicarnassus and Ovid all deal with Mezentius, and their version is largely
substantiated by Servius' commentary on the *Aeneid* (1.259). In this account,

Mezentius assisted Turnus against Aeneas but was eventually killed in a later battle, not by Aeneas but by his son Ascanius. Some of these writers say that Mezentius demanded from either the Rutulians or Aeneas the '*primitiae*', or first-fruits, of the vintage, which the Latini apparently usually consecrated to Jupiter. This showed more contempt for the gods.

In the end, though, Virgil's impious Mezentius is carefully contrived, by and large, to represent the opposite values to those championed by *pius* Aeneas. He represents the atrocities of the civil wars, carnage and bloodshed which Aeneas' descendants will eventually bring to an end under the reign of Augustus. But it is not quite so simple. Virgil's Mezentius is an ambivalent and paradoxical character: his one redeeming factor is his role as father, and the heartfelt *pietas* and grief he shows to his slain son, Lausus. It is an instance of *pietas* which gives Aeneas, his killer, pause for thought as he, no doubt, reflects on his son, who is also enveloped and vulnerable in the fog of war. Aeneas also recognizes the *patria pietas* exhibited by Lausus before he kills him (821–24), a virtue which sets him apart from his bloodthirsty father. There is a characteristic which disruptively brings the two warriors together: both share a profound fatherly devotion to their sons. Just as Aeneas gives way to *furor* at the end of the poem when he kills Turnus, so Mezentius is able to discard his characteristic *furor* to mourn his son. As we shall see in Book 12, war has a habit of turning things – not least emotions – on their head.

Book 11

Aeneas, distressed by the deaths of Pallas and his other comrades, still offers a sacrifice to the gods, comprising spoils taken from Mezentius. He and his men bury the bodies of their slain companions, Aeneas himself assiduously attending to the funeral rites of Pallas.

Messengers from the Latin camp then approach Aeneas, imploring him to allow them to bury their dead. Aeneas grants their request, telling them that it is only Turnus who should be fighting him and that the Latins and Trojans should seek peace. In a deeply emotional scene, Aeneas and his men set fire to the bodies of their comrades, throw spoils taken from the corpses of the Latins into the flames and offer sacrifices. Elsewhere, the Latins do the same for their fallen, and some women cry out that only Turnus should be suffering, since it is only he who seeks war. King Latinus calls a council of the city's chiefs, at which it is felt by some that the problem should be settled by a duel between Aeneas and Turnus alone. Turnus tells Latinus that he is happy to fight Aeneas in single combat.

Meanwhile, the Trojans are marching on the city. Turnus takes advantage of the ensuing panic to urge the Latins to take up arms, and he prepares himself for battle. The Latins are joined by the legendary warrior Camilla and her Volscians, who take over the defence of the city against the approaching Trojan horsemen, while Turnus rides off to ambush Aeneas, who is taking a different route through the forest.

Virgil tells us Camilla's interesting history. When King Metabus fled his city into exile, he took the infant Camilla with him. Approaching a river that he could not safely cross, encumbered as he was with his daughter, he lashed her to a lance and hurled her across, having prayed to the goddess Diana to keep her safe. The girl was subsequently raised in the wilderness and became Diana's favorite: a fellow virgin whose only true love was of weapons.

The Trojans finally reach the city, and the battle begins. Camilla is the fiercest warrior on the field, and she slays countless Trojans until she is finally killed by Arruns. Arruns is only able to kill Camilla because he has prayed to Apollo to help him end her attack. Now Diana seeks vengeance by sending her sentinel, Opis, to slay Arruns. Having lost Camilla, and unable to restrain the Trojan army, the Latins scatter. Camilla's closest companion, Acca, sends word to Turnus of the events taking place, and Turnus is forced to abandon his ambush and return to the city only moments before Aeneas passes by. Book 11 ends with both men returning to their respective camps on the outskirts of Laurentum to prepare themselves for the next day's battle.

Book 12

This opens with Turnus only too aware that the war has turned against the Latins, and realizing that he now must keep his pledge and fight Aeneas in a duel. King Latinus begs Turnus to reconsider and seek peace with the Trojans, while a distraught Queen Amata pleads with him to defect. But Turnus won't back down: 'The war will be decided by our blood; the bride Lavinia will be won upon that field' (107–09). Aeneas sends word that he will indeed duel with Turnus.

The next day, the Trojans and Latins congregate to watch the contest. Aeneas and Turnus agree to the terms of the duel and offer sacrifices to the gods. Juno, fearing that Turnus will be killed, calls on Juturna, Turnus' sister, to help. Juturna disguises herself as Camers, a Latin warrior, and moves through the Latin ranks, inciting them by telling them that they should not allow their honour to rest on just one life. Her ploy works: Tolumnius assumes the role as their new leader and hurls his lance at the Trojans. It kills a young warrior, and the Trojan army rushes the Latins. The battle resumes in earnest, and King Latinus retreats to mourn the treaty that is now in tatters.

Aeneas implores his men to stand down and leave him to do the battling, but he is hit in the leg by an arrow and is forced to retire for medical attention. Turnus, heartened by this, starts on a killing spree. Aeneas, back at the camp, is impatient to return to the battle, but the physician, Iapyx, cannot remove the arrow from his leg. Venus, concerned by her son's pain, sends a healing balm to mend his wound. Recovered, Aeneas embraces Ascanius and returns to battle.

Aeneas and Turnus both slay a great many warriors, although Juturna is able to distract Aeneas momentarily by riding around in Turnus' chariot while Aeneas, believing his foe to be inside it, pursues her. Eventually, Venus urges Aeneas to move towards the unguarded Latin city. He pledges to lay waste to the city if the battle is not resolved that day. Queen Amata, terrified at the sight of the approaching Trojans – and believing that her beloved Turnus has been killed – hangs herself.

The tragedy that he has wrought finally dawns on Turnus, and he calls for Aeneas to meet him on the field to decide the battle once and for all. The fight begins by both men throwing their spears. They then rush toward each other with drawn swords. Turnus' sword breaks, forcing him to retreat, and Aeneas pursues him, fighting back the pain from the arrow wound. Aeneas, unable to catch Turnus, notices his spear embedded in an olive tree and struggles to free it. Meanwhile, Juturna – disguised as Turnus' charioteer, returns her brother's blade to him. Angered by this interference, Venus helps Aeneas remove his spear from the tree.

Jupiter, himself angry at this persistent meddling in mortal affairs, summons Juno. She knows, he says, that Aeneas is destined to win, so why must she persist in staving off the inevitable? Jupiter tells her that the end has come. In return, Juno asks that the Latins be able to keep their name and customs, and Jupiter, smiling, says that he will allow the customs to be blended and the Latins to keep their name: 'You will see a race arise from this that, mingled with the blood of the Ausonians, will be past men, even past gods, in piety; no other nation will pay you such honour' (1113–17).

Jupiter sends down one of the Furies to frighten Turnus into submission. Juturna, realizing that there is nothing more that she can do to help her brother, flees into the depths of the river, moaning in despair. Aeneas then hurls his spear at the fallen Turnus, and it pierces his thigh. Aeneas approaches Turnus to end his life, but Turnus pleads for mercy, for the sake of his father. Aeneas is moved, and for a moment considers sparing him, but then he notices Pallas' belt slung across Turnus' shoulders. *Pietas* leaves the scene as *pius* Aeneas plunges his sword into Turnus' chest. The dead man's soul, 'indignant, fled away to the shades below'.

We have already noted how this is not a particularly good example of what were to become the Romans sparing the defeated, as promised by Anchises in the underworld. Virgil has, nevertheless, successfully turned the Trojans – losers at Troy – into victors in Italy, a status which obviously sat much more comfortably with Virgil's portrayal of Augustus, their most famous descendant. We perhaps can see in Aeneas' slaying of Turnus a tacit warning by Virgil – to Augustus – that nothing is predictable in war: even the dutiful Aeneas can snap, overcome by *furor*, despite being an upholder of the clemency to be shown to the defeated and a paragon of *pietas* and *iustitia*.

We have to wait until Dionysius of Halicarnassus (*c.* 60 – after 7 BCE) before we know how Aeneas died. After he had fallen in battle against the Etruscans near the River Numicus, his body could not be found, and he was thereafter worshipped as a local god called, according to Livy, Juppiter Indiges.

Aeneas had completed his divinely sanctioned job. So had Virgil; he had completed the brief given to him by Augustus to produce a poem of national relevance and importance, inextricably linking Augustus genealogically to Aeneas and the Trojans. Aeneas married Lavinia and settled down in Lavinium (or Laurentum) for the next three years. It was now left to Ascanius (Iulus) to establish and rule Alba Longa, which he did for thirty-three years, and ultimately – through Romulus – found a city we know as Rome.

To make this all the more plausible, Virgil peppers his mythical epic with historical events which would have resonated with, and would have been instantly recognizable to, reader and audience: the conquest of Greece (as better-late-than-never revenge for Troy); the inexorable expansion of Rome; the curse of Carthage inflicted on Aeneas – and Rome – by the scorned Dido down among the deadmen; the rise and rise of Julius Caesar; and the glory that was Augustus, his grandnephew. Moreover, the fabulous Shield of Aeneas showcases Augustus' crowning achievement: the victory at Actium over civil warmonger Mark Antony and that doomy monster, the licentious, exotic and all-things-unRoman Cleopatra VII.

Chapter 6

The Romulus and Remus Foundation Myth

There is much that is confusing, controversial and inconsistent about the legends and myth relating to the foundation of Rome by Romulus. As we have seen, the gaping disconnect between the putative dates of the sack of Troy and Aeneas's escape and lengthy journey to Italy, and the now canonical dating of the foundation of Rome to 753 BCE (thanks to Varro, who reconciled the work of Eratosthenes of Cyrene, who calculated the date of the fall of Troy, and Timaeus of Tauromenium, who did likewise for the founding of Rome), only serves to complicate the issue further. The 371-year, fourteen-generation gap demands that a significant suspension of belief is needed, because the Romans, it seems, were not going to let the gap get in the way of two great stories of national interest, however big their chronological shortcomings.

There is no agreement on the etymology of the name 'Rome'. Many go for the obvious similarity with Romulus. Jean-Jacques Rousseau (1712–78) suggested the Greek 'ῥώμη' (rhōmē), meaning 'strength' or 'vigour'.

Early Rome was not entirely Roman: the Tarquins (Rome's fifth and seventh kings) were Etruscan, for example. Early Rome was initially a conglomeration of separate settlements perched on Rome's hills, but by the fifth century BCE they had merged to become one city strong enough to exert its power militarily over the surrounding lands of the Sabine, Etruscan and Latin tribes. As was the Roman way, the tribes' customs, rites and gods were absorbed and repurposed. The foundation myth, while not actually featuring war, is entirely predicated on belligerence: founding Rome implied conflict over territory with neighbouring tribes such as the Samnites and Etruscans, while the survival of Rome depended on the defence of the city from unneighbourly incursions and the expansion of the city's boundaries into adjacent territories at the expense of their neighbours' lands. We will see the mythical wars which this caused in later chapters.

The Trojan factor, of course, involves the famous descriptions of Aeneas' Mediterranean meanderings in search of a 'Rome' he can call home. But, as touched on above, the 'evidence' for a Trojan lineage was well established by the time Virgil embarked on his commission to endow Augustus with a Trojan heritage, demonstrating the keenness the colonizing Greeks had to associate with southern Italy and at the same time facilitating and adding credence to Virgil's story. As noted above, in the fifth century BCE, Hellanicus of Lesbos tells us that Aeneas named Rome after a Trojan woman called Rhomê who was tired of wandering the seas and burnt the Trojans' boats to reintroduce a degree of stability to the exiles' lives. Plutarch, in his life of Romulus (2.1), has Rhomê as the wife of Aeneas and of Anchises, or the granddaughter of Heracles. In 400 BCE, Damastes of Sigeum repeated the story, followed by Aristotle, who called the destination Latineon. Timaeus of Tauromeneum in Sicily (c. 356–260 BCE) made Aeneas the founder of both Rome and Lavinium. Other versions have Aeneas as the founder, or Romulus as son of Zeus, or else the friend/wife, daughter or granddaughter of Aeneas, or Aeneas as son of Odysseus or of Latinus, or Romulus and Remus as sons or grandsons of Aeneas.

Other Greek logographers extend the foundation by a couple of generations to make the founder Rhomos (the Greek eponym for Rome) – the son or grandson of Aeneas. This is corroborated in part by Xenagoras in the third century BCE, who says that Odysseus and Circe had three sons – Rhomos, Anteias and Ardeias – who went on the found cities named after themselves. According to Dionysus (1.73), Naevius and Ennius, who had access to 'ancient accounts preserved in the sacred tablets' in their primary research, then made Rhomus (Romulus) the grandson of Aeneas by Ilia, a Trojan woman (Servius, *ad Aeneid* 1.273 and 6.777). The complexity increases with Alcimus (c. 350 BCE), who makes Rhomus found Rome as the grandson of Romulus and the great grandson of Aeneas and Tyrrhenia. Callias of Syracuse (c. 300 BCE) has it that Rhomê married Latinus, the king of the Aborigines, by whom she had three sons – Rhomus, Rhomylos and Telegonos – who founded a city named after their mother.

Whatever the case, Aeneas' son founded Alba Longa and the dynasty of kings all bearing the additional name Silvius. The eleventh was Proca, father of Numitor and Amulius. Romulus (which means 'forceful', from *rhome*, 'strength') and Remus (which means 'cautious', from *remorari* – 'to hold back') were now safe for posterity.

The earliest reference to the two as twins comes from the Greek Diocles of Peparethus, according to Plutarch (*Romulus* 3 and 8), whose work was for the most part accepted by Fabius Pictor, Rome's first historian. Rhomos developed into a more Roman-Etruscan sounding Remus. Remus was disposed of early in the legend, and the rest is history, or legend, allowing Romulus to become the founder and first king of Rome. By 296 BCE, Romulus and Remus were sufficiently embedded in Roman legend to inspire the *lupa* statue, the Capitoline Wolf, with the she-wolf suckling the twins, while a silver coin minted in 269 BCE, bearing the inscription *Romanum*, had the same scene depicted. The name 'Faustulus' was later claimed by a Roman family: Sextus Pompeius Fostlus issued a silver denarius in about 140 BCE that showed the twins and she-wolf, with Faustulus to their left. The Capitoline Wolf is a late sixth/early fifth-century BCE Etruscan bronze to which a Roman sculptor added the twins to make it truly Roman, a representation of the foundation myth and a good example of the eclectic nature of Roman culture. The original twins were destroyed and replaced with copies during the Renaissance.

The city of Siena is said to have been founded by Senius and Aschius, two sons of Remus and thus nephews of Romulus. Records from the sixteenth century tell us that after their father's murder by Romulus, they supposedly fled Rome – one riding on a black horse and the other on a white one, giving rise to the colours on the Balzana, the coat of arms of Siena. They took with them the statue of the she-wolf suckling the infants, the Capitoline Wolf, which they stole from the Temple of Apollo in Rome, thus establishing that symbol for Siena. A variant of the legend holds that the brothers were protected by the gods with a white cloud during the day and a dark cloud at night. The Porta Camollia, in the walls of Siena, is said to have been named after a soldier sent to bring the brothers back to Rome, but who elected to stay instead. One function of the legend is to endow the Sienese with a noble and ancient ancestry, in much the same way as Rome itself had sought such a pedigree with the foundation story in the *Aeneid*. Every great city needs a plausible foundation story.

The famous *lupa* and Romulus and Remus mosaic found at Aldborough (Isurium Brigantum) in northern England is in Leeds City Museum and dates from *circa* 300 CE. It demonstrates how popular the iconic symbol was, even at the edge of empire, even after the best part of 1,000 years.

This was all at a time when nascent Roman historiography demanded a viable foundation story. Cato's *Origines* from about 170 BCE saw the start of a historiographical process of filling in the gaps in detail, but there are several sources that we now rely on.

Livy (59 BCE–17 CE), in his Book 1, sketches out Aeneas' flight from Troy and his eventful journey to Italy, up to the birth of Romulus and Remus, the founding of Rome and the seven kings.

Strabo (63 BCE–*c.* 24 CE) says that there is also an older story which tells of Rome being an Arcadian colony founded by Evander. Strabo also writes that Lucius Coelius Antipater believed that Rome was founded by Greeks. He was primarily a jurist (fl. 123 BCE) but none of his juridical writings have survived. He wrote a history of the Second Punic War, and composed annals which were epitomized by Brutus. Antipater followed the Greek history of Silenus Calatinus, and borrowed from the *Origines* of Cato the Elder. He is occasionally quoted by Livy, who sometimes suspects his accuracy.

Virgil (70–19 BCE) recounts in the *Aeneid* the circuitous journey of Aeneas and the wars in Italy, leading to the eventual founding, all the while linking Augustus to this glorious event and his divine descent from Venus, mother of Aeneas.

The *Fasti* of Ovid (43 BCE–17 CE) gives a month-by-month six-month calendar of sacred rites and festivals and their origins, and contains a complete account of the twins' story, including a tale in which the ghost of Remus appears to Faustulus and his wife, Acca Larentia. Ovid's *Metamorphoses* tells a number of legendary stories, culminating in the deification of Julius Caesar and an encomium to Augustus.

There are also fragments of the works of the prodigious polymath Varro (116–27 BCE) and the second-century CE epitome by Festus of the history written by Verrius Flaccus, an imperial teacher.

Dionysius of Halicarnassus (fl. around 28 BCE) cites, among others in his *Roman Antiquities*, the lost histories of Quintus Fabius Pictor, Lucius Calpurnius Piso, Cato the Elder and Lucius Cincius Alimentus; he also mentions Valerius Antias and Claudius Quadrigarius (both around 80 BCE). Dionysius asserts that the people who came to the lands that later became the city of Rome were: first, the Aborigines, who expelled the Sicels and were from Arcadia; then the Pelasgians, who came from Thessaly; third, those who arrived in Italy with Evander from the city of Pallantium in Arcadia; after them, the Epeans from Elis and Pheneats from Pheneus, who were part of the army commanded by Heracles, but opted to stay there while they were returning from the expedition at the Erytheia; they were then joined by some Trojans; finally, there were the Trojans who had escaped with Aeneas from Ilium, Dardanus and the other Trojan cities. Dionysius mentions that the Trojans were also Greek people who were originally from the Peloponnese. He adds that even Romans say that the Pallantium was founded by Greeks from Pallantium of Arcadia, about sixty years before the Trojan War, and that the leader was Evander. Later, sixteen generations after the Trojan War, the Albans merged these places into one settlement, surrounding them with a wall and a ditch. The Albans were a blended nation composed of all the above peoples, who, having lost their national identities, came to be known by one common name: Latins, after Latinus, who had been the king of the country. The leaders of the colony were the twin brothers, Romulus and Remus.

Plutarch's *Life of Romulus* (46 – after 120 CE) has chapters on Numa, Publius Valerius Publicola (one of the first consuls) and Coriolanus; his *Roman Questions* describes Roman customs and ritual. Plutarch refers to the version by Diodes of Peparethus, 'and Fabius Pictor follows him in most points'. Essentially, this is the version which is most generally accepted and known to us (Plutarch, *Romulus* 3; trans. Bernadotte Perrin):

> 'The descendants of Aeneas reigned as kings in Alba, and the succession devolved at length upon two brothers, Numitor and Amulius. Amulius divided the whole inheritance into two parts, setting the treasures and the gold which had been brought from Troy over against the kingdom, and Numitor chose the kingdom. Amulius, then, in possession of the treasure, and made more powerful by it than Numitor, easily took the kingdom away from his brother, and fearing lest that brother's daughter should have children, made her a priestess of Vesta, bound to live unwedded and a virgin all her days.'

Plutarch adds a caveat and explains away the mythical nature of the foundation (*Romulus* 8; trans. Bernadotte Perrin):

> 'Although most of these particulars are related by Fabius [Pictor] and Diodes of Peparethus, who seems to have been the first to publish a "Founding of Rome", some are suspicious of their fictitious and fabulous quality; but we should not be incredulous when we see what a poet fortune sometimes is, and when we reflect that the Roman state would not have attained to its present power, had it not been of a divine origin, and one which was attended by great marvels.'

Plutarch offers more detail about the survival of the twins (*Romulus* 4; adapted from the translation by Bernadotte Perrin):

> 'Now there was a wild fig-tree nearby, which they called Ruminalis, either from Romulus, as is generally thought, or because cud-chewing, or ruminating, animals spent the noon-tide there for the sake of the shade, or best of all, from the suckling of the babes there; for the ancient Romans called the teat "ruma", and a certain goddess, who is thought

to preside over the rearing of young children, is still called Rumilia, in sacrificing to whom no wine is used, and libations of milk are poured over her victims. Here, then, the babies lay, and the she-wolf gave them suck, and a woodpecker came to help in feeding them and to watch over them. Now these creatures are considered sacred to Mars, and the woodpecker is held in especial veneration and honour by the Latins, and this was the chief reason why the mother was believed when she declared that Mars was the father of her babies. And yet it is said that she was deceived into doing this, and was really deflowered by Amulius himself, who came to her in armour and raped her.'

The Roman History by Cassius Dio mentions an oracle that had predicted Amulius' death by a son of Numitor as the reason the Alban king expelled the twins.

The *Origo Gentis Romanae* contains a number of versions of the story, including one which describes a woodpecker (*picus*) fetching the boys food when they were exposed (as depicted in the painting by Peter Paul Rubens, *c.* 1616, now in the Capitoline Museums), and a fable in which Remus founds a city named Remuria, 5 miles from Rome, and outlives Romulus. In some legends Picus was once a Latin king and was married to the nymph Canens.

Primary sources were scant for the Romans, so the systematic plundering of past historians was crucial. The historians mentioned above plundered selectively, picking out the episodes which suited their own agendas or made the best stories. In short, they were to some extent rewriting history, omitting bits and inventing bits – modifying and embroidering their sources. Livy himself explains (Praefatio *Ab urbe condita*; trans. Aubrey de Sélincourt, 1960):

'In history you have a record of the infinite variety of human experience plainly set out for all to see; and in that record you can find for yourself and your country both examples and warnings; fine things to take as models, base things, rotten through and through, to avoid.

'I hope my passion for Rome's past has not impaired my judgement, for I do honestly believe that no country has ever been greater or purer than ours or richer in good citizens and noble deeds.'

One legend has it that Acca had twelve sons, and when one of them died, Romulus took his place, and with the remaining eleven founded the college of the Arval brothers, Fratres Arvales, thus providing a neat link between Romulus and a revered Roman institution.

The Romulus myth became an accepted and revered part of Roman life and a major tourist attraction, with visits available to the Lupercal, worship to the deified Romulus-Quirinus at the 'shepherd's hut' or dramatizations and copies of the *Fasti* and other accounts for sale. Romulus became the direct ancestor of Rome's first Imperial dynasty under Augustus, with not a little help from Aeneas.

Why would the Romans not be eager to imbibe the exciting and colourful Greek, semi-exotic myths and fuse them with their own legends? By comparison with the Greeks, Roman myths and legends were thus far somewhat monochrome, one-dimensional, humdrum and unromantic, devoid of the drama of a good Greek myth, populated as it might be with tragic heroes, squabbling gods, thunderbolts, romance, a thriving Hell under the earth, fake news, metamorphoses galore, bad parents, incest, bestiality, gender confusion and sexual deviants. So, over time, imbibe they did, forging a link between the refugee Trojans under Aeneas and Romulus and Remus in a mythology which, while never devoid of native Roman elements, was unmistakably Hellenocentric. After all, we have noted how by the time of Augustus, Greek culture eventually permeated into all aspects of Roman life, while Greece and all things Greek were becoming increasingly ubiquitous. Success on the battlefield, overseas expansion, an enlightened immigration policy and the ability to foster and appreciate foreigners and their cultures all conspired to empower this.

So what were the details of this myth or legend which stars Romulus and Remus? Like many of the stories adumbrating the foundation and early progress of Rome, it starts with a rape – that of Rhea Silvia by war god Mars. A fragment from Ennius (*Annales* 44–45) tells how she dreamed she succumbed to a god-like figure (Mars), and later, when trying to find her sister, her father appeared to her and pronounced, 'Sorrows, my daughter, you must first endure; then from the river fortune will return.' In this version, Rhea – all too aware of the punishment that awaited her as a damaged Vestal – drowned and married Anio, a river god. But the real 'fortune' that came out of this myth was the survival of her abandoned and exposed sons, Romulus and Remus. Ovid elaborates on this by having Rhea's breasts seductively exposed; Mars cannot resist, and proceeds to rape her, as described in what must be one of the tersest verses in Latin literature: '*Mars videt hanc, visamque cupit, potiturque cupita*' – 'Mars sees her, likes what he sees and takes what he likes' (*Fasti* 3.21). While no consolation to Rhea, it's over in an Ovidian flash, its terseness worryingly reminiscent of Caesar's coldly militaristic 'I came, I saw, I conquered' – '*Veni, vidi, vici*' – written in 47 BCE, according to Appian, in a triumphant letter to the Senate after his victory at the Battle of Zela.

Livy says that Rhea was raped by an unknown man, but 'declared Mars to be the father of her illegitimate offspring, either because she really thought that to be the case, or because it was less shameful to have committed such an offence with a god'.

Another version holds that she was raped by her uncle, Amulius, anonymized by his full armour. Rhea Silvia was the daughter of Numitor, the former king deposed by his younger brother Amulius when he appropriated the Alban treasury. She had not long before been elevated by Amulius to the position of Vestal Virgin, one of the holiest of offices in Rome and certainly the most honourable for a woman. Normally, her violation would have led to entombment and an agonizingly slow, terrifying and claustrophobic death, but the implication of an Olympian may have conferred mitigation and clemency, and Mars was certainly not to be angered by the execution of Rhea. When Amulius bestowed the sacred office on his niece, he was motivated by fear of a rising young grandson – the thirty-year celibacy rule which the Vestals observed effectively ensuring that the line of Numitor had no heirs; he also slew Numitor's son for the same reason. Another factor was Amulius' hatred towards Numitor, his brother.

Romulus and Remus were born of the rape in Alba Longa, near to the future site of Rome. Although Apulius had ordered their death, the servant charged with this had shown sympathy; they were exposed and left to fend for themselves, while Rhea was imprisoned. Amulius believed that this mercy shown to Rhea would save him and his city from retribution by the gods.

However, the god Tiberinus, Father of the River, intervened and ensured the twins' safety by calming the river and having their basket snag in the roots of a nearby tree, the Ruminal fig tree. This tree was at the base of the Palatine Hill in the Velabrum swamp. The boys survived and were suckled by a she-wolf (*lupa*), in a cave now known as the Lupercal, and later adopted by Faustulus, a shepherd. The story is added more poignancy because *lupa* is Latin slang for a prostitute.

Plutarch has a different version. In his *Life of Romulus*, he tells the story of Tarchetius, the cruel king of Alba Longa. A huge phallus rose from his hearth and took off, flying around the house; oracular consultation revealed that this was Mars showing his anger, impatient for Tarchetius to produce a successor to the throne by way of a virgin and the phallus. Mars demanded a virgin for the phallus because any child born of this coupling would excel in virtue, fortune and strength. Attempts by Tarchetius to persuade his daughter to have sex with the phallus failed when she refused, so he ordered a slave girl to take her place. Both girls were imprisoned, but Tarchetius' plan to execute them was foiled by Vesta, who forbad the murders. The sentence was commuted to imprisonment, during which the girls were set the task of weaving a piece of cloth; upon completion of this task, they were to be given in marriage. However, to foil this, everything they wove by day was, by order of Tarchetius, unpicked that night. Romulus and Remus were duly born. Tarchetius abandoned the twins to a Teratius, with orders to drown them – only for them to be rescued and nurtured by the she-wolf, *lupa*, fed solids by a woodpecker and adopted by a cowherd.

In Livy's canonical version, Romulus and Remus lived a rural early life in Faustulus' hut, tending grazing flocks, oblivious of their true identities and slowly building up, through their popularity and natural leadership skills, a band of rebel rustic followers. Already, Romulus and Remus were exhibiting qualities much revered by the Romans: hard work on the land and an aptitude for battlefield skills. This is how Plutarch describes their early adulthood (*Romulus* 6; adapted from the translation by Bernadotte Perrin):

'Well, the noble size and beauty of their bodies, even when they were infants, was a sign of their natural disposition; and when they grew up, they were both of them courageous and manly, with spirits which courted apparent danger, and a daring which nothing could terrify. But Romulus seemed to exercise his judgement more, and to have political sagacity, while in his dealings with their neighbours in matters pertaining to herding and hunting, he gave them the impression that he was born to command rather than to obey. With their equals or inferiors they were therefore on friendly terms, but they looked down upon the overseers, bailiffs, and chief herdsmen of the king, believing them to be no better men than themselves, and disregarded both their threats and their anger. They also applied themselves to generous occupations and pursuits, scorning laziness and idleness, preferring exercise, hunting, running, driving off robbers, capturing thieves, and rescuing the oppressed from violence. For these things, indeed, they were famous far and near.'

As they grew older, the rift between Amulius and Numitor rumbled on; the twins were embroiled in a spat over some cattle raiding between shepherds who were supporters of Amulius. Remus was taken prisoner in an ambush during the feast of Lupercalia and brought to Alba Longa, by which time both his grandfather and the king suspected his true identity. Romulus, meanwhile, planned to spring his brother, at which time both the boys learned their real identities and joined forces with Numitor to restore him to the throne. King Amulius still believed that Rhea Silvia's children were dead and did not recognize Remus or Romulus. Romulus freed his brother, and in the process killed King Amulius; Numitor was reinstated as king when the brothers rejected the citizens' offer of the crown of Alba Longa. The twins decided to build a city of their own. Their legendary partnership anticipated the historical Roman double magistracy of the consulship, as well as the strength inherent in the patrician and plebeian interrelationship on which the strength of the Republic was based until its decline and fall in the first century BCE.

Romulus, wasting no time in demonstrating his alpha male credentials, established Rome's swift light cavalry, the *celeres* (actually a fourth-century BCE invention). This force epitomized the Roman way of war and served the growing empire well for centuries: Romulus named the first commander Celer, meaning 'swift'. The origin of this myth probably lies in a piece of history in which, at the Battle of Imbrinium in 325 BCE, Lucius Papirius Cursor took up the dictatorship to deal with the troublesome Samnites who had installed a garrison in Greek Neapolis, but he was detained in Rome, attending to his auspices. In his absence, the *magister equitum*, one Quintus Fabius Maximus Rullianus, disobeyed orders and attacked the Samnites at Imbrinium with a headlong cavalry charge. The subsequent rout accounted for 20,000 Samnite dead. Rullianus was condemned to death by Cursor for disobeying orders, only to be saved by the intercession of the Senate, and went on to have an astonishingly successful military career.

Being brothers, Romulus and Remus fell out, unable to agree whether to call this new city Roma or Remora, or on which of Rome's seven hills they should build the city. Romulus wanted the Palatine Hill, overlooking the Lupercal with all its connotations; Remus went for the Aventine Hill. To break the deadlock, they agreed to seek the gods' advice through augury. Remus first saw six lucky-looking birds, only to be challenged by Romulus, who spotted twelve auspicious birds and claimed divine approval. Romulus asserted that he was the clear winner by six birds, but Remus argued that since he saw his birds first, he had won. In the end, the forceful nature of Romulus won out over a yielding, cautious and conflict-averse Remus.

This spat of course only worsened matters between the siblings. Romulus began to dig trenches and build walls and gates around the Palatine Hill, marking out the extent of his city. These were not just for routine defensive purposes. Throughout their history, the Romans religiously defined the sacred inviolability of their city walls when establishing a new settlement. Let anyone scale the walls at their peril – such an act was tantamount to sacrilege and was treasonable. Friends and allies came in by the gate; only trouble-making enemies scaled the walls. Remus must have been incensed because, uncharacteristically, he ridiculed the wall and his brother's city before finally jumping over it, perhaps partly in jest. But Romulus did not see the funny side of it and Remus was slain by Celer, master of works, with a well-aimed spade to the head. Romulus thundered, 'so perish anyone else who jumps over my walls' (Livy, 1.7). Rome, then, was clearly founded on aggressive expansionism and violence, all part of a divinely underwritten plan for the establishment of Romulus' new city. Woe betide anyone who had the temerity to threaten the city walls or got in the way of Roman expansion; ancient history, not myth, was to demonstrate the reality of this threat for many enemies of Rome.

We can perhaps begin to understand Remus' huge indiscretion and Romulus' rage when we see just how important city walls were to the Romans. Plutarch describes in a meticulous way how the walls are constructed, with rigorous observance of sacred procedures. He tells us Romulus was not just building his defensive walls, he was laying down the very foundations of Rome's religion (Plutarch, *Romulus* 11; trans. Bernadotte Perrin):

'Romulus buried Remus, together with his foster-fathers, in the Remonia, and then set himself to building his city, after summoning from Tuscany men who prescribed all the details in accordance with certain sacred ordinances and writings, and taught them to him as in a religious rite. A circular trench was dug around what is now the Comitium, and in this were deposited first-fruits of all things the use of which was sanctioned by custom as good and by nature as necessary; and finally, every man brought a small portion of the soil of his native land, and these were cast in among the first-fruits and mingled with them. They call this trench, as they do the heavens, by the name of "mundus". Then, taking this as a centre, they marked out the city in a circle round it. And the founder, having shod a plough with a brazen ploughshare, and having yoked to it a bull and a cow, himself drove a deep furrow round the boundary lines, while those who followed after him had to turn the clods, which the plough threw up, inwards towards the city, and suffer no clod to lie turned outwards. With this line they mark out the course of the wall, and it is called, by contraction, '"pomerium", that is "post murum", behind or next the wall. And where they purposed to put in a gate, there they took the share out of the ground, lifted the plough over, and left a vacant space. And this is the reason why they regard all the wall as sacred except the gates; but if they held the gates sacred, it would not be possible, without religious scruples, to bring into and send out of the city things which are necessary, and yet unclean.'

Remus' new-found spontaneity, and agility, cost him his life. Over time, and certainly by the time Livy came to write his *Ab Urbe Condita*, Celer was airbrushed out of this particular myth and the Romans preferred to call Romulus sole founder and to elide him into the role of murderer, guilty of the heinous sin of fratricide – a sin and a crime all so frequent in the late first-century BCE civil wars when sons slew fathers and brothers slew brothers. The shocking allusion would not have been lost on Livy's audience.

We can perhaps identify another *post-eventum* historical link with the later-construed myth, which happened thirty-five years after Imbrinium at the Battle of Sentinum in the Third Samnite War. When the armies clashed, on the right, Fabius wore down the Samnites and Gauls by carrying out a successful head-on assault. Things were very different on the left, however, where Fabius' right-hand man, the impetuous Publius Decius Mus (the son of the consul of 340 BC), incautiously played all his cards at the outset; he paid the price when his troops were overcome by a charge of Gallic chariots. Decius despaired and 'devoted' himself, as his father had done at the Battle of Mount Vesuvius, charging headlong into the ranks of Gauls to his death and consigning himself to the gods of the underworld – a textbook *devotio*. His valour and sacrifice had the desired effect when the Romans regrouped and mounted a counter-attack, supported by reserves from Fabius' army. His sacrifice saved Rome, just as the death of Remus allowed the foundation of Rome on the Palatine. After Sentinum, a temple dedicated to Victoria was erected on the Palatine.

City built, Plutarch records that Romulus set about establishing its institutions, the patronage system, government, military and religious traditions, reigning for many years as its first king (*Romulus* 13; adapted from the translation by Bernadotte Perrin):

'Romulus divided all the multitude that were of age to bear arms into military companies, each company consisting of three thousand infantry and three hundred horsemen. Such a company was called a "legion",

because the warlike were *selected* out of all. In the second place, he
treated the others as a people, and this multitude was called "populus";
a hundred of them, who were the most eminent, he appointed to be
councillors, calling the individuals themselves "patricians", and their
body a "senate". Now the word "senate" means literally a Council
of Elders, and the councillors were called "patricians", as some say,
because they were fathers of lawful children; or rather, according to
others, because they could tell who their own fathers were, which
could not be said of many of those who first streamed into the city;
according to others still, from "patronage", which was their word for
the protection of inferiors, and is so to this day.'

These sturdy Roman pillars of civilization, as seen in historical Rome, the
very *mos maiorum* encapsulated in buildings, institutions and laws – the way
the ancestors did things – are divided up between the kings: Romulus –
the Senate, the Curiate assembly and the cavalry; Numa – the calendar and
priesthoods; Hostilius – treason trials and religious procedures for making
peace; Ancus Marcius – religious procedures for declaring war, Rome's first
prison, aqueduct and bridge; Tarquinius Priscus – Rome's first stone walls
and the annual games; Servus Tullius – the census, the system of tribes
and the hierarchial centuriate assembly; Tarquinius Superbus – the Roman
sewer (or at least part of it). Here, then, we have a kind of Rome by numbers
– everything Roman neatly accounted for in the misty myths of Rome.

Livy and his fellow historians go on to tell us what happens next, as
described in the following chapters here. We are still not in the historical
world and remain largely mythological until the early years of the Republic,
traditionally founded in 509 BCE. After that, the rest is ancient history.

Chapter 7

Abduction, Rape and Murdering Your Daughter – All in the Name of History

O nce Rome was established by Romulus, a number of mythical or semi-mythical events were said to have taken place to describe and explain the early history of Rome, to lionize its values and morals and to add a veneer of historiocity to its early days. The title of this chapter reveals the nature and characteristics of much of this mythology, leaving us to conclude that the early days of Rome were founded on kidnapping, ethnic cleansing of a sort, sexual violence and filicide.

Rape in the early history of Rome

'According to Roman myth, the city of Rome was founded upon a series of sexual violations of women.'

(Helen Morales, *Classical Mythology –
A Very Short Introduction*, p.86)

Although normal behaviour and laws are, conveniently for the perpetrators, often suspended during times of war, it will still be useful to look at what the norms were in cases of rape and violent sexual abuse in Greece and early Rome. Rape, from a legal standpoint, was complicated. The male Greek gods were portrayed unashamedly as serial rapists, raping with impunity; Zeus uses non-consensual sex not just for sexual gratification, but to demonstrate and exert his virility and omnipotence. If you were to ask him why he raped, he may well have glibly replied, 'Because I can, and I get away with it.' Some men, and many victorious soldiers, would have sympathized with this. Rampant victorious Greek and Roman soldiers would have needed little encouragement to rape and loot, but if they did need reassurance then they had to look no further than their gods or legends to sanction their brutish behaviour. Livy swerves around the issue, mitigating the three episodes under discussion here as being for the benefit of the state, with the perpetrators acting in the national interest, emphasizing the long-term socio–political benefits.

The 'rape' of the Sabine women allowed Rome a blended population in which (further) violence and conflict was ultimately avoided and the Romans and Sabines eventually coexisted peacefully. The rape of that paragon of feminine virtue, Lucretia – by the king's son, no less – led to the overthrow of the monarchy and the establishment of the Republic.

In Ovid, cases of rape and sexual violence appear frequently in the *Metamorphoses*, although there are also episodes of rape in Ovid's earlier and later works: in the *Metamorphoses* there are more than fifty episodes of rape and attempted rape. Unsurprisingly, rape victims are more often than not female and their rapists are most likely to be male; however, Ovid gives us one very graphic tale of the attempted rape of Hermaphroditus by a nymph, Salmacis. In the *Metamorphoses*, male rapists by and large appear to go unpunished, and it seems that it is often the victims of rape who are slurred and stigmatized or penalized for the violation. Not much change there, then, after more than 2,000 years.

L.A. Champanis addresses the issue of rape in Ovid in *Female Changes: The Violation and Violence of Women in Ovid's Matamorphoses* (abstract, 2012):

> 'While his personal values may not necessarily be reflected in his works and his readers may never know the "true" intentions behind the poem, the Metamorphoses does hold up a mirror to the negative treatment of women and exposes the gender inequalities that existed during Ovid's time. As a poet, however, Ovid's conceived role is to entertain his audience and despite his somewhat problematic treatment of women and rape victims, he does just that.'

The vocabulary only confuses the issue: classical 'rape' was not what we today understand to be rape, revolving around the issue of consent.[1] The Greek verb *harpazein* meant 'to carry off' or 'abduct', as *raptare* did in Latin. To convey the connotative meaning of non-consensual sexual violation, the Greeks added *bia* – 'with force'. Forced sex in Latin was usually expressed as *stuprum*, 'fornication', with the addition of *cum vi* or *per vim*, 'with violent force'. *Raptus ad stuprum* was abduction with a view to committing a sex crime. The legendary 'rape of the Sabine women' was, literally, the 'abduction of the Sabine women', an undisguised and shameless act of nation-building, although no doubt the actual raping, as we understand it, took place when the Romans got the Sabine women and girls home. To honour the (reluctant and involuntary) role played by women in this early example of empire-building and ethnic cleansing of sorts, the thirty individual political wards of the new Rome were triumphantly named after thirty of the Sabine women.

Moreover, in Greece and Rome, women came under the definition of property, because, legally speaking in Rome at least, they were under the power of a man (*patria potestas*) or guardian. The rape of a woman was a property crime, committed against the man who owned the woman. If this was the case in everyday, normal civilian life, what chance did the vanquished woman have in war after a siege? Xenophon sums this up thus (*Cyrus* 7.5.73):

'It is a law established for all time among all men that when a city is taken in war, the people and property of the inhabitants belong to the captors.'

In wars fought by the Greeks and Romans, and well before that, particularly in the often repellent postcript to sieges, the systematic rape of women, men and children on the losing side was, as Xenophon says, par for the course, with the odious assumption that it was an expectation, a duty even. It has been so, to a greater or lesser extent, ever since.[2]

Wherever there is power, wherever there is war, then sex is never far away. Powerful men and women can often transmit a sexual attraction. Horace reminds us that from time immemorial, even pre-Helen of Troy, 'cunts were an abominable *casus belli*' (*Satires* 1.3.107) – '*nam fuit ante Helenam cunnus taeterrima belli causa*'. In war, rape is frequently a terrible by-product of victory, of the subjugation of enemy territory or of the raising of a siege; war permits and fosters horizontal collaboration and fraternization with the enemy.

And so to fledgling Rome, where, in legend, the Sabine women were abducted (and raped), that epitome of wifely chastity, Lucretia, was raped and Verginia was slain by her own father to obviate the very real prospect of being raped.

The Rape of the Sabine Women

Romulus had established Rome as a socio-political entity; he would not have been surprised to discover that his new city was surrounded by enemies who were nervous about Rome's territorial intentions. They, no doubt, expected a spot of land-grabbing. What they did not bargain for was grabbing, on an industrial scale, of their women. The reality was that Romulus not only had a territorial problem, he also had had an existentialist one, and that problem was women, or the lack thereof. As we have seen, Livy uses rape, or the threat of rape, as a vehicle to explain some of the most momentous events in Roman history. The first, and most famous, episode was the 'rape' – or rather abduction – of the Sabine women in 750 BCE. The insurgent Romans needed women to prolong their race, otherwise they would soon be extinct. So they took what they found, married them and produced the required progeny.

Initially, the Romans tried to persuade the Sabines to surrender their women, but not surprisingly, the Sabines were less than keen: why would they give up their sisters and daughters? No doubt, they were also concerned about the emergence of a rival nation right on their doorstep. This refusal left the Romans with an urgent survival problem. Subsequently, Romulus announced a festival and games, the festival of the Consualia, and invited the people of the neighboring cities to attend. Many did, including the Caeninenses, Crustumini and Antemnates, but in particular the Sabines, who came in their droves.

According to Plutarch, the Consualia was founded by Romulus himself. Romulus had discovered an altar of a god called Consus hidden underground. This god was said to have been either a god of counsel or the Equestrian Neptune. To celebrate the discovery, Romulus established the Consualia, a day of sacrifices, public games and celebrations.[3] At a prearranged signal, the Romans began to snatch and carry off the marriageable women among their guests in what has ever since been known as the rape of the Sabine women.

But, as noted, 'rape' is clearly a misnomer here; it signifies an abduction rather than anything to do with sexual violation. Livy makes it clear that no sexual assault took place. On the contrary, Romulus offered them free choice and promised civic and property rights to the women. According to Livy (1.9), he spoke to them individually, explaining that:

'What was done was owing to the pride of their fathers, who had refused to grant the privilege of marriage to their neighbours; but notwithstanding, they should be joined in lawful wedlock, participate in all their possessions and civil privileges, and, than which nothing can be dearer to the human heart, in their common children.'

The women relented, complied and married Roman men, but the local tribes remained implacable: the king of the Caeninenses invaded Rome's territory, only to be confronted by Romulus and the Romans. Romulus killed the king and routed his army. He went on to attack Caenina and captured it on the first assault. Returning to Rome, he dedicated a temple to Jupiter Feretrius (according to Livy, the first temple dedicated in Rome) and offered the spoils of the enemy king as *spolia opima*. According to the *Fasti Triumphales*, Romulus celebrated a triumph over the Caeninenses on 1 March 752 BCE.

The Antemnates then invaded Roman territory, but were also repulsed and their town was captured. The *Fasti Triumphales* tell us that Romulus celebrated a second triumph in 752 BCE over the Antemnates. The Crustumini also started a war, but they too were defeated and their town taken. Roman colonists were duly sent to Antemnae and Crustumerium by Romulus, and many citizens of those towns migrated to Rome, particularly the families of the captured Sabine women.

The Sabines themselves finally declared war, led into battle by their king, Titus Tatius. Tatius almost succeeded in capturing Rome, thanks to the treason of Tarpeia, daughter of Spurius Tarpeius, Roman governor of the citadel on the Capitoline Hill (see below). The Romans attacked the Sabines, who now held the citadel. The Roman advance was led by Hostus Hostilius, the Sabine defence by Mettus Curtius. Hostus fell in battle, and the Roman line gave way and retreated to the gate of the Palatium. However, Romulus rallied his men by promising to build a temple to Jupiter Stator on the site. Mettus Curtius was unhorsed and fled on foot, and the Romans appeared on the verge of victory. At this point, however, the courageous and resolute Sabine women became involved, led by Hersilia, wife of Romulus, and as described by Plutarch (*Romulus* 14), 'as they were preparing to renew the battle, they were checked by a sight that was wonderful to behold and a spectacle that passes description'. Livy (1.13) takes up the story:

> '[They], from the outrage on whom the war originated, with hair dishevelled and garments torn, the timidity of their sex being overcome by such dreadful scenes, had the courage to throw themselves amid the flying weapons, and making a rush across, to part the incensed armies, and vent their fury; imploring their fathers on the one side, their husbands on the other, "that as fathers-in-law and sons-in-law they would not contaminate each other with impious blood, nor stain their offspring with parricide, the one their grandchildren, the other their children. If you are dissatisfied with the match between you, if with our marriages, turn your resentment against us; we are the cause of war, we of wounds and of bloodshed to our husbands and parents. It were better that we perish than live widowed or fatherless without one or other of you."'

Ironically, this courageous peace-making intervention served to strengthen the military might of the newly forged Roman state: bad news perhaps for the women, but compensated for by an enlightened improvement in women's rights, according to Plutarch (*Romulus* 19–20; adapted from the translation by Bernadotte Perrin):

'Agreements were made that such women as wished to do so might continue to live with their husbands, exempt, as aforesaid, from all labour and all drudgery except spinning; also that the city should be inhabited by Romans and Sabines in common; and that the city should be called Rome, from Romulus, but all its citizens Quirites, from the native city of Tatius; and that Romulus and Tatius should be joint kings and leaders of the army. The place where these agreements were made is to this day called Comitium, from the Roman word "conire", or "coire", to come together. The city thus doubled in its numbers, a hundred of the Sabines were added by election to the Patricii, and the legions were enlarged to six thousand infantry and six hundred cavalry. The people, too, were arranged in three bodies, the first called Ramnenses, from Romulus; the second Tatienses, from Tatius; and the third Lucerenses, from the grove into which many went for refuge, when a general asylum was offered, and then became citizens.'

Dionysius (2.31.1) and Plutarch (*Romulus* 14.1) posit alternative reasons for the Roman decision to abduct the Sabine women. The first is that Romulus simply used it as a pretext for war; the second that the rape was the consequence of Romulus' policy to bring neighbouring tribes under his sway by peaceful alliances, acting as he did having been snubbed in his attempts to achieve this through marriage, *conubium*.

A vision of Romulus appears to Proculus Julius

This myth substantiates the claims the Romans made to link the *gens Julia* with Julius Caesar. Livy (1.16) tells us that Romulus, around 716 BCE, was officiating at a public review of the army at Palus Caprae when he was enveloped in mist during a sudden, violent storm. When the mist had cleared, Romulus was nowhere to be seen: the king had gone. Some nobles claimed that he had been carried off into the sky by a divine force; the plebs believed him now to be a god. Nevertheless, the more sceptical among the people believed that, under cover of the mist, the nobles had killed and dismembered him. Proculus, a shrewd man according to Livy, told the people that at dawn, a vision of Romulus descended from the sky and predicted that Rome and Roman power would rule the world. Livy is not alone in being surprised that both the plebs and the army were so gullible as to believe this.

Plutarch, in his *Life of Romulus*, offers a variant, saying Proculus, a friend of the king, was a Roman colonist from the city of Alba. Before testifying to the Senate, he had sworn a sacred oath and then told the assembly that Romulus had descended from the sky before his very eyes. Proculus added that he had asked Romulus why he had left them as he did so suddenly, leaving so many in mourning and suspicious about the circumstances of his disappearance. Romulus explained that it was the will of the gods; he had come to earth to build a city destined to be the greatest known to man, and now his work was done. Rome, with 'self-restraint' and 'valour', Romulus said, was destined to be the most powerful force on earth. Finally, he told Proculus that he would always watch over the people of Rome as Quirinus. This was enough, along with a divine force that came over the people, to make them abandon their anxieties.

The Rape of Lucretia

The rape of Lucretia by regal Sextus Tarquinius (Tarquin), and her subsequent suicide (*c.* 510 BCE), firmly roots brutish rape and matronly *pudicitia* and valour in the traditional foundation story of Rome and its movement from monarchy to Republic. Tarquin was the third and youngest son of the last king of Rome, the tyrannical Lucius Tarquinius Superbus. Tarquinius Superbus was besieging Ardea, a Rutulian city, but it could not be taken by force, so the Roman army lay encamped beneath its walls. Meanwhile, the king's sons, and their cousin, Lucius Tarquinius Collatinus, the son of Egerius, were feasting together.

Through a blend of legend and historical fact, brought to us by the historians Livy and Dionysius of Halicarnassus, we learn that Lucretia was the daughter of Spurius Lucretius Tricipitinus and the wife of Lucius Tarquinius Collatinus, a relative of Lucius Tarquinius Priscus, the fifth king of Rome. In around 510 BCE, while Collatinus was assisting the king at the siege of Ardea, his son, Sextus Tarquinius, was in Collatina on official business. He went to the home of Lucretia, intent on having sex with her; she, unaware of his foul intentions, received him with the usual courtesies accorded guests and kinsmen. With utter disregard for his reciprocal obligations as a guest and a relative, he inveigled his way into her bedroom and offered her a stark choice: submit to him now and he would marry her, making her his queen, or refuse and he would kill her with his sword. Lucretia resisted. To Lucretia, death was preferable to defilement by rape (which was also an act of adultery). Sextus Tarquinius piled on the pressure, adding that he would kill her and one of her male slaves, laying the bodies together in the bed to give the impression that she had been found *in flagrante* with the slave. His right to kill her with impunity for catching her in the act would be unnegotiable, since he was a relative.

However, for a *matrona*, adultery alone was a bad enough stain, which would be made doubly shameful by consorting with a slave. Lucretia could not bear to allow such calumny to circulate after her death, so she relented and gave herself to Sextus Tarquinius.

Lucretia's credentials as a model of probity had been established at an earlier stage of the siege, when, during a drinking session which included Tarquinius and Collatinus, bets were laid as to the virtuousness of each man's wife. A drink-fuelled decision was made to ride back to Rome and Collatia, 23 miles south of the capital, to establish whose wife was the most virtuous by visiting them unannounced. The wives of the princes were found enjoying a sumptuous dinner party (*in convivio luxuque*), where the wine was flowing freely. Upon reaching Collatia, despite the lateness of the hour, Lucretia was found working away at the wool by lamplight, surrounded by her maids in the hall. The essence of good matronly conduct was there for all to see, and it left no doubt as to who had won the wager; Lucretia was manifestly more virtuous. To the Romans of Livy's time, working the wool (*lanificium*) was synonymous with sexual propriety (*pudicitia*), a throwback to the times when homespun fabric was an essential facet of domestic life. According to Ovid, Lucretia was working on a cloak for Collatinus.[4] Fatefully, Lucretia's beauty and virtue had not escaped the notice of Sextus Tarquinius (*cum forma tum spectate castitas*).[5]

Lucretia's body may have been defiled, but, she protested, her mind remained pure (*corpus est tantum violatum, animus insons*). Despite absolute forgiveness from her father and husband (ironically, two of the four people who would have made up the domestic court had there been a charge of adultery), she resolved to commit suicide – but only after she secured her husband's promise to kill Sextus Tarquinius in revenge. Lucretia stabbed herself, her final words asserting that her name would never be used scandalously by any unchaste woman (*inpudica*) seeking to avoid due punishment.

To a good Roman *matrona*, adultery was the last word in defilement, polluting not just the perpetrator but any children too. Lucretia, brave and virtuous, was inextricably linked with Rome's proud early beginnings. She would rather die than be raped, but she would rather be raped than compromise her reputation and her *pudicitia*. Rome, like Lucretia, had been compromised and violated by the Tarquins. Her noble reaction, and the ensuing vengeful act of defeating the kings and abolishing the monarchy to establish the Republic, symbolizes Rome's honourable struggle against regal tyranny. Some 500 years later, Livy makes her an unimpeachable exemplar of feminine virtue in his Augustan Rome, a city now beset by increasing adultery, decreasing marriage and rampant divorce. The rape of a proud and virtuous woman was the catalyst for a major constitutional change, just as the abduction of the Sabine women had ensured the survival of Rome. After Lucretia's suicide, Lucus Iunius Brutus, her uncle, drew the dagger from her breast and swore an oath of vengeance against Tarquinius and all his family.

Brutus convened the *comitia curiata* and levelled a number of charges against the king and his family: the callous and savage rape of Lucretia – whose body was there to see on the dais – the king's tyranny and the slave labour of the plebeians in the ditches and sewers of Rome. He reminded the assembly that Tarquinius Superbus had come to rule by the murder of Servius Tullius, his wife's father and penultimate king of Rome, with the complicity of his wife, Tullia, who now fled to the camp at Ardea.

Brutus then initiated a debate on the form of government Rome ought to have. In summary, he proposed the banishment of the Tarquins from all the territories of Rome and the appointment of an *interrex* to nominate new magistrates and conduct an election. A republican form of government was the consensus, with two consuls replacing a king; the consuls would execute the will of a patrician Senate. Spurius Lucretius was elected *interrex* and proposed Brutus and Collatinus (both related by blood to Rome's fifth king, Lucius Tarquinius Priscus) as the first two consuls. That choice was ratified by the *curiae*, as was the establishment of the Republic. The monarchy was over while Lucretia's body was still warm, displayed in the Forum.

Brutus, leaving Lucretius in command of the city, marched with a force of armed men to the Roman army camped at Ardea. The king fled before Brutus' arrival. The army received Brutus as a hero, while the king's sons were expelled from the camp. Tarquinius Superbus, meanwhile, was refused entry at Rome, and went with his family into exile at Caere, in what became known as the Regifugium.

Brutus' first act after the expulsion of Lucius Tarquinius Superbus was to bring the people to swear an oath – the Oath of Brutus – never to allow any man again to be king in Rome (Livy 1.59):

> 'By this guiltless blood before the kingly injustice I swear – you and the gods as my witnesses – I make myself the one who will prosecute, by what force I am able, Lucius Tarquinius Superbus along with his wicked wife and the whole house of his freeborn children by sword, by fire, by any means hence, so that neither they nor any one else be allowed to rule Rome.'

There were inevitably attempts to reinstate the monarchy. First, Tarquinius sent ambassadors to the Senate to request the return of his family's personal effects, which had been seized in the coup. But while the Senate debated his request, the ambassadors met in secret with and converted a number of the leading men of Rome to the royal cause, in what is known as the Tarquinian conspiracy. The conspirators included two of Brutus' brothers-in-law and his sons Titus and Tiberius. The conspiracy was discovered and the conspirators executed. Although the Senate had initially agreed to Tarquin's request for his goods, the decision was revoked after the discovery of the conspiracy and the royal property was given over to the Roman people.

The *matronae* who witnessed the suicide of Lucretia were filled with so much horror and compassion that they lamented that they would rather die a thousand deaths in defence of their liberty than suffer such outrages to be committed by the tyrants.

The inflammatory display of Lucretia's body in the Forum at Collatia by Lucius Junius Brutus, and the subsequent public clamour for justice, would have reminded Livy's audience of the equally revolutionary and sordid spectacle of Julius Caesar's neglected, discarded corpse after his assassination – in which, of course, another Brutus was implicated. Before Livy, Cicero had used the rape of Lucretia to illustrate that Tarquinius was guilty of a breach of eternal law and that he was morally guilty, despite the fact that there was no contemporary written law relating to adultery. In the *De Republica*, he describes Lucretia as 'a chaste and noble woman' ('*mulierque pudens et nobilis*').[6] In the second century CE, Martial – albeit cynically – makes Lucretia an exemplar of *gravitas* and chastity.[7] However, in *De Civitate Dei* 1, Augustine questioned whether Lucretia ought to have carried out the wrong that was suicide over an event of which she had no control.

Lucretia became an icon, but it seems that many Roman men considered her qualities and virtues to be more masculine than feminine. She is defeminized by both Ovid and Valerius Maximus, who ascribe masculine qualities to her and her actions when praising her. To Ovid she is a *matrona* with a manly spirit (*animi matron virilis*), and to Valerius Maximus she is 'the leader in Roman sexual propriety' ('*dux Romanae pudicitiae*'), who, by a wicked twist of fate, possesses a man's spirit in a female body'.[8,9] *Dux* usually describes a man; in two instances where Roman writers used it to describe a woman, it signifies powerful, disturbing and regal foreign women – Dido and Boudica. Apart from being reminiscent of three Roman taboos (monarchy, women and foreigners), the implication is that Lucretia and her actions were almost too good to be those of a woman. Lucretia is not the only Roman woman to be denied her true gender by male writers.[10]

What then did Lucretia's audacious and selfless act achieve politically? Publius Valerius Poplicola (or Publicola; d. 503 BCE) was one of the four Roman aristocrats who spearheaded the overthrow of the monarchy, along with Lucius Junius Brutus (the king's newphew), Lucius Tarquinius Collatinus and Spurius Lucretius Tricipitinus. While the king, Lucius Tarquinius Superbus, was away campaigning in Ardea, the four men mustered the youth of Collatia, then went to Rome where Brutus, then Tribunus Celerum (Tribune of the Knights), summoned the people to the Forum and urged them to rise up against the king. The people voted to depose Tarquinius and barred the gates of Rome against him; he was the seventh and last king of Rome. To replace the monarchy they established a republic, together with the office of consul. Brutus and Collatinus were elected the first consuls. The Tribune of the Knights was commander of the king's personal bodyguard, the Celeres, and was second only to the king, with the authority to pass laws, known as *lex tribunicia*, and to preside over the *comitia curiata*.

Together with some disaffected monarchists of the Aquillii and Vitellii families, the exiled Tarquins, as we have seen, plotted to assassinate the consuls. Valerius was informed of the plot by a slave, Vindicius. He personally investigated the conspiracy, infiltrating the Aquillius estate and finding incriminating evidence, based on which the consuls held a public trial. The conspirators, including two of Brutus' sons, were found guilty and executed. Valerius played a leading role in the trial.

But all was not well amongst the rebels. After the trial, Brutus demanded that his colleague Collatinus (Lucretia's widower) resign the consulship and go into exile, as he was a member of the hated royal family. Collatinus was thunderstruck by this betrayal, as he had been one of the leaders of the rebellion following the death of his wife. He resigned nevertheless, to be replaced by Valerius.

After the death of Brutus, Valerius was the sole surviving consul. Spurius Lucretius was chosen to replace Brutus, but he died after only a few days, to be followed by Marcus Horatius Pulvillus. When Valerius began to build a new house at the top of the Velian Hill, it soon became apparent that it could be seen from the Senate house and rumours began to circulate that he intended to re-establish the monarchy, with himself as king. Valerius immediately stopped building, and demolished the structure in a single night. Addressing an assembly of the people, he made his lictors lower their *fasces* as a mark of humility, and to remove their axes (Livy 1.58; 2.20): 'I have just liberated Rome, bravely, but now I am slandered, as if I were an Aquillius or a Vitellian. I am the bitterest enemy of the former kings, so I shouldn't be accused of wanting to be king.' In order to allay suspicions, he started rebuilding his house at the foot of the hill. In later days, the Temple of Victory stood on the site.

In honour of his humility and for his deferential behaviour to the people of Rome, Valerius received the surname Poplicola, meaning 'one who looks after the people'. Before the impending elections, Valerius filled up the ranks of the Senate, which had been severely depleted as a result of the revolution and the subsequent war. The consul also promulgated new laws, including the right of appeal (*provocatio*) from the decisions of a magistrate, and demanding the forfeiture of all the rights of anyone convicted of plotting to restore the monarchy. Poplicola was elected consul three more times, in 508, 507 and 504 BCE. Horatius was his colleague again in 507, while his colleague in 508 and 504 was Titus Lucretius Tricipitinus. He was the first consul ever to be re-elected.

Publius Valerius Poplicola died in 503 BCE, shortly after passing the consulship to his successors, Agrippa Menenius Lanatus and Publius Postumius Tubertus. Livy records that at the time of his death, he was considered 'by universal consent to be the ablest man in Rome, in the arts both of peace and war'. He was never a rich man, and so was buried at public expense and was mourned by the Roman *matronae* just like Brutus before him. Poplicola was at the forefront of the political upheaval which saw the monarchy replaced by the Republic; he helped in the revolution itself and then he went on to champion and develop the democratic measures which replaced the tyranny of the Tarquins. Lucretia had not died in vain.

The Murder of Verginia

The murder of Verginia in 449 BCE had not dissimilar causes and ramifications. Her death occurred at a flashpoint of the Conflict of the Orders – the struggle between the patricians and the plebeians during the decemvirate, an ultimately unsuccessful attempt to reorganize Roman administration and codify the law (which found voice as the enduring 'Twelve Tables'), while all other magistracies were suspended and decisions were not subject to appeal. In this case, the actions of Verginia's father, Verginius, provoked a secession of the plebeians, precipitated the abolition of the decemvirate and caused the restoration of the consulship and tribunate of the peoples – and, with it, the right of appeal. The decemvirs had become increasingly tyrannical, and refused to give up power even though their tenure was limited to two years. This undemocratic behaviour smacked of despotism and was eerily reminiscent of the dreaded rule of the kings, who had been overthrown sixty years earlier – due, in no small part, to Lucretia. Members of the second decemvirate either committed suicide or were exiled.

Appius Claudius, a decemvir, set his eye on young Verginia. His attempts to bribe her and win her favour with promises fell flat; Verginia was from a humble, honourable and principled family. Although she was already betrothed to Lucius Icilius, Claudius contrived a plan where Marcus Claudius – 'the decemvir's pimp' – claimed that Verginia was really his slave, and that she had been illegally adopted by Lucius Verginius. One day, Marcus Claudius attempted to abduct Verginia while she was on her way to school, but a shocked and outraged crowd gathered to help the girl. Claudius insisted that the matter be dealt with before a judge, namely Appius, in court; in the meantime, Verginia would be held with Claudius while her father rushed back to the hearing from active service. When not away with the army, he was a butcher in one of the stalls of the Tabernae Novae. An enraged Lucius Icilius then arrived, threatening to die rather than betray his fiancée; Appius relented, and allowed Verginia to go home. Despite attempts by Appius to have Verginius arrested before he could reach Rome, the distraught father arrived in Rome. The next morning, he gathered his supporters and led his daughter into the Forum; he was in mourning, she in rags, attended by *matronae*. Appius, to everyone's astonishment, ruled in favour of Marcus Claudius and that Verginia was indeed his slave. Livy tells us that the supportive women in the crowd were 'more effective with their silent tears than words could be'.

Appius Claudius had brought an armed escort with him and accused the citizens of sedition. The supporters of Verginius left the Forum rather than cause any violence, but Verginius begged to question his daughter himself. Claudius agreed, but the incident ended tragically when Verginius, exercising his right as *paterfamilias*, grabbed a butcher's knife and, at the Shrine of Venus Cloacina, stabbed Verginia to liberate her from the shame (*stuprum*) which a marriage to Appius Claudius would inevitably have brought. Verginius said: 'I set her free' ('*in libertatem vindico*'; Livy, 3.44–48; *Confessio Amantis* 7, 5131–5306; RR 5589–5658).

Verginius and Icilius were arrested, but their supporters returned to attack the lictors and destroy their *fasces*. This led to the overthrow of the decemviri and the re-establishment of the Roman Republic. Verginius cursed Appius; the women indignantly demanded to know if this was their reward for raising children and remaining chaste (*pudicitiae praemia*). According to Livy, 'the grief of women' (*muliebris dolor*) was much more powerful, their grief so much deeper, due to their lack of restraint.

The story, as related by Livy and Dionysius of Halicarnassus, is significant on a number of levels.[11] Firstly, it reinforces the traditional Roman values of chastity and virtue we saw in Lucretia. The aptly named Verginia, like her predecessor, became a symbol of Roman *pudicitia* – Livy himself remarks on the striking similarities between the two women's circumstances. Secondly, the story demonstrates an early example of the special qualities and dynamics women exerted when they resorted to public demonstrations. The infrequency of such behaviour generally, along with their silent but plangent support, their *dolor* and their *pudicitia*, was influential (although ultimately unsuccessful). Thirdly, it serves as an example of a father exerting the power legally invested in him as a father (his *patria potestas*). As *paterfamilias*, under Roman law, Verginius had an absolute obligation to preserve the integrity of his family, including defending the chastity of his daughters; when this was compromised, he had little option other than to kill his daughter to preserve her *pudicitia*. Ironically, this law was enshrined in the 'Twelve Tables' – one of the legislators for which was Appius Claudius. Fourthly, the consequences of this episode were, as in the case of Lucretia, highly significant politically and socially: the public demonstration that ensued led to the abolition of the highly unpopular and increasingly tyrannical decemvirs. Finally, Verginia was a symbol of liberty; if she had lived, she would have forever been under the undesirable and coercive control of Appius Claudius, but her father's actions allowed her to escape that dreadful fate. She was liberated in death: *libertatem vindicare*.

The tale re-emerges in several works, including Chaucer's 'The Physician's Tale' in the *Canterbury Tales* and Thomas Babington Macaulay's *Lays of*

Ancient Rome. John Webster and Thomas Heywood sum up the influence of Lucretia and Verginia very neatly in their seventeenth-century play *Appius and Virginia*:

> 'Two ladies fair, but most unfortunate
> Have in their ruins rais'd declining Rome,
> Lucretia and Virginia, both renowned
> For chastity.'

Chaucer's version is altogether more gruesome. Virginius goes home and tells his daughter that he intends to kill her rather than give her to Claudius (203–30). Verginia pleads for her life and laments her death, as Jeptha's daughter lamented her death (238–50). Virginius then beheads his daughter and sends her head to Appius (251–59). The people throw Appius into prison, where he hangs himself, and they order Marcus Claudius to be hanged too, but Virginius intervenes and he is exiled instead (260–76).

Lucretia and Verginia were two women who paid for their *pudicitia* with their lives, symbols of virtue who helped to change the course of Roman history. They were also women who, like Rome itself, had been vindicated and defended by men against the tyrannical abuse of power; 'The rape of women became the history of the state,' as Joshel puts it.

There was another Verginia, a determined and plucky woman who reinforced the importance of *pudicitia* in 296 BCE. Fabius Rullianis had set up a shrine to Patrician Chastity (*Pudicitia Patricia*), exclusive to *univira*, one-man patrician women. However, when the patrician Verginia married the plebeian Lucius Volumnius Flamma, she found herself excluded from the cult. Not to be outdone, she set up a parallel shrine in her husband's house in the Vicus Longus, on the grounds that *pudicitia* was classless; in doing so, she provided one of the first examples of the fight for women's social justice in Rome.

Ironically, the following year saw plague, prodigies, and an outburst of *stuprum* amongst a number of patrician women who had allegedly resorted to prostitution. This was considered serious enough to warrant consultation of the Sibylline Books by Fabius Gurges (one of the curile aediles), in order to divine the appropriate official reaction. The patrician prostitutes were fined, and the proceeds (indicative of the scale of the scandal) were used to build the Temple of Venus Obsequens (The Temple of Obedient Venus). The reason for this mass conversion of *matronae* to *meretrix* (prostitute) is unclear, but it is possible that it was an early bid for marriage reform that would increase freedom for women.

These were by no means the only legendary women whom Livy associates with conflict and war, as the following shows.

Hersilia was the Sabine wife of Romulus. She was the only woman who was not a virgin from all those abducted during the rape of the Sabine women. Plutarch says that she was kindnapped by mistake. We learn from Livy's description that she was Rome's first female diplomat and woman military advisor. Romulus was jubilant at his victory over the army of the Antemnates, but Hersilia was mobbed by entreaties for clemency from the captured Antemnate women. Consequently, she implored Romulus to show mercy and take them on as citizens of Rome, an act which would have the advantage of strengthening the state and easing the shortage of women. He was only too happy to do this, thus performing one of the first acts of extending Roman citizenship to the vanquished – a policy which was to serve Rome well for centuries to come.

Dionysius, Macrobius and Plutarch (*Romulus* 14.7–8), meanwhile, say Hersilia was the wife of Hostus Hostilius, a Roman champion under Romulus. This would make her the grandmother of Tullus Hostilius, the third king of Rome. As with Romulus (who became the god Quirinus), she was deified after her death, as Hora Quirini, as we hear in Ovid's *Metamorphoses* (14.829–51):

> 'At once Hersilia and the virgin child
> of Thaumas, went together up the hill
> of Romulus. Descending through thin air
> there came a star, and then Hersilia
> her tresses glowing fiery in the light,
> rose with that star, as it returned through air.
> And her the founder of the Roman state [Romulus]
> received with dear, familiar hands. He changed
> her old time form and with the form her name.
> He called her Hora and let her become
> a goddess, now the mate of Quirinus.'

Titus Tatius (d. 748 BCE) was the Sabine king of Cures who attacked Rome after the rape of the Sabine women, aided by the treacherous **Tarpeia**, Vestal Virgin daughter (in Propertius' version) of Spurius Tarpeius, the commander of the Roman citadel. This relationship in essence gave her 'access all areas'. After their women had been famously seized and abducted by the Romans, according to Livy, the Sabines declared war on Rome. They were aided in their assault on Rome by Tarpeia, who opened the city gates to them, having gone outside the walls to fetch water for a sacrifice. Why she betrayed Rome is open to dispute. Some say that she was bribed by Tatius, with the promise of receiving what the Sabine soldiers wore on their shield arms, their left arms. Tarpeia could only see their shiny gold bracelets (*armillae*) and bejewelled rings; the Sabines, unfortunately for her, saw it very differently and crushed her to death with their shields, *scuta congesta*, which were also on their left arms.

Others give an aetiological explanation and maintain that the Sabines killed Tarpeia by pushing her off a 25-metre-high cliff on the Capitol which later took her name (*Rupes Tarpeia*, or *Saxum Tarpeium*) and became notorious as a place of terrible execution for murderers, traitors and the mentally and physically disabled. To be hurled off the Tarpeian Rock was a fate worse than mere death, carrying with it the stigma of shame. The standard method of execution in ancient Rome was by strangulation in the Tullianum. The rock was reserved for the most notorious traitors and as a place of unofficial, extra-legal executions. The Latin proverb *arx Tarpeia Capitoli proxima*, 'The Tarpeian Rock is close to the Capitol', means one's fall from grace can happen very quickly. Tarpeia became a byword in the Roman world for greed and treachery: Propertius, for example, talks of Tarpeia's 'shameful tomb'.

Propertius deals with Tarpeia in Book 4 quite differently. She is smitten with love for Titus Tatius as he rides out resplendent in his armour, and betrays the Romans, not from a lust for jewellery but in order to offer her hand in marriage to the king. The outcome, however, is just the same – she dies, and deservedly so, in the eyes of Propertius. Treachery and unpatriotic behaviour were inexcusable whatever their cause. Propertius piles on Tarpeia's guilt and moral deficiency by making her a Vestal Virgin, supposedly pledged to chastity and the honourable guardians of Rome's safety through the flame of Vesta. While all was well with the Vestals, all was said to be well with Rome; trouble with the Vestals presaged trouble for Rome.

We have already seen how the Sabine women, by now Roman wives and mothers, were in the thick of it again later when they conducted some desperate but effective diplomacy. Titus Tatius had declared war on Rome in the aftermath of the rape of the Sabine women. After he captured the citadel on the Capitoline Hill, assisted by the treachery of Tarpeia, the Sabines and Romans joined battle.

One of the two magnificant statues of war god **Mars** in the Yorkshire Museum in York. (*Courtesy of York Museums Trust*)

Bellona presenting the reins of his horses to Mars, by Louis Jean François Lagrenée (1766), in the Princeton University Art Museum. Possibly it refers to a passage from the Latin writer Claudian: '*Fer galleam Bellona mihi, nexusque rotarum tende Pavor.*' (*Source: http://www.the-athenaeum.org/art/full.php?ID=140334*)

Bellona, the goddess of war – Waterloo Station. The Victory Arch, built of Portland Stone, commemorates the London and South Western Railway and the Southern Railway men who gave their lives in the First and Second World Wars. It features figures representing war and peace, beneath a statue of Britannia.

A colossal statue of the Roman goddess **Juno Sospita** (the Saviour). She wears a goatskin over her head and torso. It is probably from a temple in the Forum Olitorium, Rome, in the second century CE. (*Courtesy of Vatican Museums, Rome*)

The Witch Erichtho by John Hamilton Mortimer ARA (1740–1779). Detail from 'Sextus Pompeius consulting Erichtho before the Battle of Pharsalia'. (*Source/Photographer: Flickr: Playing Futures: Applied Nomadology, 2012-01-05*)

Mithras sacrificing the bull (100–200 CE), Borghése Collection, purchased by the Louvre in 1807 and on display in the Gallery du temps au Louvre-Lens. (*Author: Serge Ottaviani*)

An eighteenth-century depiction of the sacking of Troy by Johann Georg Trautmann (1713–1769). From the collections of the granddukes of Baden, Karlsruhe. (*Source/ Photographer: http://www. zeller.de/*)

Sinon as a prisoner before the walls of Troy, in the Vergilius Romanus, fifth century CE.

Laocoön and his sons, also known as the Laocoön Group. Marble copy after an Hellenistic original from *c*. 200 BCE. Found in the Baths of Trajan, Rome, 1506. (*Courtesy of Early First Century BCE Collection, Vatican Museums, Museo Pio-Clementino, Octagon, Laocoön Hall. Source/ Photographer: Marie-Lan Nguyen, 2009*)

Aeneas tells Dido about the fall of Troy by Pierre-Narcisse Guérin (*c.* 1815); Georgia Regents University.

The death of Dido (1631) by Guercino (1591–1666). (*http://www.galleriaborghese. it/spada/it/didone.htm*)

Aeneas's flight from Troy (1598), by Federico Barocci (1535–1612); Galleria Borghese, Rome. Based on *Aeneid* 2.671–729: in the sack of Troy, Aeneas flees the burning city with his young son, Ascanius, at his side and carries on his shoulders his father, Anchises, who clutches the family's household gods.

Aeneas and his family fleeing burning Troy (1654) by Henry Gibbs (1631–1713); Tate Gallery, London. Aeneas' wife, Creusa, who in Virgil merely falls behind and is lost, is here shown being captured by a Greek soldier. This last detail is rare, if not unique, in representations of this scene.

Landscape with Aeneas at Delos (1672), by Claude Lorrain (1600–1682); National Gallery, London.

Aeneas at the court of Latinus (c. 1661–63), by Ferdinand Bol (1616–1680); Rijksmuseum, Amsterdam.

Nisus and Euryalus, by Jean–Baptiste Roman (1792–1835); Louvre Museum Department of Sculptures, Richelieu, lower ground floor, Cour Puget. Marble, exhibited at the 1827 Salon. (*Source / Photographer: Jastrow, 2007*)

The doctor Iapyx heals Aeneas, who is wounded in one leg (with his mother, Venus, and his son, Ascanius, who is weeping). Ancient Roman fresco from the House of Sirico in Pompeii, Italy; mid-first century. On display at the Museo Archeologico Nazionale, Naples.

Virgil Aeneid: Allecto maddens Queen Amata, by Master of Gruninger Workshop. From the First Crespin Lyons edition of Virgil's works, 1529, containing the woodcuts prepared for the Johan Gruninger Strasbourg edition of Virgil (1502), but on fine continental vélin and therefore with a dark rich tone. This edition is rightly acclaimed for its magnificent series of woodcut illustrations by the anonymous Late Master of the Grüninger Workshop.

The death of Pallas, by Jacques Henri Sablet (1749–1803); Museum of Fine Arts, Houston.

The death of Turnus, after Pietro da Cortona (1597–1669).

The Capitoline wolf at Siena Duomo. Legend has it that Siena was founded by Senius and Aschius, two sons of Remus. When they fled Rome, they took the statue of the lupa, she-wolf, to Siena; it became a symbol of the town. (*Photographer: Petar Milošević*)

Romulus and Remus sheltered by Faustulus, 1643, by Pietro da Cortona (1596–1669); Louvre Museum, Paris.

The shepherd Faustulus bringing Romulus and Remus to his wife (1654), by Nicolas Mignard (1606–1668); Dallas Museum of Art.

Faustulus (detail), as seen in the Font de Mussa mosaic at Museu de Prehistòria de València.

The rape of the Sabine women (1583), by Giambologna, in the Loggia dei Lanzi in Florence. (*Photo by Thermos*)

Rape of the Sabine women (between 1627 and 1629), by Pietro da Cortona (1596–1669); Capitoline Museums, Rome.

The rape of the Sabines – the Abduction (1870).

The rape of the Sabines: the Invasion (1871). Some depictions of the abduction event show the Sabine women as being willing participants. 'The Rape of the Sabines: The Invasion', by Charles Christian Nahl (1818–1878), is one of them; Crocker Art Museum, Sacramento, California.

The intervention of the Sabine women (1799), by Jacques-Louis David (1748–1825); Louvre Museum, Paris. The rape of the Sabine women has been portrayed in paintings by Bolgna, Poussin, Rubens and David, who conveys a later scene, after the abduction, when the Sabine women, now grown to love their husbands and to be mothers of their children, intervene when their families attack the Romans, pleading with both sides to make peace.

Tarquinius finding Lucretia at Work (1633), by Willem de Poorter (1608–1668); Musée des Augustins, Toulouse.

Tarquin and Lucretia (1571), by Titian (*c.* 1488/90–1576); Fitzwilliam Gallery, Cambridge. The head and hand entering from the left belong to a male slave. In Livy's version, Tarquin threatened Lucretia that if she did not yield to him, he would kill both Lucretia and the slave and then claim to have caught them during the act of adultery.

The Oath of Brutus (1771), by Jacques-Antoine Beaufort (1721–1784); Musee Municipale Frédéric Blandin, Nevers, France. Lucretia lies dead and rather discarded in the gloomy background, while the heroic men preen themselves and strut in the foreground: Brutus, Lucretia's father, Valerius and Collatinus.

The Oath of the Horatii (1786), by Jacques-Louis David (1748–1825); The Louvre, Paris. The oath of the Horatii involved a conflict between the Romans and the Albans. Rather than continue a full-scale war, the adversaries elected representative combatants to settle their dispute. The Romans chose the Horatii and the Albans another trio of brothers, the Curatii. In the painting we watch the Horatii taking an oath to defend Rome.

Mucius Scaevola in the presence of Lars Porsena (1640), by Matthias Stom (fl. 1615–1649). (*Art Gallery of New South Wales, Australia*)

Verginius murders his daughter, Virginia;
Walker Art Gallery, Liverpool. This wonderful
statue languishes in the gallery cafeteria; there
is no plaque to tell anyone what it is, although
information is available on request.

The sacrificial death of Marcus Curtius
(1550), by Paolo Veronese (1528–1588);
Kunsthistorisches Museum, Vienna. Blue
pencil.svg wikidata:Q95569. (*Photographer:
Kunsthistorisches Museum Wien, Bilddatenbank*)

**Cloelia passing the
Tiber** (between 1630
and 1640); Peter Paul
Rubens (1577–1640);
Louvre Museum,
Richelieu, second
floor, room 21.
Formerly attributed
to Abraham van
Diepenbeeck
(1596–1675).

Horatius Cocles defending the bridge (*c.* 1642/43), by Charles Le Brun (1619–1690). (*Dulwich Picture Gallery*)

Jean Bardin: Tullia drives over the corpse of her father (1765); Landesmuseum Mainz. (*Source/Photographer: http://galatea.univ-tlse2.fr/pictura/UtpicturaServeur/GenerateurNotice.php?numnotice=A5287*)

The Battle of Actium, 2 September 31 BC (1672), by Lorenzo A. Castro (fl. 1664–1700). (*National Maritime Museum, London*)

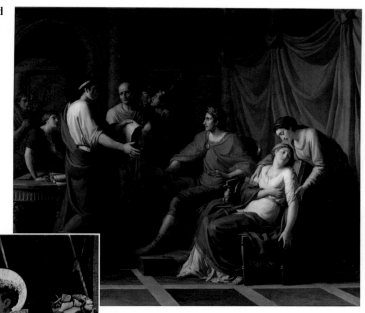

Virgil reading the Aeneid to Augustus and Octavia (1787), by Jean-Joseph Taillasson (1745–1809); National Gallery, London. (*Source/Photographer: National Gallery, London. Uploaded to Wikipedia by Neddyseagoon, 24 November 2006*)

The meeting of Erasmus and St Maurice (between *c*. 1520 and *c*. 1524), by Mathias Grünewald (c. 1475/80–1528); Alte Pinakothek, Munich.

The Battle of the Milvian Bridge (between 1520 and 1524), by Giulio Romano (1499–1546); Vatican City, Apostolic Palace.

During the reign of Tullus Hostilius around 642 BCE, in the war with Alba Longa, **Camilla**, the fiancée of one of Rome's enemies, one of the Curiatii, made the mistake of mourning his death after he was slain by one of her three brothers (the Horatii), two of whom also died in the fight. It had been agreed by the two enemies that fighting a costly war between their armies would leave the door open for an Etruscan invasion. Sabine dictator Mettius Fufetius proposed to Tullus Hostilius that the conflict should be settled by a fight to the death between the Roman Horatii triplets and their Alban counterparts, also triplets, known as the Curiatii. They met on the battlefield between the lines as the two armies and their countrymen looked on.

The Horatii inflicted wounds on all three Curiatii, but two of the Romans were killed in the act. That left their brother Publius alone and surrounded by the three wounded Curiatii. Publius realized he stood no chance against all three of his enemies together, despite their injuries, so he ran across the battlefield, causing the Albans to chase him, each as fast as their wounds would allow. Publius' plan worked: he saw that the Curiatii had become separated from each other, so he turned and attacked the first and least-injured Curiatius and slew him. Despite the Albans urging the two surviving Curiatii to regroup, Horatius caught up to the second Curiatius and killed him as his surviving brother, helpless, looked on. This last Curiatius was physically spent from his wounds and the chase. Publius declared that he had killed the first two Curiatii in revenge for his fallen brothers. He would kill this last one for Rome and their rule over Alba Longa. Thus, he thrust his sword into the Alban's throat and took the armour of his slain enemies as the spoils of his victory. Afterwards, the Alban dictator Mettius honoured the treaty and Alba Longa briefly accepted Roman rule.

The victorious brother returned to Rome triumphant with the booty and the blood-soaked cloak of his sister's fiancé, a cloak Camilla had made for him. She was demonstrably distraught, bewailing her fiancé's death. Publius was appalled and had no hesitation in stabbing Camilla to death, telling her:

'Take your childlike love to your betrothed; you have no thought for your brothers living or dead, nor for your country; any woman who mourns an enemy of Rome will die like this.'

Her father sanctioned the sororicide, adding that he would have killed her himself had her brother not (Livy 1.24–26). Publius – at one and the same time a murderer and a national hero – was put on trial for *perduellio* and condemned to death, but appealed to one of the popular assemblies.

Perduellio was the capital offence of high treason as set down in the 'Twelve Tables'; those convicted were subject to death, either by being hanged from the *arbor infelix* or thrown from the Tarpeian Rock. Their families were not allowed to mourn them and their houses were razed.

King Tullus Hostilius said:

> 'In accordance with the law I appoint duumvirs to pass judgment upon Horatius for treason [perduellio]. The dread formula of the law ran thus: "Let the duumvirs pronounce him guilty of treason; if he shall appeal from the duumvirs, let the appeal be tried; if the duumvirs win, let the lictor veil his head, let [the lictor] suspend him with a rope from a barren tree [*arbor infelix*]; let [the lictor] scourge him either within or without the pomerium."'

Even though the duumvirs found Horatius guilty, Horatius was acquitted when he appealed to the people. In defence of his son, Horatius' father, also Publius, spoke of the recent victory and entreated them to spare his last surviving son (his fourth son, a brother of the Horatii, had also died). The assembly was persuaded and Publius' sentence was commuted. This trial was the source of the later Roman tradition of allowing the condemned to appeal their sentences to the people.

Publius the elder was required to offer a sacrifice to atone for his son's crime. The spoils of the victory were hung in a place that became known as *Pila Horatia*. A wooden beam was erected on the slope of the Oppian Hill, which was called the *Sororium Tigillum* (Sister's Beam). It symbolized a yoke, under which Publius the younger was made to pass, and remained standing long after his death. Publius was seen by the Romans to embody country before life and patriotism before sentimentality.

Cloelia is described by Livy (2.13) as '*dux*' in her brave escapade, an epithet, as we have seen, usually reserved for men. She demonstrated conspicuous bravery and military sagacity when Lars Porsena, the Etruscan king, took Roman hostages as part of the peace treaty which ended the war between Rome and Clusium in 508 BCE. Lars Porsena came into contact and conflict with Rome after the overthrowing of the monarchy there in 509 BCE, resulting in the exile of the last king of Rome, Lucius Tarquinius Superbus. The deposed monarch, whose family was of Etruscan origin, tried and failed to retake the throne a number of times before appealing to Porsena for assistance. Lars Porsena duly agreed to help.

One of Porsena's hostages was a young woman named Cloelia, who managed to flee the Clusian camp on horseback at the head of a group of Roman girls. According to Valerius Maximus, she then swam across the Tiber back to the Romans. Porsena demanded that she be returned, to which the Romans consented. When she arrived back at Clusium, Porsena was so impressed by her bravery that he allowed her go free and to choose half the remaining hostages to be liberated with her. She picked the Roman boys, knowing that they could continue the war against the enemies of Rome. The Romans voted Cloelia an honour usually reserved for men: an equestrian statue, located at the top of the Via Sacra.

It was women too who averted the Volscian attack on Rome led by Gaius Marcius Coriolanus in 491 BCE. Coriolanus was an arch aristocrat who believed that it was wrong to grant any political concessions to the plebeians. The Volscian war brought about a famine in Rome because so many men had been recruited into the army that the fields and crops were neglected. The price of grain rose to the point where many of the plebeians were in danger of starving. Coriolanus gave incendiary speeches in the Senate, advocating that relief be withdrawn from the plebeians unless they agreed to the abolition of the Tribunate of the Plebs and gave up other concessions they had extracted from their secession. The Plebeian Tribunes, Brutus and Sicinius, recommended that Coriolanus be thrown to his death from the Tarpeian Rock, but allies in the Senate protected him. Sicinius then ordered that Coriolanus be brought to trial. He was condemned and sentenced to perpetual banishment, and then went to the Volscian city of Antium, to the house of Tullus Aufidius, previously a deadly enemy, offered his services and urged him to renew the war on Rome. Aufidius readily agreed to the alliance. Coriolanus led the Volscians to reconquer all of the cities they had lost in the recent war with Rome, and then led them to a camp 5 miles from the city.

Coriolanus and the Volscians marched on Rome and besieged the city. The Romans sent an embassy made up of family and friends of Corliolanus, offering to rescind his banishment if he would call off his attack. Coriolanus insisted on conditions that were so favourable to the Volscians that he knew the Romans could not accept them. It appeared that Rome would have to give in. However, when envoys, augurs and priests had failed to appease Coriolanus, the women of Rome – *ingens mulierum agmen*, 'a mighty column of women' – began to congregate at various temples to the Gods and pray for deliverance.

Their leader was Valeria, the sister of the eminent statesman and co-
founder of the Republic, Publius Valerius Publicola, (d. 503 BCE). Valeria
gathered the women around her and bid them go to the house of Corliolanus,
where they found his mother **Veturia** (confusingly called Volumnia by
Plutarch) and her daughter-in-law Volumnia (yet more confusingly called
Vergilia by Plutarch and Virgilia by Shakespeare), Coriolanius' wife, with the
children on their mother's knee. They persuaded them to go into the siege
lines with Coriolanus' two young sons and implore him to withdraw, saying,
'where men failed to defend the city with their swords, women may be more
successful with their tears and pleas.' Moved by the unexpected appearance
of his close family, and by an angry and impassioned Veturia, who appealed
to his duty as a son and to Rome, Coriolanus relented and withdrew his army.
Veturia's success was, no doubt, assured when she reminded Coriolanus how
much she had sacrificed for him over the years, providing an education and
remaining a *univira*, a one-man woman, after his father's death, thus making
her mother, father, nurse, teacher and sister to him.

The Romans honoured Veturia for her courage, patriotism and strength in
a crisis; she had succeeded where all men before her had failed. She became
a model of Roman female virtue. A temple to divine Fortuna was built in
honour of Veturia and the other women. She did not ask for any special
favours or honours, except that a temple be built as a monument of Female
Fortune. Plutarch (*Life of Corialanus* 37) wrote:

> 'The senate, much commending their public spirit, caused the temple
> to be built and a statue set up in it at the public charge; they, however,
> made up a sum among themselves, for a second image of Fortune,
> which the Romans say uttered, as it was being put up "Blessed of the
> gods, O women, is your gift."'

In Shakespeare's *Coriolanus*, Coriolanus' mother appears as Volumnia, while
Volumnia appears as Virgilia.

The Pons Sublicius is the earliest known bridge to be built in ancient
Rome, spanning the Tiber near the Forum Boarium downstream from
the Tiber Island, near the foot of the Aventine Hill. Legend has it that its
construction was ordered by Ancus Marcius around 642 BCE. The Sublicius
bridge was later deemed so sacred that alterations or repairs could not be
made before sacrifices were given by the *pontifex maximus* – an ancient
equivalent to a protected listed building.

Publius Horatius Cocles made the bridge eternally famous. After the overthrow of the Roman monarchy in 509 BCE and the establishment of the Roman Republic, as we have seen, Tarquinius sought military aid from the Etruscan king of Clusium, Lars Porsena. Porsena led his army against Rome, concentrating his forces on the Etruscan (west) side of the Tiber, and stormed and took the Janiculum Hill with all its materiel. Porsena posted an Etruscan garrison to hold it, then made for the Pons Sublicius, the only bridge then spanning the Tiber.

Things soon started to go badly for the Romans, who waited in the Naevian Meadow between Porsena and the bridge. The Tarquins commanded the Etruscan left wing, facing the Roman troops under Spurius Lartius and Titus Herminius. Octavius Mamilius commanded the Etruscan right right wing, made up of rebel Latins; they faced Romans under Marcus Valerius Volusus and Titus Lucretius Tricipitinus. Porsena commanded the centre, facing the two Roman consuls. Porsena outnumbered the Romans, and his plan was to intimidate them into retreat.

When battle eventually ensued, the Etruscan right wing was successful in wounding Valerius and Lucretius, the commanders of the Roman left wing. After both were carried from the field, the Romans began to panic and made for the bridge, with the enemy in pursuit. However, a certain Horatius saved the day; he was a junior officer 'on guard at the bridge when he saw the Janiculum taken by a sudden assault and the enemy rushing down from it to the river'.[12] Horatius was a patrician aristocrat who could claim descent from one of the Horatii who had fought the Curiatii of Alba Longa. His agnomen 'Cocles' came from the fact he had lost an eye in battle (an abbreviation of Cyclops?).[13] Aided and abetted by Spurius Lartius and Titus Herminius, the three valiant defenders withstood sword and spear attacks, holding the bridge until all the Roman troops had crossed.[14] Horatius then sought to buy further time and halt the attack by defending the opposite end of the bridge while the Roman soldiers destroyed the bridge, by so doing blocking the Etruscans' advance and saving Rome.

Livy's account of the event omits any battle, but does tell us that Horatius' 'own men, a panic-struck mob, were deserting their posts and throwing away their arms'.[15] Dionysius gives more detail (perhaps too much detail at times!):

'Herminius and Lartius, their weapons now rendered useless by the continual blows they received, began to retreat gradually. They ordered Horatius to retreat with them, but he stood his ground. Understanding the threat to Rome if the enemy were to cross the river, he ordered his men to destroy the bridge. The enemy was shocked not only by Horatius' suicidal last stand, but also by his decision to use a pile of bodies as a shield wall. Horatius was struck by enemy missiles many times including a spear in the buttocks. Hearing word from his men they'd torn up the bridge, he leaped fully armed into the river and swimming across ... he emerged upon the shore without losing any of his weapons.'[16]

Horatius' action scuppered Lars Porsena's assault on the city, forcing him into a siege which ended with a peace treaty, leaving Rome safe. The story exudes good old Roman values: valour, heroism, national pride and self-sacrifice. Horatius was awarded a crown for his bravery (possibly the equivalent of our Victoria Cross). He was now disabled from his injuries, but was awarded 'as much of the public land as he himself could plow around in one day with a yoke of oxen', and each citizen of Rome was obliged to gave him one day's ration of food, and that in a time of famine. He was also honoured with a bronze statue in the Comitium.[17]

Polybius is at pains to illustrate the bravery of Horatius, to such an extent that he introduces a much more tragic ending. He uses Horatius as an example of the men who had 'devoted themselves to inevitable death ... to save the lives of other citizens. ... [H]e threw himself into the river with his armour, and there lost his life as he had designed.'[18]

Napoleon, after a battle at Clausen in the South Tyrol, nicknamed General Thomas-Alexandre Dumas 'The Horatius Cocles of the Tyrol' for his solo defence of a bridge over the River Eisack.

In the historical era, the Pons Sublicius is also where Gaius Gracchus (160/153?–121 BCE) fled to when pursued by his enemies. Two of his friends attempted to stop them at the bridge, but were themselves killed. Gracchus died violently soon after in the Grove of Furrina. His flight may have been intended to benefit from the magical powers traditionally attributed to the bridge, but they failed him.

Another myth attributed to the bridge was the Ritual of the Argei – thought to be an Etruscan magical military tactic, comparable to another in which a Gallic man and woman were buried alive in the Forum Boarium. This symbolized the ritual burying or drowning of the Greeks and Gauls which the superstitious Romans believed had a palpable negative effect on their Greek or Gallic enemies. They also carried out this form of sacrifice after major defeats. On the Ides of May, the procession of the Argei made its way from the Temple of Fors Fortuna, built by Servius Tullius, to the

Pons Sublicius. The ritual involved priests travelling to all (twenty-seven or thirty) of the shrines (*sacella*), called Argei, in the original four regions of Rome before arriving at the Pons Sublicius. The pontiffs and the magistrates carried straw effigies of bound men, also called Argei, which the Vestal Virgins threw into the Tiber. The Flaminica Dialis was dressed in mourning.

Livy got his wish that the legend be read for years to come when Macaulay wrote his poem *Horatius*, composed in 1842 as part of the *Lays of Ancient Rome*, and which, if nothing else, captures the proud spirit of Livy's description:

> "'Hew down the bridge, Sir Consul, with all the speed ye may!
> I, with two more to help me, will hold the foe in play.
> In yon strait path, a thousand may well be stopped by three:
> Now, who will stand on either hand and keep the bridge with me?" ...
> "Oh Tiber, father Tiber, to whom the Romans pray,
> A Roman's life, a Roman's arms, take thou in charge this day!"
> So he spake and, speaking, sheathed the good sword by his side,
> And, with his harness on his back, plunged headlong in the tide.'

'A Nation Once Again' was a popular Irish rebel song, written in the early to mid-1840s by Thomas Osborne Davis (1814–45) to promote Irish nationalism. First published in *The Nation* on 13 July 1844 (two years after Macaulay's *Horatius*), the first verse refers to the heroism of 'ancient freemen, For Greece and Rome who bravely stood, three hundred men and three men', referencing the 300 valiant Spartans at Thermopylae and the three defenders at the Pons Sublicius.

Horatius at the bridge figures prominently in Jessie Pope's 1915 poem *The Longest Odds* about the exploits of a Highlander who single-handedly clears an entire German trench before being killed. His actions are likewise compared to the Spartans and the Roman defenders:

> 'Horatius – the odds grow longer now –
> With two bold friends, Lars Porsena defied.
> That dauntless trio registered a vow
> To hold the bridge that stemmed the Tiber's tide.
> Their deed of valour makes our bosoms glow,
> A deed which poets and chroniclers relate.
> Three heroes held in check a bitter foe
> And saved their city from a cruel fate.

One Highlander – the longest odds of all –
One man alone, when all the rest were slain,
Carried the Maxim through the bullet squall,
And set it spitting at the foe again.
Under its hail the Germans broke, they fled.
One man, one gun, and yet they would not stay!
Riddled with shot, his comrades found him dead.
Dead? No! That Hieland laddie lives for aye.

Gaius Mucius Scaevola

The first reference to this story is a fragment from a Roman history by the mid-second-century BCE author Lucius Cassius Hemina, but Livy and Dionysius are our chief sources. As we have seen, in 508 BCE, during the war between Rome and Clusium, Lars Porsena besieged Rome. Gaius Mucius, a young Roman soldier, set off on a clandestine mission to murder Porsena. He stole into the Etruscan camp masquerading as a deserter, only to find that there were two people there similarly dressed: one was the king, standing on a raised stage addressing the troops; but who was the other one? Mucius' intelligence for the mission let him down because he misidentified his target and killed Porsena's paymaster by mistake. Mucius was duly captured and came before the real Porsena, to whom Mucius revealed his mission. Porsena threatened to have him roasted alive, but undaunted, Mucius boasted (Livy 2.12–13):

> 'I am Gaius Mucius, a citizen of Rome. I came here as an enemy to kill my enemy, and I am as ready to die as I am to kill. We Romans act bravely and, when things turn bad, we suffer bravely.'

He added that he was but one of 300 Roman youths queuing up to volunteer to assassinate Porsena, at the risk of losing their own lives.[19] 'And then "Watch", so that you see how cheap the body is to men who have their eye on great glory.' At which Mucius thrust his right hand into a fire lit for sacrifice and held it there until it was burnt off – all without giving any indication of feeling pain. As a consequence, he earned for himself and his descendants the cognomen Scaevola, meaning 'left-handed'.[20]

Porsena, astonished by the youth's bravery, dismissed him from the Etruscan camp, free to return to Rome, with the words 'Go home – you harm yourself more than me' ringing in his ears. Porsena then sent ambassadors to Rome to offer peace terms.

As a reward for effectively saving Rome, his defiance, bravery and self-sacrifice, Mucius was granted farming land on the right bank of the Tiber, which later became known as the *Mucia Prata* (Mucian Meadows).

The uplifting story of Mucius was to blame for a sadistic punishment performed in Rome's Colosseum for condemned prisoners, where they would be forced to reenact this tale. Of course, few if any of the victims would have benefitted from congenital insensitivity to pain. The most celebrated occasion of this barbaric act was at the 80 CE inauguration of the Colosseum under the emperor Titus.

Over the years there has been many a Scaevola wannabee. Dante Alighieri refers to Mucius and the sacrifice of his hand in the *The Divine Comedy*. In 'Paradiso Canto' 4.82–87, along with St Lawrence, Mucius is depicted as a person possessing the rarest and firmest of wills. Jean-Jacques Rousseau mentions in Book One of his *Confessions* that, as a child, he attempted to replicate Mucius' action by placing his hand over a chafing dish. At the age of 12, Friedrich Nietzsche, attempting to prove to his classmates at Schulpforta that the story could be true, burnt his outstretched palm over a book of burning matches without expression of pain, and was only saved from serious harm by the school's prefect.

Long after Scaevola's brave act – well into the historical period – an earthquake centred on Rome in 326 BCE had profound effects on the city and its people. A huge crater suddenly opened in the Forum, which the Romans tried unsuccessfully to fill. After much head scratching, they consulted an augur, who responded that the gods demanded the most precious thing the country had be thrown into the chasm; if they did this, the Roman nation would prevail forever. The Romans were sceptical, and struggled to think what that elusive object could be.

However, a young soldier named **Marcus Curtius** came forward and castigated them, pointing out that arms and courage were the nation's most precious possessions. Mounting his horse, fully and meticulously armed and decked out in his uniform, Marcus rode headlong into the chasm, bound for Hades. Immediately, the deep pit closed over him and Rome was saved.[21] The Lacus Curtius in the Forum was supposedly built on the site of the pit.

We have seen the catalogue of brave Roman women who exuded patriotism and exhibited the robust values on which Rome was founded. What could the Roman learn from these stories? What was Livy, Dio and the others trying to convey to their readership and audiences? Essentially, they are what might be called cautionary tales, or lessons for life, clarifying how to conduct oneself, which values to embrace and how to be a good Roman.

The abduction of the Sabine women demonstrated that, to expand one's borders and develop and succeed as a permanent power, it was sometimes necessary to take extreme and aggressive measures. Lucretia showed up the sinister side of monarchy, the evils of unfettered lust overriding duty to the state and the deplorable lack of respect shown towards virtuous women, which at the same time compromised the sanctity of the family through sexual violence and coercive power, all against a background of fiercely proud, chaste and self-respecting womanhood. Verginia was another paragon of feminine virtue, suffering a similar fate to that inflicted on Lucretia, her father tragically preserving her moral integrity and virginity in the only way he knew. Tarpeia, on the other hand, suffered the terrible death due to anyone seduced by material things and ready to betray her country to acquire them, while Cloelia exhibited good Roman (masculine) qualities in her bravery (like Lucretia) and in her attempts to save her country. The Sabine women, Hersilia, Veturia and Virgilia showed just how powerful though inconspicuous the determination of women could be in the face of dogged male beligerence. Horatius too demonstrated extreme valour in his selfless defence of and self-sacrifice for Rome, as did proud Mucius and Marcus Curtius, while Publius, one of the Horatii, demonstrated how vital absolute patriotism was to Rome and the relative flexibility of the Roman judicial system.

Soon after the kings had finally been consigned to history, Rome was beset by resurgent hill peoples and by the **First Secession of the People** – a long-running dispute between patricians and plebs, the latter demanding civil rights relating to imprisonment, cruelty and the right that creditors enjoyed to seize the property of debtors. Agrippa Menenius Lanatus (died 493 BCE) was a consul in 503 BCE, with Publius Postumius Tubertus. He had been victorious over the Sabines and was awarded a triumph, celebrated in 503 BCE. According to Livy, he also led Roman troops against the Latin town of Pometia (2.16.32–33).

Menenius was elected by the patricians in 494 BCE to persuade the plebs to end their secession. Livy says (2.32) that Menenius (drawing on an impressive knowledge of Aesop's 'The Belly and the Members', one of his *Fables*) told a tale which involved expatiating on the parts of the human anatomy and how each had its own essential function in the greater workings of the body. He used the metaphor of the self-destructive refusal of the limbs to feed the stomach to convince the plebs of the futility of secession. Soon, the other body parts became tired and unable to function, making them realize that the stomach did serve a purpose after all and that they were all entirely dependant on it. In Menenius' metaphor, the stomach represented the patrician class and the other body parts the plebs. Eventually, Livy says, an agreement was reached between the patricians and the plebs, which included creating the office of tribune of the plebs.

The Oxford Classical Dictionary says ('Menenius Lanatus, Agrippa', Andrew Drummond):

'In Livy (2.32.8 ff.), the fable apparently justifies aristocratic socio-economic power and leisure; in Dionysius of Halicarnassus (Ant. Rom. 6.86.1 ff.) it less effectively legitimizes the political dominance of the senate. The entire story, with its élitist assumptions about effective popular oratory, may have been concocted by one of the Grecizing early Roman historians (cf. Dion. Hal. Ant. Rom. 6.83.2); Menenius' role as mediator was perhaps invented on the assumption that he was of plebeian birth (Livy 2.32.8).'

Chapter 8

Warlike Women in Roman Epic

T he women described in the wars of Virgilian and later epic embrace a number of functions, defined in part by their roles in surviving Greek epic and, no doubt, non-extant Greek and Roman epic. They are *causae bellorum*, like Helen and Lavinia; they are victims of war, like Dido, who is also a *causa*; they are combatants, like Camilla and the Amazon Penthesilea; or they stoke the fires of war and impel it forward, as with witches, godesses and Furies such as Allecto and Erichtho.

Camilla

Camilla was of the Volsci tribe, the daughter of King Metabus and Casmilla.[1] When he was deposed, Metabus was chased into the wilderness by armed Volsci, carrying his infant daughter in his arms. The River Amasenus blocked his path, and, fearing for the child's life, Metabus tied her to a spear and promised the goddess Diana that Camilla would be her life-long servant, a warrior virgin. He then threw her to the other side, and swam across to retrieve her. The baby Camilla was later suckled by a mare, and once her 'first firm steps had [been] taken, her small palms were armed with a keen javelin; her sire a bow and quiver from her shoulder slung'.[2]

Camilla was raised as a child to be a huntress, appropriately enough, and lived a rural life with her father and the shepherds in the hills and woods. Virgil says that Camilla was so fleet of foot that she could run over a field of wheat without breaking the tops of the plants, or over the ocean without getting her feet wet.[3]

Camilla is the woman warrior *par excellence* – effective, successful, competent, a leader of men and women and a reliable second-in-command. She only dies when, in a momentary lapse of battlefield concentration, she is distracted by the spoils of war. Virgil suggests that she was intent on plundering the corpse of Chloreus, either to dedicate Trojan weapons in a temple or else to procure them to wear herself. Either way, the temptation has been to dismiss or diminish Camilla by comparing her to an Amazon. Amazons are exemplary warriors, but while there are undeniable parallels – both Amazons and Camilla are *bellatrices* and both expose a breast, for example – and although Virgil calls her 'Amazon', Camilla is her own woman warrior and demands to be treated as such. Homogenizing her does her little justice.[4]

We first meet her as the final warrior, a privileged position, in the parade of Italian allies in Book 7 of the *Aeneid*; she is a *bellatrix*, a woman warrior.[5] Not for her were traditional matronly pastimes, womanly wool-working, housework or baskets of wool – Camilla's forté was battling hard and speeding, fleet-footed, after the enemy. Young men and *matronae* were agog in admiration at her splendour as she rode by. Her position at the end of Virgil's procession emphasizes her martial expertise and closes the catalogue on a high note, a morale booster for the people.

She reappears in Book 11 in the thick of battle, [6] but before that a short biography describes her early childhood as a semi-feral daughter in a one-parent family living and hunting in the woods, trained by her father. As we have seen, the shadow of war informs her life right from the start when her father propels her across a river lashed to a spear to escape a pursuing foe. Camilla thus becomes a weapon of war, a metaphor for war.[7] Her beauty, however, would remain undiminished, as later she was much in demand as a wife for many a mother's son.[8]

Her battlefield prowess is second-to-none:

'She rains down from her hand volleys of pliant shafts, or whirls with tireless arm a stout battle-axe; her shoulder bears Diana's sounding arms and golden bow. Sometimes retreating when forced to flee, this maiden shoots arrows with a rearward-pointing bow as she flies.'

Her comrades are hand-picked, armed to the teeth, just like an Amazon:

'Around her move her chosen peers, Larina, virgin brave, Tarpeia, brandishing an axe of bronze, and Tulla, virgins from Italy whom the divine Camilla chose to share her glory, each a faithful servant in days of peace or war. The maids of Thrace ride along Thermodon's frozen flood, and fight with emblazoned Amazonian arms around Hippolyta; or when Penthesilea returns in triumphal chariot amid shrill shouting, and all her host of women clash the moon-shaped shield in the air.'[9]

Lavinia

Lavinia was the second wife of Aeneas. When she was widowed by Aeneas' death, Lavinia took on the role of regent until Ascanius, her stepson, was old enough to rule independently. Indeed, when he did finally assume full regal responsibility, one of his first acts was to found a new settlement in the Alban

Hills, leaving Lavinia to rule Lavinium. Livy tells us that '*tanta indoles in Lavinia erat*', she was a very gifted woman. Obviously, she was exactly that if she was able to govern in such a bellicose and unpredictably unsettled world. Significantly, Lavinia – a capable and strong woman – was instrumental in the very birth of Rome and joins that small, exclusive club, which numbers Argia, Lucretia and Verginia in its membership, of women who influenced the constitution and political history of Rome.

As a young woman, Lavinia had always been a desirable match; when she was old enough for a husband, *matura viro* (7.53), she was courted by Turnus, no less, later to be Aeneas' arch-enemy. However, her father, King Latinus, had been warned by the gods that a Latin husband was not an option and that she should marry a foreign warrior. The warning came from his own father, Faunus, in a dream oracle (*Aeneid* 7, 96–101; trans. Robert Fitzgerald):

> 'Propose no Latin alliance for your daughter
> Son of mine; distrust the bridal chamber
> Now prepared. Men from abroad will come
> And be your sons by marriage. Blood so mingled
> Lifts our name starward. Children of that stock
> Will see all earth turned Latin at their feet,
> Governed by them, as far as on his rounds.
> The Sun looks down on Ocean, East or West.'

The prophecy was reinforced when Lavinia's hair burst into flames – a literally hair-raising moment – and the seer predicted great glory for her but terrible wars for Italy; the very same *magnum bellum* announced by the Cumaean Sibyl to Aeneas in the underworld in Book 6 (*Aeneid* 7, 94–104; trans. Robert Fitzgerald):

> 'While the old king lit fires at the altars
> With a pure torch, the girl Lavinia with him,
> It seemed her long hair caught, her head-dress caught
> In crackling flame, her queenly tresses blazed,
> Her jeweled crown blazed. Mantled then in smoke
> And russet light, she scattered divine fire
> Throughout all the house. No one could hold that sight
> Anything but hair-raising, marvelous,
> And it was read by seers to mean the girl
> Would have renown and glorious days to come,
> But that she brought a great war on her people.'

Dido, Queen of Carthage

Dido is both a tragic victim of war and a potent catalyst of future war.[10] Betrayed by Aeneas and cruelly sidelined by his dedication to his mission to fight for and help found Rome, Dido is incandescent with rage, and in a pit of misery and despair, she rages, out of her mind, and rushes through the city, mad as a Bacchant. She confronts the treacherous Aeneas and promises to haunt him for eternity in a threat reminiscent of a *defixio*:

> 'When I'm gone I'll follow you into the black fire of Hell, when icy death draws out the spirit from my limbs; my ghost will be everywhere; you'll pay the price, you traitor, and I will hear about it – the news will reach me deep down among the deadmen.'

Dido had seen the future, and the future frightened her; when she made offerings to the gods on the incense-burning altars, the milk turned black and the wine she poured congealed into an obscene gore. '*Horrendus dictu*', shocking to say it, she resolved to take her own life. She can hear the ghost of Sychaeus, her late husband, and a solitary owl wails its song of death. Dido recalls the warnings of the *pious* priests who predicted that her relationship with *pius* Aeneas would all end in tears. She instructs her sister, Anna, to build a pyre and enlist the services of the remarkable Massylian priestess; she will wipe out the memory of Aeneas with her spells, and his things will burn on the pyre. By implication, Aeneas is *impious*; he is subjected to a kind of *damnatio memoriae* in which he is erased from Dido's memory, as befits a traitor. When Dido sees Aeneas' fleet departing, she curses him and his Trojans and foretells endless enmity between Carthage and the descendants of Troy, foreshadowing the Punic Wars (*Aeneid* 4.642). Dido then falls on the sword given to her by Aeneas.

Virgil's audience would have understood only too well the potency of Dido's threats: Rome did indeed pay the price for Aeneas' alleged duplicity, with three devastating Punic Wars, one of which was near terminal for Rome. Furthermore, Aeneas was indeed haunted by Dido in their frosty meeting in the underworld. The Dido episode would resonate uncomfortably with the political upheaval caused so recently to Virgil's time by Cleopatra, a foreign queen eerily reminiscent of Dido, whose facility for global power-play would be viewed as comparable to the unnatural skills of a sorceress.

Shakespeare refers to Dido twelve times in his plays: four times in *The Tempest*, twice in *Titus Andronicus*, and also in *Henry VI Part 2*, *Antony and Cleopatra*, *Hamlet*, *Romeo and Juliet*, *A Midsummer Night's Dream* and, most famously, in *The Merchant of Venice*, in Lorenzo's and Jessica's mutual wooing.

Amata

Queen Amata was Lavinia's mother, wife to King Latinus and a source of great irritation to Aeneas. He, of course, was the foreign warrior who was ordained to marry Lavinia, but this was never to be with the blessing of Amata. She is possessed by Allecto, Juno's furious stooge, and vehemently opposes the match, preferring instead the native Latin, Turnus, for a son-in-law. When she concealed Lavinia in the woods and incited the Latin women, Amata triggered the war between the Trojans and the Etruscan king Mezentius, who was allied with Turnus. When she learns of Turnus' death at the hands of Aeneas, she hangs herself.

Juturna

Juturna was a goddess of fountains, wells and springs. As devoted sister to Turnus, she – on Juno's bidding – supported him against Aeneas by giving him back his sword after he dropped it in battle, as well as whisking him from the jaws of death when it looked very likely he would be killed by Aeneas.

Callisto

The virginal nymph Callisto was an acolyte of the goddess Artemis – virginity was a prerequisite for cult membership – so Jupiter disguised himself as Artemis in order to lure Callisto into the woods to rape her. Juno, Jupiter's wife, turned Callisto into a bear and set her loose in the forest, where she gave birth to Arcas. Jupiter hid Arcas away and never revealed the true identity of his mother, with fatal consequences: Arcas went out hunting one day and shot a bear dead; that bear was Callisto, his mother, no less. Another version holds that sixteen years after her metamorphosis, Callisto, still a bear, encountered her son Arcas hunting in the forest. Just as Arcas was about to kill his own mother with his javelin, Jupiter averted the tragedy by placing mother and son amongst the stars as Ursa Major and Minor, respectively. According to Ovid,[11] Callisto, like Camilla, had no interest in wool-working; neither was she interested in having her hair styled – thus eschewing one key matronly emblem and repudiating the feminine practice of making herself look nice. Instead, Ovid calls her a *miles*, a woman soldier who arms herself with bow and arrow and a soldier of Phoebe. Callisto was, then, a kind of female *miles amoris*, a soldier of love. Sadly, her military characteristics failed to prevent her from being raped.

Atalanta

Ovid's Atalanta is a huntress and a virgin who is doomed never to lose her virginity, even though she is loved by Meleager. She excels in the hunt against the Calydonian boar and is involved in battles when on the *Argo* as the only woman passenger with Meleager, Jason and the Argonauts. Atalanta sustains an injury while fighting in a battle at Colchis. Apollonius, however, says that Atalanta was never on the *Argo* because Jason had concerns over having a woman on board with an otherwise all-male crew.[12]

We meet her again in Statius' *Thebaid*, where she is 'pacifying groves' with her bow.[13] Later in the poem, she is a victim of war. Grief-stricken, she promises her son, Parthenopaeus, as he departs for war, that when he is older she will give him *bella* and *ferrum*, wars and weapons, and will not detain or deter him with a mother's weeping.[14]

Erichtho

Witches and other female chthonic agents were stock characters in ancient epic and tragedy, with, it seems, each poet vying with their predecessors to produce the most terrifying and abhorrent cabalistic characters. Erichtho is a witch surpassing even Seneca's Medea in her repulsiveness; Erichtho is the satanic witch–queen of all witches. She is literally an 'epic' witch. Her role in Lucan's (39–65 CE) *De Bello Civili* is to prophesy the outcome of the civil war: by providing Sextus Pompey with this information, she influences the course of the war.[15]

Sextus Pompey, driven by fear, wants to know the future and the outcome of the imminent Battle of Pharsalus in 48 BCE. He rejects conventional forms of divination, electing instead to deploy the ungodly, 'the mysteries of the furious enchantress'. Being in Thessally, he is local to the world's most dreadul witches and their *herbae nocentes*, pernicious herbs. When the witches here cast their spells, even the gods above pause to take note, and can sometimes be persuaded to do the witches' will.

Wild Erichtho takes even their evil excesses to new extremes. She communes with the dead and is expert in all things eschatological; where she goes, contagion follows; she buries the living and brings the dead back to life; and she snatches burning babies from their pyres for occult research and experimentation and assaults the corpses of the dead, scooping out eyeballs and gnawing at their nails. She tears flesh from corpses crucified on crosses, harvests the black, putrid, congealed gore suppurating from the limbs of the decaying, and she steals the meat ripped off putrefying bodies by rapacious wolves. She is a serial murderess, performing crude caesarean sections on pregnant women whenever a baby is required for the pyre. She also rips the faces off young boys, and at funerals she opens the mouths of the dead with her teeth, bites their tongues and thereby communes with Hell.

She is a liminal figure, living on the outskirts of civilized society and inhabiting 'graveyards, gibbets, and the battlefields generously supplied by civil war'. She uses body parts in her grisly magic spells (*De Bello Civili* 6.538–43):

> 'When the dead are confined in a sarcophagus ... then she eagerly rages every limb. She plunges her hand into the eyes, delights at digging out the congealed eyeballs, and gnaws the pallid nails on a desiccated hand.'

She is an expert necromancer. When she surveys corpses in a battlefield (*De Bello Civili* 6.633–36):

> 'If she had tried to raise up the entire army on the field to revert to war, the laws of Erebus would have yielded, and a host – pulled from the Stygian Avernus by her terrible power – would have gone to war.'

It is precisely for these reasons that she is sought out by Sextus Pompey. Erichtho is just the witch for him; she would be a fine teacher for any of the black arts, but it is in reanimation that she excels.

Erichtho complies with Pompey's request to know the future and the outcome of Pharsalus. She wanders through an old battlefield and seeks out a cadaver with 'uninjured tissues of a stiffened lung' (6.630). She cleanses the corpse's organs and fills the body with a potion consisting of, among other things, a mixture of warm blood, 'lunar poison' and 'everything that nature wickedly bears', so as to bring the dead body back to life (6.667–71). The spirit is summoned, but, initially refuses to return to its former body (6.721–29). She then promptly threatens the whole universe by promising to summon 'that god at whose dread name earth trembles' (6.744–46). The corpse is now successfully brought back to life and delivers a profoundly bleak description of a civil war in the underworld and an ambiguous prophecy about the fate that awaits Pompey and his family.

Erichtho may well have been the inspiration for Mary Shelley's *Frankenstein* some 1,750 years later: she would have been familiar with the episode through her husband, the poet Shelley, who was a great admirer of Lucan.

Asbyte

Silius Italicus (*c*. 28–103 CE) is the author of the 12,202-line epic *Punica*, the longest surviving poem in Latin from antiquity. Book 2 opens with Hannibal dismissing Roman envoys from Saguntum and addressing his troops with a threat to Rome. The siege of Saguntum continues, during which the warrior princess Asbyte is killed by Theron, who in turn is slain by Hannibal and mutilated.[16] A Camilla-type figure, Asbyte hails from Libya and, like other warrior women, is never much bothered by traditional women's work; she is a huntress and a virgin. She is bold (*audax*), has a band of sisters to follow her in battle – only some of whom are virgins – and has the characteristics of an Amazon, including the bare right breast. Her arrows whizz into the citadel she is attacking, while one of her comrades, Harpe, saves her from certain death when she stands before the flight of an arrow loosed by Mopsus and, in mid-shout, takes it in her open mouth, from where it passes right through her. The battle rages on, but Asbyte's time on Silius' blood-soaked battlefield is short. The warrior maiden, *belligera virgo*, is targeted by Theron; she escapes one attack but returns to the fray, at which point she is tipped out of her chariot (*Punica* 197–205):

> '[A]s Asbyte tried to flee from the fight, he [Theron] sprang up to stop her, and smashed her with his club between her two temples; he spattered the shiny wheels and the reins, tangled up by the terrified horses, with the brains that gushed from her broken skull … he then cut off the head of the maiden when she rolled out of her chariot. His rage was still not sated, for he fixed her head on a long pike for all to see, and made men carry it in front of the Punic army.'

Argia

Like Polyxena in Seneca's *Troades*, Argia exhibits shades of masculine militarism as portrayed in Statius' epic *Thebaid*, written between 80 and 92 CE. Statius' narrative is, of course, familiar to us from Greek tragedy, in particular from the *Phoenissae* and the *Suppliants* by Euripides. We pick up the story where Eteocles and Polynices have slain each other in battle, and their mother, a distraught Jocasta, commits suicide. Argia is the wife of Polynices and graduates in the action of the poem from deserted (*relicta*) army wife to heroine and female warrior.

Argia was a catalyst for war well before she knew it herself. It all began with her marriage to Polynices, which Statius describes as *semina belli*, or seeds of war, contrived by Jupiter to enable him to launch the 'Seven against Thebes'. Argia is soon abandoned as Polynices heads off to his unjust war. At first she is fearful, but soon is asking her father, Adrastus, to bring on the war.[17]

The crucial moment for Argia comes in the final book of the epic when Creon, recently installed as the new tyrant of Thebes, defies all convention and the rules of war and religion by denying Argia the right to bury Polynices. Meanwhile, the Argive women, acting as ambassadors, appeal to Theseus, king of Athens, for military aid. Argia, meantime, has left for Thebes to resolve the issues over Polynices' burial, despite the possibility of a cruel death at the hands of Creon.

Argia moves from being one of the allegedly inferior sex, men being the better sex (*melior sexus*), to a *matrona virilis*, a matron with strong, masculine qualities, who has deserted her gender: *sexu relictu*. Her *virtus* is definitely not a woman's – *non feminea* – and she later 'cultivates a sudden passion for courage that is not a woman's courage' (*non femineae subitum virtutis amorem colligit Argia*).

Women generally can also exhibit *virtus*, despite its explicit connotations of manliness (*vir*) and traditional male attributes of strength and bravery, as well as of virtue. From Seneca, we hear about the conspicuous valour of Cornelia and Rutilia described as *conspecta virtus*; in the *Ad Marciam*, he spells out his belief that women are just as capable of displaying *virtutes* as men.[18] Argia's *virtus* brings her up against Creon. Her decision to defy his orders is a huge undertaking – *immane opus*. It is an *arte dolum*, a crafty strategy, and is driven by chaste love and *pietas*, a duty to her son carried out in the face of the *fulmina regni*, the thunderbolts of the king, a blood-stained king and an abominable king.

The three-times repetition of the word 'king' would have resonated with Statius' audience, still sensitively mindful of the monarchy from the early days of Rome. Argia is, therefore, linked with Lucretia and Verginia –the two virtuous females who stood up to tyranny and, in so doing, paved the way for the Roman Republic and Roman democracy. But she is better than even that: she is more than a match for the Amazons, those celebrated female warriors who became, for many, the role models for the fighting woman in classical times. Belligerent woman though she is, Argia's chutzpah is, nevertheless, founded on sound *matrona* values, as we see when she poignantly recognizes Polynices' body on the battlefield by the clothes which she herself had devotedly woven for him.[19]

The Lemnian Women

A Lemnian deed or crime is defined as one of exceptional barbarity and cruelty. The phrase originates from two shocking massacres perpetrated by the Lemnians: one was the extermination of all the men and male children on the island by their outraged women; the other was the infanticide by the men of all the children born of Athenian parents in Lemnos. The epic poet Valerius Flaccus (died *c*. 90 CE) describes the first for us, leaning heavily on a long literary tradition, writing that the Thracian men were routed by the women in this internecine war: *Thracas qui fuderat armis*.[20] The returning Thracian boats approached Lemnos laden with the spoils of war, *praemia belli*, which included livestock and foreign women. Venus – angry that the Lemnians did not pay her honour – fired up Rumour to spread the word that the Lemnian warriors were bringing back Thracian women to warm their beds. Venus intended to inflict pain on and incite the Lemnian women into a frenzy. Rumour ran from house to house, comparing the local Lemnian women's beauty, their patient chastity and their industrious wool-working as good *matronae*, with these foreign imports with painted faces. The poet describes the Lemnians as Penelopes and Lucretias, paragons of female virtue, while the Thracians are depicted as whores. Further rumours had it that the Lemnian women would be exiled, their places taken by these Thracians, which further incensed the Lemnians. They feign a welcoming homecoming for their husbands, and then retire with them to eat and make love.[21]

Venus then takes on the role of commander and incites revenge: drenched in blood, she rushes into a house clutching a still pulsating decapitated head. Venus is the first avenger: she forcibly arms the women with swords and they fall on their husbands, many of whom are paralyzed by fear at the butchery going on all around them, perpetrated by wives, mothers and daughters. Blood flows in the bedrooms and foams in the chests of the slain Lemnian men. The women add to the atrocity when they torch their houses and block the exits.

In Statius (45–96 CE), Hypsipyle's description of the carnage is even more gruesome: [22]

'And we made our way through the deserted streets of the city, concealed in the dark, finding everywhere the heaped corpses from the night's massacre, where cruel twilight had seen them slain in the sacred groves. Here were faces pressed into beds, sword-hilts erect in wounded breasts, broken fragments of huge spears, knife-rent clothes among corpses, upturned wine-bowls, entrails drenched in blood, and bloody wine spilling over the wine cups out of severed throats.'

Statius even mentions some of the women by name.

In the third century BCE, Apollonius Rhodius had given more precise reasons why Lemnos came to be ruled by women:

'Led by Jason, the Argonauts first sailed to Lemnos which was then totally devoid of men and ruled by Hypsipyle, daughter of Thoas. This came about as follows: the women of Lemnos had neglected the cult of Aphrodite. As a punishment, the goddess afflicted them with a foul smell. The men found this repellent and took up with captive women from nearby Thrace. The Lemnian women were outraged at this humiliation and proceeded to murder their fathers and husbands.'

Apollonius tells us of the Lemnians subsequent belligerence and rejection of traditionally female activities:[23]

'The Lemnian women found it easier to look after cattle, put on a suit of bronze, and plough the earth for corn rather than to devote themselves, as they had done before, to the tasks of which Athene is the patroness [handicrafts]. Nevertheless, they lived in dire dread of the Thracians ... so when they saw the Argo rowing up to the island, they immediately got ready for war ... Hypsipyle joined them, dressed in her father Thoas' armour.'

Hypsipyle, the leader, advised conciliation and provisioning the Argonauts on their ships in order to keep them at bay. Venerable old Polyxo added her wisdom and foresight, born as it was of age and experience. 'Provisioning', it seems, must also include procreation:

'Hypsipyle is right. We must accommodate these strangers ... there are many troubles worse than war that you will have to confront as time goes by. When the older ones among us have died off, how are you younger women going to face the miseries of old age without children? Will the oxen yoke themselves? Will they go out into the fields and drag the ploughshare through the unyielding fallow? Will they watch the changing seasons and harvest at the right time?'

Valerius Flaccus states it more bluntly, citing the ticking clock that is the approaching menopause: 'Venus herself wishes us to join our bodies with theirs, while our wombs still remain strong and we are not beyond childbearing age.'[24]

Many centuries earlier, in the *Libation Bearers*, Aeschylus had put the criminal actions of the Lemnian women into some sort of context, providing a benchmark for female atrocity against male:[25]

> 'Indeed the Lemnian holds first place among evils as stories go: it has long been told with groans as an abominable calamity. Men compare each new horror to Lemnian troubles; and because of a woeful deed abhorred by the gods a race has disappeared, cast out in infamy from among mortals.'

The androcide committed by the Lemnian women led to a race without men, thus introducing the need for the women to adopt traditionally male functions: working the fields instead of the wool and defending their homes in war, rather than managing the *oikos* in domestic peace. Avoiding extinction was, as with the Amazons and early Romans, a chronic problem, eased here, on the advice of the wisest of Lemnian heads, by the chance visit of the Argonauts.

The Old Woman of Bessa

The Roman novel also featured women caught up in the shadowy and disturbing world of war. Heliodorus of Emesa, in the third century CE, describes a necromancy conducted by a witch, an old woman of Bessa, in his *Aethiopica*. Calasiris, a priest of Isis, and Charicleia, the heroine of the novel, come across the aftermath of a battle between the Persians and the Egyptians, a battlefield strewn with corpses. The only living soul is an elderly Egyptian woman mourning her dead son. She invites the couple to spend the night there with her. During the night, Charicleia witnesses a shocking scene: the old woman digs a trench, lights two pyres on either side and places the body of her son between them. She pours libations into the trench and throws in a male effigy made from dough. Shaking, and in a trance, the old woman cuts her arm with a sword and drips her blood into the trench, uttering wild and exotic prayers to the moon. She chants into her son's ear and makes him stand up, then questions him about the fate of her other son, his brother. The corpse at first says nothing, but because his mother persists, rebukes her for sinning against nature and breaking the law when she should have been organizing his burial. He reveals not only that his brother is dead, but that she too will soon die violently because of her life of unlawful practice.

Before collapsing again, the corpse reveals the awful truth that the necromancy had been witnessed not only by a priest beloved by the gods, but also by a young girl who has travelled to the ends of the earth looking for her lover. A happy outcome is promised for both. The old mother is outraged by this intrusion and, while pursuing Calasiris and Charicleia, is fatally impaled on a spear.[26] The old woman exemplifies the victims of war: in this case, a mother bereft of her two sons slain in battle is so desperate for news of the one who is missing that she resorts to the black arts in a necromancy with the other.

Chapter 9

Trojan Heroes

Nisus and Euryalus

We met this pair of warriors in the coverage of Book 9 of the *Aeneid*. Their night raid is one our earliest descriptions of guerrilla warfare; their zeal and competitiveness is first showcased in the Book 5 (286ff) footrace at the funeral games in honour of Anchises, in which a spot of gamesmanship allows Euryalus to win. Nisus, in the lead, slips in the blood shed from the cattle sacrificed during the religious rituals that preceded the race. Seeing that he cannot recover his lead, he trips Salius (then in second place) to allow Euryalus to cross the line first. Nisus thus demonstrates that he is willing to sacrifice his own honour in order to help Euryalus win, but the gesture demonstrates not only his loyalty but a willingness to cheat. The incident is an ominous prelude to what later befalls the pair on their night raid. Loyalty, bravery, camaraderie and an *amor* are their hallmarks – fitting companions to *pius* Aeneas in the quest for Rome. The dishonest act in the race tells us that sometimes, as in the heat of battle, it is necessary to act with dishonour to achieve victory.

Although their military skills are paramount here, their mutual love and affection invites parallels with the Greek custom of *paiderastia*. However, by describing their love as *pius*, Virgil endorses it as honourable and consistent with Roman values of *virtus*.

The younger Euryalus knew little else in his life other than war and displacement: he was trained as a fighter by his battle-hardened father, Opheltes, of whom he speaks with pride. Nisus, though, is the elder and more experienced of the two. He is swift of foot and a good shot (*acerrimus*) in the use of the javelin (*iaculum*) and arrows.

The night raid picks up major themes of the epic, such as the transition from boyhood to manhood – also present in the characters of Ascanius, Pallas and Lausus – and the waste of young lives in war. Nisus and Euryalus' killing spree through the camp of the Rutuli is one of Virgil's most brutal descriptions of combat, not least when Nisus decapitates Remus, along with Lamyrus, Lamus and Serranus. The floral similes used to describe Euryalus' death – 'as when a richly hued flower is cut down by the plough and withers as it dies, or when the rains beat down the poppy's head, weighed down on slack neck' – recalls the death of Gorgytion in the *Iliad*.

Achates

Achates was a true and constant companion of Aeneas, more often than not tagged as 'good, faithful Achates' (*fidus Achates*), a symbol of camaraderie and one part of a good, trusty friendship. Upon reaching Carthage Achates accompanied Aeneas on their scouting mission. However, despite his importance to Aeneas, he has only four spoken lines in the entire epic.[1]

The Aeneads (Αἰνειάδαι) were the friends, family and companions of Aeneas, fellow exiles and refugees who fled from Troy after the Trojan War disaster. They include Achates; Acmon, son of Clytius (son of Aeolus); Anchises; Creusa, wife of Aeneas and mother of Ascanius; Ascanius; Iapyx; Mimas; Misenus, Aeneas' trumpeter; Sergestus; and Achaemenides, one of Odysseus' crew the Aeneads picked up in Sicily (strictly speaking not an Aenead, as he was not Trojan but Greek).

Cydon and Clytius

There are three warriors by the name of Clytius mentioned in the *Aeneid*: there is one of the sons of Aeolus, who followed Aeneas to Italy and was killed by Turnus (*Aeneid* 9.744); Clytius, father of Euneus and one of those killed in the battle between Aeneas and Turnus (11.666); and Clytius, a young soldier in Turnus' army who was Cydon's lover and was killed by Aeneas (10.325):

'Cydon, wast by the Trojan stroke o'erthrown, while following in ill-omened haste the steps of Clytius, thy last joy, whose round cheek wore its youthful golden down: soon hadst thou lain in death, unheeding of thy fancies fond which ever turned to youth.'

Virgil *Aeneid* 9.744f; trans. T.E. Williams

Erulus

Erulus was a king of Praeneste blessed at birth with three souls (*animae*) by his mother, the goddess Feronia, who also handily increased threefold his ability to defend himself by giving him three sets of arms. Erulus may be modelled on the mythological figure Geryon.

Virgil tells his story through the Arcadian king Evander, founder of Pallantium, who forges an alliance with the Trojan exiles. Evander bemoans that the frailty of old age keeps him from fighting alongside Aeneas, and reminisces about the warlike deeds of his youth (*Aeneid* 8.560–67; trans. Robert Fitzgerald):

> 'If only Jupiter would give me back
> The past years and the man I was, when I
> Cut down the front rank by Praeneste's wall
> And won the fight and burned the piles of shields!
> I had dispatched to Hell with this right hand
> King Erulus, to whom Feronia,
> His mother, gave three lives at birth – a thing
> To chill the blood – three sets of arms to fight with,
> So that he had to be brought down three times.
> Yet this hand took his lives that day, took all,
> And each time took his arms.'

Evander

Evander was a hero from Arcadia in Greece who introduced the Greek pantheon, laws and alphabet to Italy, where he founded the city of Pallantium on the future site of Rome, sixty years before the Trojan War. He also established the festival of the Lupercalia. Evander was deified after his death and an altar was erected to him on the Aventine Hill.

Evander is a key player in *Aeneid* 8–12: before the Trojan War, Evander took a group of men to a city he founded in Italy near the Tiber, which he named Pallantium in honour of his Arcadian ancestor, Pallas.

Evander built the Great Altar of Hercules in the Forum Boarium. In *Aeneid* 8, where Aeneas and his followers first come upon Evander and his people, they were venerating Hercules for dispatching the giant Cacus. Virgil's audience would have related this scene to the same Great Altar of Hercules in the Forum Boarium of their own day, one of many scenarios in the *Aeneid* that Virgil used to link the heroic past with the age of Augustus. The archaic altar was destroyed in the Great Fire of Rome in 64 CE.

Evander helped Aeneas in his war against Turnus and the Rutuli. Evander had known Aeneas' father, Anchises, before the Trojan War, and shares a common ancestry through Atlas with Aeneas' family.

Helenus

Helenus was in the Trojan army led by his brother Hector that beat the Greeks back from the plains west of Troy and attacked their camp in the *Iliad*.

In the final year of the Trojan War, Helenus competed against his brother Deiphobus for the hand of Helen of Troy after the death of their brother Paris – but Helen went to Deiphobus. Disgruntled over his loss, Helenus retreated to Mount Ida, where Odysseus later captured him. He then betrayed the Trojans when he told the Greek forces how they might take Troy. He said that they would win if they stole the Trojan Palladium, brought the bones of Pelops to Troy and persuaded Neoptolemus and Philoctetes to join the Greeks in the war.

Helenus, having escaped Troy after its fall to found a new city, prophesied Aeneas' founding of Rome when he and his followers stopped at Buthrotum in Book 3 of the *Aeneid* (459–63; trans. H.R. Fairclough):

> 'The nations of Italy, the wars to come, how you are to flee or face each toil, she [the Cumaean Sibyl] will unfold to you; and, reverently besought, she will grant you a prosperous voyage. These are the warnings that you are permitted to hear from my voice. Go, then, and by your deeds exalt Troy in greatness unto heaven!'

Laocoön

Laocoön is pivotal to Rome's foundation myth, as much so as the abduction of Helen, because it was his actions which led to the Trojan horse gaining access to Troy, the subsequent sacking of the city and Aeneas' flight. According to Virgil, Laocoön cautioned the Trojans against taking in the horse, but to no avail; they opted instead to be taken in by the duplicity of Sinon. Virgil gives Laocoön the famous line '*Equō nē crēdite, Teucrī Quidquid id est, timeō Danaōs et dōna ferentēs*', 'Do not trust the Horse, Trojans. Whatever it is, I fear the Greeks even when bearing gifts.' This line usually survives as 'Beware of Greeks bearing gifts.'

An incensed Laocoön hurled his spear at the horse, causing the pro-Greek goddess Minerva to dispatch sea-serpents to strangle Laocoön and his two sons, Antiphantes and Thymbraeus. Virgil graphically describes the circumstances of Laocoön's terrible death (*Aeneid* 2.267–96; trans. John Dryden):

'Laocoon, Neptune's priest by lot that year,
  With solemn pomp then sacrific'd a steer;
  When, dreadful to behold, from sea we spied
  Two serpents, rank'd abreast, the seas divide,
  And smoothly sweep along the swelling tide.
  Their flaming crests above the waves they show;
  Their bellies seem to burn the seas below;
  Their speckled tails advance to steer their course,
  And on the sounding shore the flying billows force.
  And now the strand, and now the plain they held;
  Their ardent eyes with bloody streaks were fill'd;
  Their nimble tongues they brandish'd as they came,
  And lick'd their hissing jaws, that sputter'd flame.
  We fled amaz'd; their destin'd way they take,
  And to Laocoon and his children make;
  And first around the tender boys they wind,
  Then with their sharpen'd fangs their limbs and bodies grind
  The wretched father, running to their aid
  With pious haste, but vain, they next invade;
  Twice round his waist their winding volumes roll'd;
  And twice about his gasping throat they fold.
  The priest thus doubly chok'd, their crests divide,
  And tow'ring o'er his head in triumph ride.
  With both his hands he labors at the knots;
  His holy fillets the blue venom blots;
  His roaring fills the flitting air around.
  Thus, when an ox receives a glancing wound,
  He breaks his bands, the fatal altar flies,
  And with loud bellowings breaks the yielding skies.
  Their tasks perform'd, the serpents quit their prey.'

Palinurus

Palinurus features as Aeneas' trusty and experienced navigator in Book 3 (202; 595). Later, in Book 5, having set sail from Carthage, he advised Aeneas to delay sailing to Italy and to shelter from a terrible storm on Sicily, where they hold the funeral games honouring Aeneas' father, Anchises. After leaving Sicily for Italy, Palinurus, at the helm and leading the fleet, was singled out as the one whom the gods would sacrifice to guarantee safe passage to Italy for the rest of the Trojans (5'840): '*unum pro multis dabitur caput*', 'one single life shall be offered to save many'. Doped by the god of sleep, he falls overboard. Aeneas took over the helm and, unaware of the gods' influence, accused Palinurus of complacency (5.870–71): 'You, Palinurus, placed too much trust in the sky and the ocean's calm. You'll lie naked and dead on the sands of an unknown seashore.'

The next time the pair met they were in the underworld, where Palinurus was waiting for burial so that he can cross the River Styx. Aeneas asked how it came to be that he died despite a prophecy from Apollo that he would reach Italy unscathed. Palinurus responded that he survived the sea and was washed ashore after four days near Velia, where he was killed by natives and left unburied. The Cumaean Sibyl predicted that locals would build him a burial mound, which would be named Cape Palinuro in his honour (6.337–83).

Sinon

Sinon feigned to have deserted the Greeks and, as a Trojan prisoner of war, revealed to his captors that the giant wooden horse the Greeks had left behind was intended as a gift to the gods to ensure their safe voyage home. He told them that the horse was made so big deliberately so that the Trojans would not be able to move it into their city, because if they did the Trojans would be invincible to later Greek invasions. His duplicity convinced the Trojans, who brought it into the city against the advice of Cassandra and, as we have seen, Laocoön. The belly of the horse, of course, was filled with Greek soldiers, who, as night fell, spilled from the horse and opened the city gates, thus sealing the fate of Troy.

Chapter 10

Horace and Propertius

As already mentioned, the Augustan poets – which for our purposes formed a kind of côterie, with Virgil, Propertius, Horace and Ovid among their number at different times – were all, to some extent, poets of national interest, caught up in the Augustan propaganda machine which obliged them to subscribe to and promote the Augustan political agenda. An important facet of this was the idea that Augustus, through Julius Caesar, was a descendant of both Romulus and Aeneas – a notion which they were obliged to reinforce in their poetry by referencing various aspects of the foundation myths and the wars fought in their name. Indeed, Virgil and Horace were part of that privileged set which circulated around Maecenas, who in turn was, for the most part, very close to Augustus as his first minister with a responsibility for the arts. We have seen how Virgil, and will see how Ovid, interwove panegyric for Augustus into their poetry, implicitly endorsing the wars the *princeps* fought to get Rome to where it was. We have also seen how the wars fought by Aeneas and Romulus set laudable precedents for Augustus' militarism. But what about Horace and Propertius?

Horace (65–8 BCE)

Horace was a republican and fought as a military tribune on the losing side in the civil wars, defeated at the Battle of Philippi in 42 BCE. He was clearly able to live with whatever problems he may have had with this, since when courted by Augustus' right-hand man, Maecenas, he launched into a career characterized by support for the Augustan regime. He has been described by one critic as 'a master of the graceful sidestep',[1] and by Dryden as 'a well-mannered court slave'.[2] Perhaps Horace decided that, if it brought him relative peace, he could and should tolerate the Augustan administration (*Epodes* 5).

Saved by his acceptance of the amnesty Octavian offered to his defeated opponents in 39 BCE, Horace returned to Italy, only to find that his father's estate in Venusia had been impounded for the settlement of veterans. Horace, reduced to poverty and with nothing left to do, decided to become a poet[3].

He had procured the sinecure of *scriba quaestorius*, an unchallenging civil service post, one of thirty-six clerkships at the *aerarium*, or Treasury. It was about this time that he began writing his *Satires* and *Epodes*. Things started to look up for the near-destitute Horace, being gifted his Sabine farm by Maecenas soon after the publication of the first book of *Satires*.[4]

We can plainly see in the *Satires* Horace's support for Octavian's attempts to restore old-fashioned, traditional morality, defending small landowners being sucked into large estates (*latifundia*), combating debt and usury, and encouraging *novi homines* ('new men') to aspire to take their place next to the hoary old republican aristocracy.

His abhorrence of the effects of the civil wars is evident in *Epodes* 7, in which he deplores the prospect of another such conflict: Horace demands to know where the sinners (*scelesti*) are rushing off to now, grasping swords; hasn't enough blood been spilled? He demands to know what blind frenzy, fiercer force or crime is driving this – '*furorne caecos an rapit vis acrior an culpa? responsum date.*' He concludes by referencing the fratricide of Remus, which had tainted Rome ever since.

Epode 9 has Horace celebrating Octavian's victory at Actium, while *Epode* 16 returns to the poet's disgust at the depradations of civil war: he says another generation has been worn down by civil war (*teritur bellis civilibus*), and Rome is ruined by its own power.

Odes 1–3 were next on the agenda. His output between 30 and 27 BCE began to show signs that he was getting increasingly close to the Augustan regime and imbibing its ideology. In *Odes* 1 and 2, he eulogized Octavian in hyperbole that would have done Hellenistic court poetry proud. From 27–24 BCE, there are references in the *Odes* to foreign wars in Britannia (1.35), Arabia (1.29) Spain (3.8) and Parthia (2.2). When Augustus returned triumphant to Rome in 24 BCE, the fawning is there for all to see (Odes 3.14.13–16):

'Romans, all conquering Caesar is back home from the Spanish shores, who, like Hercules, was said to be after that laurel, that's bought at the price of death. May Livia rejoice in her peerless husband ... This day is a real festival day for me, it banishes gloomy moods: I will not fear riots or a violent death while Caesar's on this earth.'

Michael Grant has called *Odes* 3.1–6 'a great tribute to Augustus' principate, perhaps the greatest political poetry that has ever been written. But these *Odes* are by no means wholly political, for much other material, including abundant Greek and Roman mythology, is woven into their dense, compact, resplendent texture.'[5]

By around 20 BCE, Augustus was commissioning more and more from Horace, including celebrations of the military achievements of close relatives Drusus and Tiberius.[6] The pièce de résistance – for Augustus – was the commissioning in 17 BCE of the *Carmen Saeculare*. The hymn was sung by a chorus of twenty-seven maidens and youths on the occasion of the Ludi Saeculares (Secular Games), which celebrated the end of one *saeculum* (typically 110 years) and the beginning of another. The song takes the form of a prayer addressed to Apollo and Diana, in which Apollo is a surrogate for and patron of Augustus, for whom a new temple on the Palatine had recently been consecrated. As such it chimed nicely with Augustus' programme of religious reform, reintroducing the old–style reverence of the Olympian gods.

In the hymn, Horace urges Diana to make Augustus' new legislation on marriage and the family effective, with wives delivering more children – the '*lex Iulia de maritandis ordinibus*' of 18 BCE encouraged marriage and imposed penalties on celibacy. We hear a retelling of the Trojan foundation myth in which the refugees from faraway Ilium reached the Tuscan shore with orders to change their home and their city, under '*castus*' (pious) Aeneas, the unscathed survivor from the flames of Troy who trod a path to freedom, sure to gain more than he'd lost. Apollo and Diana are beseeched to show virtue, grant peace and quiet to the old, give children and wealth to the people of Romulus and, echoing Virgil, let Augustus, a war winner, be merciful to beaten foes.[7]

Where else do we find evidence of Horace's use of war mythology? We have already discussed the important role Castor and Pollux play as divinities in Roman war-related mythology. After their star role after the Battle of Lake Regillus (499 BCE), the twins continued to appear in the Forum as harbingers of Roman military victories. They had their Temple of the Dioscuri for their cult, and the great military spectacle and feast day of the Dioskouroi, when 5,000 or so young men would be led by two impersonators of the heroes through the streets of Rome. In Horace, they appear in several contexts connected with the deification of Augustus and crop up in passages linked with apotheosis.[8]

In Horace's *Odes*, Castor and Pollux share the stage with Augustus, indicative of the relatively nuanced approach Horace takes to the rule of Augustus, and, ironically, how his wars and battles were sold as a necessary price to pay if peace was to break out under his sway. The Dioscuri represent belligerence through Castor's horsemanship and pugilistic skills (2.25–27), but also pacification with their sea-calming abilities and their safeguarding of sailors at sea (27–28). Romulus is cited as a paradigm of rule by war (his Sabine wars, for example), while Numa's reign is an *exemplum* of peaceful rule: '*quietum/Pompili regnum*' (33–34). Livy corroborates for us that it is Numa's policy to temper the bellicose nature of the early Romans. Livy (1.19.1) says that Numa, a civilizer, wanted to 'found anew with justice and laws and customs' ('*iure ... legibusque ac moribus de integro condere*') a city that had been 'founded on force and arms' ('conditam vi et armis'). In order to do this, he had to mollify the warlike Romans by urging peace over war (1.19.2):

> 'And since he realised that it was impossible to become accustomed to these things while wars were raging (for military service brutalized the mind), thinking that a warlike people should be softened by not using arms, he dedicated a temple to Janus at the foot of the Argiletum as a barometer of peace and war: when open it would signify that the state was at war, and closed it signified that all the peoples around were pacified.'

Livy adds that Numa feared 'that in a warlike state there would be more Romuluses than Numas' – '*in civitate bellicosa plures Romuli quam Numae similes*'.

Horace also refers to Julius Caesar and his divine status (46–48), 'the Julian star glitters among all of them, just as the moon does among the lesser lights', anticipating the future deification of Augustus and thereby connecting the *gens Julia* with the placatory powers of the Dioscuri. The final stanza describes the dual role that Augustus and Jupiter will share in their universal reign over the world (57–60), while the reference to sullied groves is, according to one critic:[9]

> 'a hint of Augustus' desire to raise the standards of sexual behavior, a theme repeatedly stressed in the Roman *Odes* (3.1–6), and which was to become official policy in 18–17 BC.'

In *Odes* 3.3, Horace confirms and reinforces these sentiments. The strong and good ruler, Augustus, will not be swayed by the malicious, morally bankrupt mob, and will not be seduced by tyranny. The sea storm reminds us of the Dioscuri, while Pollux himself is referenced as an example of one who has crossed from mortality to immortality by apotheosis, and thus recalls Augustus. Through Juno, Horace delivers an unequivocal message to Augustus that 'the Romans should turn their aggression outward. By redirecting the Romans away from civil war and toward wars abroad and peace at home, Augustus can bring stability to warlike Rome just as the Dioscuri soothe raging storms.'[10]

Indeed, it is with the 'Roman Odes' (3.1–6) – as they have since been called by H.T. Plüss in 1882 – that Horace finds his most fluent expression of admiration for Augustus' regime, his celebration of the new age and of Augustus's lineage, stretching back to Aeneas and Venus.

Their theme is the lionization of Roman virtues and the glory that is Rome under Augustus. Ode 3.5, for example, explicitly identifies Augustus as a new-age Jupiter who is determined to restore in Horace's Rome the prestige of past Roman heroes like Marcus Atilius Regulus, whose story takes up the second half of the poem.

The following is a short summary of some of the poems in *Odes* 3 and their themes:

1: The poet as priest of the Muses sings new poems to a new generation. Men must realize that they are all subject to Fate and the gods, and that the road to happiness and serenity is to restrict desires and be content with frugality.

2: A poem more famous for its *dulce et decorum est pro patria mori*, this describes a Roman youth who is encouraged to terrify 'wild Parthians' with his spear under the walls – a scene watched both by the Parthian king's mother or wife, and, with some trepidation, by a *virgo* – the bride of the king or of a Parthian prince. This bride is anxious that her prince (or king) does not provoke the Roman into violent action, likened as he is to a ferocious lion, capable of extreme carnage. She sees caution as the best option that is open to her Parthian. The lesson to be learnt, though, according to Horace, is that 'it is sweet and fitting to die for one's country' – although there is no escaping death anyway, even when a soldier flees the battlefield. The young Roman soldier is idealized and his fate is declared to be sweet and glorious (*dulce et decorum*). True *virtus* is the path to heaven, and discretion is vital to the safety of all.

3: The just man is fearless and can attain divine status. Juno's speech permits the deification of Romulus on condition that Troy never rises again.

4: The poet recalls his boyhood and claims that he owes his life to the protection of the Muses, who likewise refresh Augustus now that his military campaigns are over. The Giants threatened to overthrow the

Olympians, but were unable to defeat the gods; force is wicked without wisdom.

5: Augustus will be declared a god after the defeat of Britain and Parthia. The disgrace of Roman soldiers marrying Parthian wives is contrasted with the heroism of Regulus, who rejected the pleas of his friends to stay and kept his oath to return to his torturers in Carthage and certain death.

6: Rome must rebuild the temples and the relationship with the gods which underwrites Roman rule. Impiety brings ruin; sexual immorality is now pervasive in Rome. In the old days, young people were virtuous and disciplined, whereas the contemporary generation is permissive, with worse to come.

In short, Horace bewails the prevailing immorality and contempt for the traditional religions, and recommends a swift resumption of a simpler, less permissive, venal and materialistic way of life – all consistent with Augustus' programme of moral reform and revivification.

To these we can add the following, which exhibit similar sentiments:

16: The key to wealth is not excess of gold but limiting desires to the 'little which is sufficient'.

24: This poem idealizes the simple life of Scythian and Getan nomads and, in contrast, paints a miserable picture of contemporary Rome, with feckless youth and corrupt parents (24.17–34; trans. J. Connington):

> 'There the step-dame keeps her hand From guilty plots, from blood of orphans clean; There no downed wives command Their feeble lords, or on adulterers lean. Theirs are dowries not of gold, Their parents' worth, their own pure chastity, True to one, to others cold; They dare not sin, or, if they dare, they die. O, whoe'er has heart and head To stay our plague of blood, our civic brawls, Would he that his name be read "Father of Rome" on lofty pedestals, Let him chain this lawless will, And be our children's hero! cursed spite! Living worth we envy still, Then seek it with strain'd eyes, when snatch'd from sight. What can sad laments avail Unless sharp justice kill the taint of sin?'

Money and self-indulgence are bad when they destroy the moral fibre of the Roman people.

25: The poet is in a state of ecstasy brought on by Bacchus and proposes to celebrate the deification of Augustus.

Elsewhere in the Odes, we see praise for Augustus in 1.2, where Horace concludes the poem by wishing Augustus a long and triumphant life as *pater atque princeps*, enjoying *magnos triumphos* (1.2.49–50). Meanwhile, 1.4, 1.6 and 1.7 are what have been called 'Parade Odes', where Horace eulogizes Augustus' policies, which are bringing civil unity and harmonisation. In poem 6, we read of a peerless Augustus, while poem 7 tells of the emperor's mercy and reconciliatory actions.

Propertius (50/45–c. 15 BCE)

Propertius, like Horace, was scarred by the toxic years of the Republic and by the civil wars with which it became synonymous in its final years. Like Virgil and Horace, he and his family were forced to surrender land when Octavian grabbed and reallocated other people's property amongst his veterans in 41 BCE. But Propertius' wounds were inflicted by events which went much deeper than even that.

His political attitude will have been formed, no doubt, from a childhood living in Asis (modern Assisi), a mere 15 miles from war-torn Perusia, where he will have witnessed the death and destruction caused by Octavian's siege of Perusia (41/40 BCE); his family suffered badly, with at least one relative killed. In the end, Octavian exterminated the Perusian senate, 300 or so innocent men whose only crime was that their city had been commandeered by outside forces. According to Suetonius (*Life of Augustus* 15):

> 'After the fall of the city Augustus took vengeance on crowds of prisoners and returned the same answer to all who sued for pardon or tried to explain their presence among the rebels. It was simply: "You must die!" According to some historians, he chose 300 prisoners of equestrian or senatorial rank, and offered them on the Ides of March at the altar of the God Julius, as human sacrifices.'

The town was then razed, except, according to Dio, for the Temple of Hephaistos and the statue of Hera.

Propertius, then, had good reason to reject not just war but also Augustan moral and political values generally. The poet is much more interested in a *pax amoris* than any *pax Romana*. His main war poems comprise 1.21, 1.22, 2.7, 2.10 and 3.1–5. While there is praise for Augustus' achievements, there is always a suspicion that, for whatever reason, the poet was, on occasions, being somewhat disingenuous and that his true feelings were in fact informed by his unhappy experience of Octavian's depradations in the Perusine War.

The two interrelated closing poems of the *Monobiblos* see Propertius suspend his treatment of things amatory to comment on the effects of war. In 1.21 we read of the tragic impact the death of Gallus has on his family, while 1.22 opens with reference to the horrors of Octavian's actions at Perusia, where the words '*Romana discordia*' figure prominently:

> 'If the Perusine tombs of our country are known to you, funerals in Italy's hard times, when Roman discord hunted her citizens (This was especially painful for me, my Etruscan soil – you allowed my neighbour's limbs to go abandoned, no earth covers his poor bones) – neighbouring Umbria, below Perusia on the plain bore me, fertile Umbria, productive land.'

For Propertius, the 'Roman discord' was clearly personal.

Propertius, Tibullus and Ovid, and others, cliché and chorus 'make love not war' in direct opposition to what was expected of them as men and citizens of imperial, expansionist and bellicose Rome: instead of donning greaves and shields, and spending the best part of their lives guarding or acquiring far-flung foreign parts, they assumed the mantle of pacifist and poet, versifying in a life of *otium* in a cosmopolitan Rome. Anagrammatically, they had joined the army of *Amor*, not the army of *Roma*. The soldier of love was fighting endless battles with his mistress in a war of love, the objective of his quasi-military service. She is the enemy, the other half of the conflict, the *sine qua non* of the poet's military service and of the battles he was fighting; she is his *causa belli*. The poets actually allowed themselves to be dominated by their women (their *dominae*), and even to be enslaved by them in *servitium amoris*. Their *cursus honorum* and military career was *militia amoris*; they languished, locked out, humiliated and rejected, on the doorstep of a capricious woman, *exclusus amator*. To traditional conservative Romans, good Roman *militia* were being supplanted by feeble, lovelorn 'soldiers', who were under the control of women rather than centurions.

This had been the case for a number of years in the first century BCE before the love elegists came on the scene. Among the flourishing côteries anxious to imbibe and parade Hellenism and other exotic influences, we can recognize such poets as Licinius Calvus, Varro of Atax, Valerius Cato, Furius Bibaculus, Helvius Cinna, Cornificius, Ticidas and, most famously, Catullus. Collectively, they went under the name of *poetae novi* (new poets), *neoteroi* (the new poets), *delicata iuventus* (pleasure-seeking youths) or *Cantores Euphorionis*.

To most Romans, war was an unquestioned and unquestionable fact of life. It had been a constant since the foundation of the city in 753 BCE and was credited with getting the Romans to the place they were in the first century BCE: a truly supreme power and successful expansionist civilization dominating the Mediterranean region and further afield. Catullus, though, managed to dodge the military life and only had to endure two years on the staff of propraetor C. Memmius, governor of Bithynia, in 57–56 BCE. No doubt others were equally successful draft-dodgers.

This unconventional, un-Roman way of life pursued by the outré poets would have been expected to foster not only outrage amongst conservatives, but also a pacifist, anti-war attitude amongst its adherents. Propertius, we have observed, indignantly demanded to know: 'why should I breed sons for Rome's triumphs? No blood of mine will ever produce a soldier.'[11] However, it was not always as simple as that. Catullus, as noted above, thirty-five years or so earlier – as unconventional as any of the new poets – had, surprisingly perhaps, taken the establishment line that marriage and procreation was very much a duty.

The motifs of *miles* and *militia amoris* which we find in Propertius and Tibullus, and in Horace and Ovid, are themselves indicative of pacifism. For a Roman to fight in the war of love as a soldier of love was at once the abnegation and rejection of the conventional Roman way, the Augustan way – namely, pursuing the *cursus honorum* according to the *mos maiorum* – and also a vocalization of the fact that the only war to be fought was the war of love: in short, a regular military career was rejected in favour of pacifism.

Propertius could not be clearer about his position and his pacifistic leanings when he exclaims, 'I'm not naturally suited to glory or for arms; Love's is the only warfare which the Fates have planned for me.' Propertius must instead serve under Venus (4.1.37). A victory over Cynthia is likened to a triumph (2.14.23ff), complete with booty. In poem 3.6, we find an incredulous Propertius demanding to know from Postumus just how he can bear to leave Galla, his wife, crying her eyes out, 'and follow the soldier's trade, behind Caesar's flags'? 'What good is Parthian plunder', he asks, when his wife's tears go unheeded? He curses 'any man who prefers the arms of the camp to those awaiting him in his bed'.

Propertius introduces mythology into the device when he associates himself with such famous warriors as Achilles and wild Hector (2.22.34). He suggests Paris fought his biggest battles on Helen's knee (3.8.32).

Sex episodes with Cynthia are lengthy *Iliads*, the ultimate war story in Propertius' day (2.1.13). Ovid redresses the balance between the sexes in the *Ars Amatoria* (3.1–4), which, in Books 1–2, offered advice aimed at men chasing women. He refers to women, mock-heroically, as Amazons and Penthesilea; these are the subject of his tuition in Book 3. By 'arming' women, he nevertheless realizes he is effectively betraying his own sex, his comrades in arms (3.667f).

In 2.10, we get an apparent *volte face*. Propertius tells his readers and audiences that he is changing course, literally; he has finished with Cynthia-inspired verse and will now sing about wars and in praise of Augustus. It didn't last long: by 2.13a he is back writing about Cynthia. We got a hint of his inconsistency in 2.1, where a paean to Maecenas – and by extension, Augustus – turns from a poem replete with Greek mythology and references to war to one proclaiming Cythia as his inspiration. In 3.11 he is much the same, with Augustus ultimately dominating over a catalogue of enemies, predominantly Cleopatra, whom he masquerades as a metaphor for Cynthia.

It is in Propertius' Book 4 where we find much of his work on war-related myth, the book which more than the first three demonstrate the tensions he must have felt to celebrate Augustus, succumb to Augustan pressure and indulge Maecenas. At the same time, he has to fulfil his desire to be the *Callimachus Romanus*, explaining the origin of Roman rites, deities and names of ancient places, just as Callimachus did in the *Aitia* (4.1.57, 67–70). Propertius accordingly gives us five aetiological poems (4.2, 4.4, 4.6, 4.9 and 4.10), one of which is his *aition* on the foundation myth of Tarpeia. In the same book, we also find him turning his hand to national, political poetry by celebrating Actium and urging revenge on the standard-stealing Parthians at Crassus' Carrhae disaster.

Propertius, ambivalent again, opens his fourth book with a poem which is intended to firmly establish his patriotic credentials, an opening shot which could not have failed to please Augustus and his image people. We are guided round Propertius' Rome in all its modern architectural splendour, with him pointing out the whereabouts of the ancient city's structures and edifices before the time of its foundation. In fact, it seems that we are transported back into Ovid's 'Golden Age', where simple rusticity and a bucolic air prevail. Augustus' Trojan lineage is mentioned as soon as line 2 by way of a reference to Aeneas; then the old festivals which Augustus was trying to revive loom large. Honest simplicity and unpretentious living were the hallmarks of this ancient Rome. Propertius's real history (our legend) begins with the fall of Troy and Aeneas' flight with father on back – the first demonstration of *pietas* – then we fast-forward with reference to a resurgent Troy and the modern fruits that have come from the milk of the *lupa*, nursemaid to the state of Rome.

This is what Propertius tells us he is concerned with now. Self-deprecatingly, he announces his launch into soaring patriotic verse in service to his country. 'Fall Troy, and Trojan Rome arise!' is his theme; aetiology now is the name of his game. But we have been here before. Propertius is merely going through another false start, as he did before when announcing a move away from love poetry to national poetry. As before (2.10 and 3.11), the plan soon peters out and Book 4 still manages to include two Cynthia poems.

In going aetiological, Propertius had made the decision to be seen to be associated with the Augustan regime – he would now, or at least his intention was to, expatiate on Roman history, the *mos maiorum*, the very ideal Augustus was determined to promote. The *princeps* would have had little interest in the poet's love elegies or in a woman called Cynthia, but he would have encouraged anything which celebrated old-fashioned Roman moral rectitude and which deplored and denigrated a traitorous woman called Tarpeia. Propertius may have seen how inimical his love poetry might have been viewed in official propaganda and image-obsessed circles, and so decided to add historical respectability to his poetic offer. We shall see in the next chapter how Ovid had a similar wake-up call.

Propertius' version of the Tarpeia myth is unique among the extant renderings when he ascribes her treason to passionate love for Tatius, Rome's Sabine enemy. His version shows her desperate to be Tatius' lover and queen, not the opportunist winner of a few golden trinkets. Propertius' Tarpeia is driven by passion, not by the usual material gain. This is not surprising, given that Propertius was primarily a love poet, so the poem may well be an attempt by him to chime with Augustus' programme of moral reform by exposing the untenable, un-Roman things done in the name of love and uncontrollable passion.

We have seen in an earlier chapter how Propertius deals with the myth surrounding the traitor Tarpeia (4.4), but it is perhaps important that we emphasize one aspect of his version, a version in which, like Varro,[12] Propertius designates Tarpeia as one of the serving Vestal Virgins of the day. On one level this association with one of the most sacred offices in ancient Rome serves to accentuate the enormity of Tarpeia's crime – a woman so sacred in a position so revered turning to treason and prepared to betray the state as a victim to immoderate passion. It also alerts us to the horror Propertius felt at Tarpeia's odious treason and treachery – despite his overarching anti-war sentiments. We must, however, remember that, in the words of A.E. Watts, 'Propertius makes inconsistency into a fine art', on the basis of the poet's prayers 'for the success of Roman arms' in 2.7 and 3.4.[13]

However, on another level, Propertius shows a degree of sympathy towards the traitor. In the first place, alone of all the extant sources, he gives her a voice, allowing her – in a monologue which occupies one-third of the poem – to articulate her side of the story and to voice the emotional torment she is patently enduring. She is no naïve fool: she tries to rationalize her dilemma, to reconcile her desires for Tatius with the price at which this comes – an abdication of her duty to her *patria*, her homeland, a total abnegation of *pietas* and a need for *amor* over *Roma*. She evokes a precedent for her action when the Sabine women were abducted and became peacemakers in the war between the Sabines and Rome. Likewise, her longed-for marriage to Tatius will forge a pacifying link between the two adversaries as the battling evaporates and peace prevails.

Propertius, of course, was well qualified to describe such an anguished struggle – his experiences with the whimsical and fickle Cynthia will have seen to that. Ultimately, though, Propertius' sympathetic portrayal of Tarpeia's emotional turmoil here may be an indication of what was in reality a vapid and uncomfortable attempt at being a good and compliant Augustan poet.

The situation is blurred further by the fact that the legendary Tarpeia has always been an ambivalent character, despite her association with the terrible fate which awaited anyone on a one-way ticket up to the notorious rock. After her famous fall, Tarpeia was buried in a tomb which was venerated well enough by the Roman people; and under Augustus, her portrait features on two coins and on the frieze in the Basilica Aemilia, as restored by Augustus. Her elevation to Vestal Virginity also suggests that before the Tatius episode in her life, she was a woman of some standing. So again, Propertius may have chosen Tarpeia as an *aetion* because she represented ambiguity and ambivalence, and reflected the poet's own insecurity in relation to his alliance to the Augustan regime.

It important to understand the significance of Tarpeia's designation as a Vestal Virgin here and the enormity of her crime in the context of her office. Vesta was the goddess of the hearth, traditionally attended by virgin priestesses, the Vestal Virgins, who kept the sacred flame, *ignis inextinctus*, alight in the Temple of Vesta. This flame symbolized the nourishment of the Roman state; the head Vestal, *Virgo Vestalis Maxima*, symbolized the wife of the old Roman kings (represented in turn by the *Pontifex Maximus*) while the others, the College, were the symbolic daughters of the king. The kings were said to originate from sparks in the ground. Any Vestal careless enough to allow the flame to go out was whipped; tending the flame occupied the Vestals for around eight hours every day. As already stated, the Vestals' virginity embodied the safety of Rome. Rome was safe while their virginity and integrity remained intact; when it was violated, Rome was under threat.

Romulus and Remus, we have seen, were reputedly the offspring of Rhea Silvia, a Vestal Virgin, and Mars. In the early Republic, there was possibly just one Vestal Virgin, but this increased to a college of six, of various ages. Recruitment took place every five or so years: candidates were originally elected by lot from a group of about twenty aged between 6 and 10. They served for thirty years (ten in an apprenticeship, ten as a Vestal and ten as a teacher), after which they were let go, given dowries and were free to marry should they so wish. Not many did. To be considered for election, the parents of candidates not only had to be alive, but their pedigree had to be above question. In 19 CE, when two girls were competing for one vacancy, the unsuccessful candidate was the one whose parents had divorced;[14] the successful girl's mother was a *univira*. The candidates themselves must have had neither a speech impediment nor a hearing defect.[15] Initiation bore similarities to the regular marriage ceremony, with initiates delivered to the Pontifex Maximus; they wore a red headdress (the *flammeum*) and the six braids.[16]

As well as keeping the flame alight, and thereby ensuring the endurance of the Roman state and the purity of public sacrifices, the Vestal Virgins had a number of exclusive festal responsibilities.[17] In mid-May, they threw straw figures (*argei*) into the Tiber from the Pons Sublicius. In June, the *penus* – their storehouse, symbolizing the storehouse of the state – was· opened for women to bring offerings at the Vestalia on 9 June; the blood from the slaughtered 'October horse' was stored in the *penus* in October. Calves' foetuses were ripped from the wombs of thirty-one slaughtered cows in April at the festival of Fordicidia, cremated, and their ashes stored in the *penus* until the Pales (21 April), when they were scattered to purify the people; people ritually jumped over a mixture of the blood and the ashes which had been poured over burning straw at the feast of Parilia. *Mola salsa* were made in May ready for the Vestalia and the Lupercalia on 15 February – an instance of the Vestals' special dispensation to help in the preparation of sacrifices, hence our word immolation. They each carried a *sescepita* – a sacrificial knife. On 15 June, they ritually swept and cleansed their temple.

During the Vestalia, donkeys were celebrated to mark their valuable role in the making of bread, a staple food in Rome. The donkey was Vesta's saviour when Priapus attempted to rape her: this accounts for the presence of a donkey in some depictions of the goddess. Its sexual prowess forms part of the fertility paradox that surrounds the Vestals, as does the phallus which is sometimes shown in the flames of their fire. In a more secular context, both Julius Caesar and Augustus deposited their wills with the Vestals.[18] The fact that Vestals, as virgins, enjoyed privileges reserved for married women, *matronae*, and for men highlights even further the sexual ambiguity of their status and throws into relief their vulnerability and the fragility of their reputation.

Vestals received a payment upon joining and a yearly stipend thereafter; as much as two million sesterces were paid out – twice the dowry of a rich girl. The remuneration came to be as much a bribe as anything, given the increasing difficulty in finding candidates. If a Vestal died intestate, then the estate went to the treasury, supposedly to pay for sacrifices. However, Vestals could make wills and they were free to dispose of their property.

The last-known *vestalis maxima* was Coelia Concordia, appointed in 380 CE. The Vestals were finally disbanded in 394 CE, but not before ten or so had been entombed alive, the awful penalty for a Vestal who lost her virginity (*incestum*) or was suspected of having lost it. The entombment took place in a cellar under the Campus Sceleratus, while the male partner was flogged to death in the Comitium like a slave, *sub furca*. The rationale behind entombment was that Vesta would still be able to rescue the 'Virgin' if she was innocent. Vesta never did. Plutarch wonders if entombment was decided upon because the Romans thought it somehow inappropriate that one charged with looking after the flame should be cremated, or that one so sacrosanct should be murdered.[19] He graphically describes the solemn process where the condemned Vestal is bound and gagged, then carried to her subterranean prison in a curtained litter. She is unbound and, after a prayer, the Pontifex Maximus puts her on a ladder which leads to the small chamber below. The ladder is hauled up, the entrance closed and covered with earth. The chamber has a bed, lamp, bread, water, milk and oil. To Plutarch, this is the most shocking spectacle in the world; when it occurs, it is the most horrific day Rome has ever seen.[20]

Propertius links Tarpeia's Vestal Virginity to her treason, her shocking wickedness: he asks how a single death could be enough to recompense for her betrayal of Vesta, and therefore of Rome. He has Tarpeia herself admit in her valedictory how she has shamed the symbolic hills of Rome, and Rome itself and Vesta, by her wickedness, and how great a reproach she will become to Italy's girls – a traitress chosen as servant to the virgin flame. Even Tatius, after giving the order to bury her under his soldiers' shields on his bed, places her fate in the context of her virginity when he asserts that her death was a fitting dowry for her treachery.

Paradoxically, Propertius has Vesta, happy guardian of the all-important Trojan flame, fan the flames of Tarpeia's guilt and implant more torches of passion in her bones. The flame and fire imagery represents a powerful confusion in which the elemental flames of Troy were brought by the exiles to Italy from the conflagration that was their city, only to be transplanted into Tarpeia in her bid to confound the successful founding of Rome.[21]

Poem 6, to the Temple of Palatine Apollo, is the high-point of Propertius' panegyric to Augustus. Here we find an all-conquering Augustus, descended from Alba Longa ('*Longa mundi servator ab Alba*'), greater even than his Trojan ancestors. Apollo urges him to deliver Rome from fear as its protector. Actium was duly won and Julius Caesar, his 'father', was amazed, and from the comet released by Venus proclaimed: 'I am a god: and this shows evidence of my race.' At 4.11.60, Augustus too is a god.

Chapter 11

Ovid

Publius Ovidius Naso (43 BCE–17/18 CE), or Ovid, was roughly contemporary with Virgil and Horace. He was one of Rome's consummate storytellers, and would have been caught up in the same hopeful surge of propaganda that Augustus was using to sell a new world based on peace and a return to traditional Roman values, founded on the *mos maiorum* and Roman religion, to a cautious Roman people fearing a return to the bloody civil wars of recent years. Ovid's work includes much on myth and religion, not least the epic *Metamorphoses*, while the *Fasti* gives us the origin and protocol involved in the Roman festivals of the first six months of the old Roman calendar, the legends of the gods and the origin of many Roman festivals and rituals.[1] It is with the *Metamorphoses* and the *Fasti* that Ovid introduces panegyric into his work – partly in order to be seen and heard to be celebrating Augustus and his achievements, his *res gestae*, but with more than an attempt at the same time to receive pardon for his tactless *carmen et error* and rehabilitation back into the Roman society he missed so much. Ovid's panegyric often involves reference to the divine origins of the *princeps* and his genealogical links to Aeneas, Romulus and the foundation of Rome. The *Metamorphoses* concludes with the apotheoses of Romulus and Julius Caesar and looks forward to the apotheosis of Augustus himself.

Indeed, Ovid would have us believe that, like Virgil, he was all set to write about Roman war when a well-aimed arrow from the bow of Cupid persuaded him otherwise: '*Arma gravi numero violentaque bella parabam edere, materia conveniente modis, risisse Cupido dicitur atque unum surripuisse*' – 'arms, violence, wars – I was gearing up to knock out an epic in stately measure [hexameters] when they say that Cupid chortled and pinched one of my feet [leaving him with elegiac couplets].'[2] The allusion to the *Aeneid* is unmissable, but it is to women, love and sex that Cupid steers Ovid, as evidenced by much of his output: the *Amores*, *Ars Amatoria*, *Heroides*, *Remedia Amoris* and *Medicamina Faciei* (Women's Make-up). Buried somewhere in these *carmina* is the *error* which saw man-about-town Ovid exiled to bleak Tomis on the edge of empire in 8 CE to repent at leisure. What that blunder was exactly we can only speculate, but it presumably entailed an indiscretion which did not chime with Augustus' programme of moral reform and his fight against surging levels of adultery and divorce. The emperor's exiling of wayward daughter Julia was another high-profile example he felt obliged to make in defence of his moral reformation.

Julia is alleged to have said that being pregnant allowed her to pursue her extra-maritial affairs without fear of getting pregnant: 'I never take on a passenger unless the ship is full.' Unfortunately for Julia, another less-accommodating ship was to take her into insular exile on Pandateria, modern-day Ventotene in the Tyrhennian Sea, for her adulterous behaviour.

Augustus could only take so much. He had to choose between his responsibility to Rome's moral health or to Julia. He first denounced Julia and her permissive behaviour to the Senate, and then he had her arrested for adultery and treason and annulled her marriage. Her very public fornication was the last straw and reflected very badly on him, on the state and on his ability to govern the state. To a sensationalist Velleius Paterculus, a storm erupted in Augustus' *domus*, 'disgusting to describe, repellent to remember'. Augustus had found out about his daughter's all-too-public and wilful fornication (Paterculus, 2.100):

> 'Julia … scandalously left nothing lustful or lavish undone that a woman could when prostituting herself, and quantified her good fortune by her dissolute sin, claiming she could rightfully do whatever she liked.'

According to Seneca, whose vocubulary and imagery is even more immoderate, Julia's sins were, for Augustus, 'sores', which when excised, felt as if he was cutting off his own limbs; limbs which, Tityos–like, kept growing back. Julia's nocturnal adventures had even involved prostitution and, ironically, sex on the statue of Marysas in the Forum – a symbol of liberty and freedom of speech. More galling for Augustus must have been the report that Julia regularly fornicated on the very Rostra on which he had delivered his moral legislation, which, among other things, criminalized adultery with a sentence of island exile. Thus did Julia arrive on the island of Pandateria, which Augustus made even more attractive by rendering it an alcohol-free zone! Julia may not have been totally without male company on her island, though, if Suetonius' story that she gave birth to a child there is to be believed. Augustus, exercising his rights as *paterfamilias*, had the baby exposed, left outside in the elements to die.[3]

Velleius Paterculus describes Julia as 'stained by sex or excess', adding a list of her lovers.[4] Seneca says she had 'adulterers by the herd'; Pliny the

Elder calls her 'the epitome of licentiousness' with her night-time frolics on the statue of Marsyas, which groans under the weight of her lewdness. Cassius Dio records 'night-time orgies and drinking parties in the Forum, even on the Rostra'. Seneca reminds us that the Rostra was the very place where Augustus had delivered his moral legislation, restoring family values and outlawing adultery, the Leges Juliae; Julia had chosen to prostitute herself there.[5]

Love poetry, then, was to be the order of the day for Ovid. Nevertheless, as noted, the *Metamorphoses* and the *Fasti* still provide us with a fertile source of Roman myth that is war-related.

The *Metamorphoses*

After more than thirteen books full of stories of change taken largely from Greek mythology, Ovid eventually brings us to his version of the Aeneas foundation myth, which starts with the founding and the fall of Troy and the wanderings of Aeneas, takes us through the wars in Latium, the deifications of Aeneas and Romulus, fighting the Sabines, a parade of the Alban kings and through to the deification of Julius Caesar, culminating in Ovid's *encomium* to Augustus at the end of Book 15, the climax of the 11,995-line poem. On this highly entertaining, often scurrilous and colourful journey towards the deification of Julius Caesar, Ovid takes on the not insubstantial task of chronicalling the history of the world from its prehistory and creation, governed by what has been called 'a loose mythico–historical framework'; for Ovid, the sum total of human experience is his canvas. Denis Feeney neatly described the *Metamorphoses* when he mentioned 'the kaleidoscopic variety of the poem, its baffling shifts in register and mood, its manifold layers of irony and self-consciousness'.[6] What it succeeds in doing is providing another impressive vehicle for the Aeneas foundation myth, which, as with Virgil, has as its pinnacle the inextricable link between Aeneas, Julius Caesar and Augustus.

While some consider the final books of the *Metamorphoses* an attempt by Ovid to raise the tone of his poem to a higher, more epic level, culminating in the apotheosis of Julius Caesar – for example L.P. Wilkinson, *Ovid Recalled* (Cambridge, 1955), p.221; and H. Fränkel, *A Poet Between Two Worlds* (Berkeley, 1945), pp.10506 – it should be pointed out that others – in particular G. Galinsky, 'The Cipus Episode in Ovid's Metamorphoses' (15.565–621) and B. Otis, *Ovid as an Epic Poet* – see Ovid not only as anti-Augustan (as he indeed seems to be in the love poems) but, as with Galinsky on Cipus, displaying absurd and grotesque flattery and 'the most telling indication of the lack of sincerity in Ovid's attitude to Augustan themes' (pp.181–82). Whatever the case, Ovid may well be hiding his true feelings regarding the Principate in order to offer some special pleading to placate an increasingly impatient Augustus or, in the exilic poems, secure a much longed-for return to civilization.

If there is any consistent theme it is, of course, the numerous tales of transformation, of delightful transmogrifications one after the other – many of which (not surprisingly for Ovid) feature love in all its manifestations, and rather a lot of rape.[7] Ovid makes this focus on the mutability of the world clear from the word go: '*In nova fert animus mutatas dicere formas / corpora*' ('I mean to speak of forms changed into new bodies'). But otherwise there is little cohesion, with Ovid flying off at tangents, jumping arbitrarily from one tale of change to another, giving his own take on what were to him established and traditional myths. What follows is a paraphrase of the key parts of the *Metamorphoses* which are relevant to militaristic Roman mythology.

Book 13: 399–428, The fall of Troy

Troy fell to the Greeks, and with it Priam. Hecuba, Priam's distraught wife, gave up the ghost, lost her human form and filled the air of an alien country, where the long Hellespont narrows to a strait, with strange barking.

Troy burned; Jove's altar was soaking up old Priam's thin stream of blood; and Cassandra, the head priestess of Apollo, dragged along by her hair, stretched out her arms in vain to the heavens. The Trojan women, embracing the statues of their nation's gods while they still could, and thronging the burning temples, were snatched away by the victorious Greeks as prizes well worth having. The infant Astyanax was hurled down from a tower of Troy, the very one from which he used to watch his father, Hector, whom Andromache, his mother, pointed out to him, fighting for him and protecting the ancestral kingdom. Now Boreas, the north wind, urged the triumphant Greeks on their way, and the sails flapped in a favourable breeze.

The Trojan women wailed, kissing their native earth, abandoning their burning houses: 'Farewell Troy ! We are taken against our will.' The last to embark – a pitiable sight – was Hecuba, discovered among the tombs of her sons, where she clung to their graves, trying to kiss their remains when Ulysses dragged her away. Yet she did manage to empty one tomb and carried away Hector's ashes, leaving a scanty offering to the dead: shreds of her grey hair and tears.

The wooden horse is conspicuous by its absence – Virgil's tour de force in Book 2 of the *Aeneid* was too recent and had stolen the show. Instead, Ovid leans heavily on Euripides' *Hecuba* for his version of the fall of Troy and, ultimately, the founding of Rome. Ovid's treatment is thereby more tragic, focusing on the abduction and appropriation of the Trojan women, and Hecuba in particular (429–575), as spoils of war, all too reminiscent of the 'rape' of the Sabine women. As noted, Ovid was always deeply interested in women and in female psychology, so perhaps this is a reflection of that preoccupation, imbuing the foundation myth with an ummistakably critical picture of the atrocious behaviour of the Greek victors and the utter indignity meted out to these innocent victims of war – women and children.

Ovid's readers and audiences would recognize immediately the plot of Euripides' tragedy *Hecuba* and its messages. The action of the play (first performed in 424 BCE) takes place after the fall of Troy and before the women's wretched dispersal to various parts of Greece as slaves. The chorus is made up of Trojan women already consigned to a life of endless servitude. Hecuba's double tragedy is the sacrifice of her daughter, Polyxena, on the altar of the ghost of Achilles, and the treacherous slaying of her son, Polydorus, by the Thracian king Polymestor. The chorus of women, Polyxena and Hecuba all pay the heaviest price for their gender in the aftermath of the war. They graphically describe the fate that awaits each of them, dumb with grief, husband dead and city sacked. Prayers are made to Artemis, goddess of virginity, but go unanswered. Polyxena faces her fate bravely, proudly asserting that she would rather die than live a life of servitude and rape. Shades of Lucretia will have haunted Ovid's audience and readers. Polyxena's fall from her regal status is great, as she finds herself reduced to slavery: 'it is that name of slave, so ugly, so foreign, that makes me want to die.' Her alternative is a life of abject misery and drudgery as described in lines 351–66, reminiscent of the fate Hector foresees for Andromache:

'Or should I live to be knocked down to the highest bidder, sold to a master man for cash? Sister of Hector … doing the work of a skivvy, kneading the bread and washing the floors, forced to drag out endless weary days. Me, the bride of kings compelled by some gutter slave to share his fetid bed.'

Hecuba dutifully attends to the funeral rites due to her daughter and vows revenge for the slaughter of Polydorus. She enlists the support of Agamemnon, taking full advantage of the fact that Agamemnon is obsessed with Cassandra – his concubine – and her other daughter. Hecuba lures Polymestor into a tent, where she claims her treasures are hidden: Hecuba and women from the chorus slay Polymestor's two sons and put his eyes out. Blinded and furious, he casts about for the women who have committed this 'vile act'. Justice is deemed to have been done, but Polymestor, still raging, prophesies the deaths of Hecuba by drowning and Agamemnon at the hands of his wife, Clytemnestra. The Greeks set sail with the distressed women of the Chorus to their new lives as abused slaves.

Book 13: 623–39, Aeneas sets off on his wanderings

This is where Ovid's version gathers speed, propelling us towards Sicily with its wonderful stories, the mythology of Rome itself and the death and apotheosis of Aeneas.

The fates did not allow Troy's destiny to crumble with its walls. Aeneas (*pius* as ever) took control, gathered up Troy's sacred icons and hoisted his father, Anchises, onto his shoulders. With son Ascanius and a motley band of war refugees, he set off, arriving first at the city of Apollo on Delos and then Thrace.

Book 13: 705–37, Aeneas's journey to Sicily

From Thrace they made for Crete, but plagued by Jove, they soon left, with Italy firmly in their sights. The harpy Aëllo (710) recalls *Aeneid* 3.255–57, where the Trojans cryptically learn that they will have arrived at their homeland when they eat their tables; a reference to Apollo's temple at Actium (715–16) obviously references Augustus' victory there in 31 BCE as Octavian, providing a link between Augustus and the founding of Rome and the patronage of Apollo. Next they put in at Buthrotus in Epirus – a mini-Troy, ruled by Helenus, the Trojan seer, buoyed by his prophecies for the Roman future – and then to Sicily.

Book 14: 75–100, Aeneas journeys to Cumae

After safely navigating Scylla and Charybdis, the Trojans were blown off course to the coast of Libya and, for Aeneas, into the arms of Queen Dido – the liaison ended badly with a deceived and deserted Dido stabbing herself with Aeneas's sword. Ovid gives us much more of this in *Heroides* 7.

Book 14: 101–53, Aeneas and the Sibyl of Cumae

Aeneas and his band of men finally reached Italy, landing at Cumae, where Aeneas was given permission by the 700-year-old Sibyl to descend into the underworld to locate his father's ghost in a scenario reminiscent of Aeneas' *katabasis* in *Aeneid* Book 6. A god-frenzied Sibyl cried:

'You ask great things, man of great achievements, whose hand has been tested by the sword, whose faith has been tested by the fire. But have no fear, Trojan, you will have what you desire, and, with me as your guide, you will know the halls of Elysium, and earth's strangest realm, and the likeness of your dear father. To virtue, no way is barred.'

The fabulous golden bough was duly plucked, and ancestors were reviewed, including Anchises. The trials and tribulations of yet more wars to come were revealed. A reverential Aeneas said:

'Whether you are truly a goddess, or only most beloved by the gods, you will always be like a goddess to me, and I will acknowledge myself in your debt, who have allowed me to enter the place of the dead, and having seen that place of the dead, escape it. When I reach the upper air, I will build a temple to you, for this service, and burn incense in your honour.'

Book 14: 445–82, War in Latium: Turnus asks Diomedes' help

The Trojans then sailed up the Tiber estuary, where Aeneas won the hand of King Latinus' daughter, Lavinia, and the kingdom of Latinus. But not without a battle. Turnus, who had been expecting to marry Lavinia, was naturally furious at being sidelined by the arriviste Aeneas, and war broke out between his Rutuli and the Latin-Trojan alliance, sucking in many of the local tribes on one side or another. Memories of Rome's own civil wars would have been acutely felt. The Rutilian Venulus attempted to persuade the Greek hero Diomedes to join forces, but Diomedes refused, citing the multiple metamorphoses of his men as the reason.

Book 14: 527–65, The transformation of Aeneas' ships

Turnus fired the Trojan ships, but Cybele, the sacred mother of the gods, remembering that these pines were felled on Mount Ida's summit, filled the air with the clashing throb of bronze cymbals and the shrilling of boxwood flutes. Carried through the clear air by tame lions, she cried out: 'Turnus, you hurl those firebrands, with sacrilegious hands, in vain! I will not allow the devouring fire to burn what was part of my woods and belongs to me.'

As the goddess spoke, it thundered, and after the thunder, heavy rain and leaping hail fell, and the winds, the brothers, sons of Astraeus the Titan by Aurora, troubled the air and the sea, swollen by the sudden onrush, and joined the conflict. The all-sustaining mother goddess used the force of one of them and broke the hempen cables of the Trojan ships, drove them headlong and sank them in the deep ocean.

Cybele would have had special significance, and her intervention here embellishes Ovid's foundation story in two ways: she was symbolic of the Roman victory over Carthage and she was another factor in Ovid's recurring motif of women. An early, and officially sanctioned, import from Asia Minor – or Magna Mater – she was a deity with obvious relevance to and association with women; she was a universal earth mother who looked out for all things maternal and represented rebirth and immortality through the resurrection of Attis. The couple are celebrated in Catullus 63, while Ovid describes Attis in detail in the *Fasti*.[8] Cybele was brought to Rome in 204 BCE after consultation of the *Sibylline Books* revealed that victory over the Carthaginians could be ensured by her presence – according to Livy, the *Books* decreed that any foe will be expelled if the Idaean mother was brought from Pessinus to Rome. A delegation was promptly dispatched to Phrygia to bring back a meteoric stone symbolizing the deity.[9] The stone had originally been brought from Pessinus to Pergamum by King Attalus I, and lodged in the Megalesion shrine there.[10] Publius Cornelius Scipio (the future Nasica) was the official receiver at Ostia, chosen as the noblest man (*vir optimus*) in Rome at the time. He handed the 'goddess' over to a delegation of *matronae*, who took her on to Rome. One of these was Quinta Claudia, a *matrona* whose *pudicitia* had been questioned. However, she scotched all rumours and emphatically restored her reputation that day: the boat carrying the delegation ran aground in the Tiber and soothsayers declared that it could only be refloated by a *matrona* whose reputation was above doubt. Claudia grabbed the rope and refloated the boat, and with it her reputation. The Magna Mater was duly installed in the Temple of Victory on the Palatine. She received her own temple there in 191 BCE, and games, the Ludi Megalenses, were set up in her honour.

However, once the cult was established, the Roman authorities must have wished that they had taken more care over what they had wished for. The orgiastic, frenzied rites, the eunuchs, the dancing, the self-castration and other acts of self harm by adherents – the Galli – were all quite alien and objectionable to many Romans: measures were taken to control the cult and to marginalize it as far as possible. Lucretius has a fine and vivid account of a display of Cybelean rites, where he describes the Galli as crazy eunuch priests, with their violent frenzy.[11]

Book 14: 566–80, The heron is born from Ardea's ruins

There was hope that the Rutuli, awestruck by the sight of the Trojan fleet transforming into sea-nymphs, would abandon the war. Not a bit of it – both sides now were not just seeking a kingdom as a dowry, nor a father-in-law's sceptre, nor virgin Lavinia, both sides were intent on winning and there was shame in surrender. In due course Turnus fell, and Ardea fell too, a power house while Turnus lived. Fire ravaged the city, which was reduced to ashes – all so reminiscent of Troy – but then a bird rose from the ruins, a species seen for the first time, beating at the embers with flapping wings. Its cry, its gracefulness, its pallor, everything that fitted the captured city, even its name, *ardea*, the heron, survived in the bird: and in the beating of its wings, Ardea mourns itself.

Book 14: 581–608, The deification of Aeneas

With the apotheosis of Aeneas, Ovid reinforced the divine lineage of the Trojan hero, and, in so doing, the divinity of Julius Caesar and Augustus. Venus, his mother, prevailed on Jupiter, Jupiter consented and even the implacable Juno resigned herself to the inevitable. All traces of mortality were expunged from Aeneas, leaving only the best of him. Once purified, his mother anointed his body with divine perfume, touched his lips with a mixture of sweet nectar and ambrosia, and made him a god, whom the Romans named Indiges; Aeneas the god had arrived.

Book 14: 609–22, The line of Alban kings

Ovid, in line with current thinking amongst Virgil and roughly contemporary historians such as Livy (59 BCE–17 CE) and Dionysius of Halicarnassus (*c.* 60 – after 7 BCE), saw the absolute need to fill the 400-year gulf between the accepted date of the fall of Troy and the rise of Rome. Accordingly, he gives us his version of the parade of the Alban kings.[12]

Ascanius, or Iulus, succeeded his now divine father; Silvius succeeded him (and reigned for twenty-nine years), whose son claimed the name Latinus (fifty-one years) and the sceptre. The famous Alba (thirty-nine years) followed Latinus, and then Epytus inherited. After him came Capys (twenty-eight years), and then Capetus (thirteen years). Tiberinus inherited the kingdom from them, but, after eight years, drowned in the River Albula, causing it to be called Tiber thereafter. His sons were Acrota the warrior and Remulus. Remulus was killed by a lightning bolt when trying to imitate thunder and lightning – the bolt he received was payback for his hubris. Indeed, he and his whole household were destroyed by thunder and lightning, and overwhelmed by the waters of the adjoining lake, after a reign of nineteen years. Acrota, more pious than his brother, passed the sceptre to Aventinus (reigned 854–817 BCE – thirty-seven years), who lay buried on the very hill where he reigned, and had given his name to it, the Aventine Hill. Finally, Proca ruled for twenty-three years (817–794 BCE), the father of Amulius and Numitor, great grandfather of Romulus and Remus.

Book 14: 772–804, War and reconciliation with the Sabines

Ovid next alludes to the tyrannical rule of Amulius, his coup against brother Numitor and the eventual restoration by Romulus, who went on to found Rome on the day of the feast of Pales, god of shepherds: '*festisque Palilibus urbis moenia conduntur*' (14.775). War broke out with the Sabines under Titus Tatius after the notorious and daring abduction of the womenfolk. Treacherous Tarpeia was given short shrift: '*arcisque via Tarpeia recluse dignam animam poena congestis exuit armis*' (Tarpeia who had opened a way to the citadel rightly lost her life when the shields of the enemy crushed her) – for Ovid, she only got what she deserved (14.776–77).

The Sabines attacked, aided by Juno, but were finally repulsed by an ingenious feat of engineering by the pro-Venus Ausonian Naiads, who poured yellow sulphur under their copious spring and heated the hollow channels with burning pitch to transform waters that a moment before dared to compete with Alpine coldness.

After this Romulus sallied out. The Roman soil was strewn with the Sabine dead, and with Rome's own, and the impious sword mixed the blood of son-in-law with that of father-in-law. But both sides decided enough was enough and it was agreed to call it a day, to let peace end war and allow Tatius to share the rule of Rome with Romulus.

Book 14: 805–28, The deification of Romulus

Mars caught up with Romulus, son of Ilia, as he was dispensing royal justice to his people. The king's mortal body dissolved in the atmosphere, like the lead bullet that often melted in mid-air, hurled by the broad thong of a catapult. Now he had beauty of form, and he was Quirinus, clothed in ceremonial robes, worthy of the sacred high seats of the gods.

Book 14: 829–51, The deification of his wife Hersilia

Without delay, Hersilia climbed to Romulus' hill, with Iris, the virgin daughter of Thaumas. There a star fell, gliding from sky to earth, and Hersilia, hair set alight by its fire, vanished with the star in the air. The founder of the Roman city received her in his familiar embrace – *'hanc manibus notis Romanae conditor urbis excipit'* – and altered her former body and her name, calling her Hora, a goddess like Quirinus.

Book 15: 429–52, The rise of Rome and the prophecy of Helenus recalled

Pythagoras figures large in this, the final book, as an agent of change. After a long list of examples of metamorphosis, the inexorable rise of Rome forms the culmination of a list of cities and civilizations which have prospered and then declined, from India and Troy to Thebes and Athens, via Sparta and Mycenae. Ovid exults in Rome's appearance on the world stage: *'nunc quoque Dardaniam fama est consurgere Romam, Appenninigenae quae proxima Thybridis undis mole sub ingenti rerum fundamina ponit'* – 'now word has it that Trojan Rome is rising up too, close to the waters of the Tiber whose source is in the Apennines; the foundations of a mighty city are being laid down'. Like the earlier cities, Rome is subject to change – changing as it grows: *'haec igitur formam crescendo mutat et olim inmensi caput orbis erit'* – 'Rome will soon be at the head of the world'. This is on the authority of prophets present and past, not least Helenus, who assured a tearful Aeneas among the ruins of Troy that the city would never be completely lost while Aeneas was around – *'non tota cadet te sospite Troia!'* – and working toward that foreign field with fire and steel. Helenus concluded with a vision of Rome as mistress of the world led by the soon-to-be-deified Julius Caesar, ancestor of Aeneas' son, Iulus, and grand uncle of Augustus: *'hanc alii proceres per saecula longa potentem, sed dominam rerum de sanguine natus Iuli efficiet, quo cum tellus erit usa, fruentur aetheriae sedes, caelumque erit exitus illi'* ('over time princes will give her power until one born of your Julian blood line will make her mistress of the world and when his work on earth is done the ethereal palaces and heaven will be his end').

Book 15: 564–621, The pietas of Cipus

Cipus, like Aeneas, is the embodiment of *pietas* – in this case exhibiting a complete absence of self-interest in favour of the state.[13] Returning to Rome one day, the praetor happened to glance into a stream and noticed from the reflection that he had grown horns on his head, an omen if ever there was one. With commendable presence of mind, he decided that if the omen was good it should benefit Rome, but if it was ill it should be his problem and his alone. Cipus then built altars and sacrifices to the gods. A seer who examined the entrails spilled during the sacrifice prophesied that Cipus would enter Rome and be chosen its king.

Cipus decided that living in exile is preferable to being made king (no one in Republican Rome remembered the monarchy with any affection), and devised a plan. He concealed his horns with a garland of laurel and convened a meeting of the citizens and the Roman Senate. Here, he warned that it had been prophesied that someone with horns on his head would enter Rome, be made its king and impose on the citizens Draconian laws as if they were slaves. Cipus did not reveal that he was the prophesied king, but, instead, told the people that he had delayed this pretender to the Roman throne.

His speech over, Cipus removed the garland of laurel and revealed his horns. The people were stunned by this revelation, but soon placed a festive headdress on Cipus since they could not allow him to remain in Rome without due honour. The Senate then granted Cipus lands equal to the amount that oxen could encircle in one day, and he left the city in exile. The image of Cipus' horns was carved on the gates of the city gate and his name was remembered for time immemorial.

Book 15: 745–842, The deification of Julius Caesar

Caesar in urbe sua deus est – Caesar is a god in his own city. Outstanding in war or peace, it was not so much his wars that ended in great victories, or his actions at home, or his swiftly won fame, that set him among the stars, a fiery comet; not so much any of those things as Augustus, his descendant. There was no greater achievement among Caesar's actions than that he stood father to the emperor. Is it a greater thing to have conquered the sea-going Britons; to have lead his victorious ships up the seven-mouthed flood of the papyrus-bearing Nile; to have brought the rebellious Numidians, under Juba of Cinyps, and Pontus, swollen with the name of Mithridates, under the people of Quirinus; to have earned many triumphs and celebrated few – than to have sponsored such a man, with whom, as ruler of all, the gods had richly favoured the human race? Therefore, in order for the emperor not to have been born of mortal seed, Caesar needed to be made a god.

So Ovid introduces his episode describing the deification of Julius Caesar, mingling praise for him with a dose of reflected glory on Augustus; high praise indeed for both Caesars. Venus, mother of Aeneas, was horrified at and tormented by the terrified fate she saw waiting for Caesar. But, as Jupiter told her, what the Fates decree would happen and her only consolation is that

'she, and Augustus, his "son", will ensure that he ascends to heaven as a god, and is worshipped in the temples. Augustus, as heir to his name, will carry the burden placed upon him alone, and will have us with him, in battle, as the most courageous avenger of his father's murder. Under his command, the conquered walls of besieged Mutina will sue for peace; Pharsalia will know him; Macedonian Philippi twice flow with blood; and the one who holds [Sextus] Pompey's great name, will be defeated in Sicilian waters; and a Roman general's Egyptian consort [Antony and Cleopatra], trusting, to her cost, in their marriage, will fall, her threat that our Capitol would bow to her city of Canopus, proved vain.'

Ovid then, still through Jupiter, gives us an outline of Augustus' programme of reform:

'Why list foreign countries, for you, or the nations living on either ocean shore? Wherever earth contains habitable land, it will be his: and even the sea will serve him! When the world is at peace, he will turn his mind to the civil code, and, as the most just of legislators, make law. He will direct morality by his own example, and, looking to the future ages and coming generations, he will order a son, Tiberius, born of his virtuous wife [Livia], to take his name, and his responsibilities. He will not attain his heavenly home, and the stars, his kindred, until he is old, and his years equal his merits. Meanwhile, take up Caesar's spirit from his murdered corpse, and change it into a star, so that the deified Julius may always look down from his high temple on our Capitol and forum.'

Book 15: 843–70, Ovid's celebration of Augustus

'He had hardly finished, when gentle Venus stood in the midst of the Senate, seen by no one, and took up the newly freed spirit of her Caesar from his body, and preventing it from vanishing into the air, carried it towards the glorious stars. As she carried it, she felt it glow and take fire, and loosed it from her breast: it climbed higher than the moon, and drawing behind it a fiery tail, shone as a star.

Seeing his son's good works, Julius Caesar acknowledged they were greater than his own, and delighted in being bettered by him. Though the son forbids his own actions being honoured above his father's, nevertheless fame, free and obedient to no one's orders, exalted him, despite himself, and denied him in this one thing. So great Atreus ceded the title to Agamemnon: so Theseus outdid Aegeus, and Achilles his father Peleus: and lastly, to quote an example worthy of these two, so Saturn was less than Jove'.

The climax of this *encomium* references all the Trojan-Roman agencies, mortal and immortal, which have worked together to achieve the foundation of Rome and its hegemony over the civilized world: Jupiter commands the heavenly citadels, and the kingdoms of the threefold universe; however, '*terra sub Augusto est; pater est et rector uterque*' – 'Earth is ruled by Augustus. Each is a father and a master. You gods, the friends of Aeneas, to whom fire and sword gave way; you deities of Italy; and Romulus, founder of our city; and Mars, father of Romulus; Vesta, Diana, sacred among Caesar's ancestral gods, and you, Phoebus, sharing the temple with Caesar's Vesta; you, Jupiter who hold the high Tarpeian citadel; and all you other gods, whom it is fitting and holy for a poet to invoke, I beg that the day be slow to arrive, and beyond our own lifetime, when Augustus shall rise to heaven, leaving the world he rules, and there, far off, shall listen, with favour, to our prayers!'

The *Fasti*

Nothing illustrates better the Roman predilection for order and organization, their almost obsessive need to keep records, than the *fasti*. The *fasti* also underline just how important religion was in Roman society, with *fasti* impinging on and percolating through all apects of Roman life, official and private. The *fasti* were calendarized lists: records of official and religiously sanctioned events and dates.

There are more than forty extant *fasti*. All are fragmentary, with numerous different findspots, although most come from the vicinity of Rome.

Nevertheless, we can piece together a plethora of political, social and religious information from them – a veritable goldmine of Roman records. The most important are the *Fasti Praenestini*, probably compiled by Verrius Flaccus from 6–9 CE, displayed in the forum of Praeneste, and the *Fasti Antiates Maiores*, painted on plaster between 84 and 55 BCE. Both will have been major sources for Ovid. Who would have thought that such detailed record-keeping could have provided the seedcorn for a poem, and a successful one at that? Callimachus' *Aetia*, with its explanations of the origins of customs and festivals, and perhaps even the fourth Book of Propertius – who claimed to be the Roman Callimachus – since it also deals with aetiologies of Roman customs and myths, were other important sources.

Ovid had plenty of time to work on his particular *Fasti*. It was his last work, supposedly unfinished upon his death and largely composed in the miserable exile he endured from 9 CE in faraway Tomis, a Black Sea backwater on the edge of empire that is now Constanza in Romania. The *Fasti* is an aetiological poem surviving in six books, covering January to June. Its theme is the Roman calendar, animating dry-as-dust religious records by interweaving the facts with mythic fiction and established history, adumbrating Rome's religious and political foundations and, in so doing, providing us with an indispensable record of early imperial Roman religious practice, its origins and causes, of cult and ritual and its calendarization.

Ovid's *Fasti* exemplifies the meticulous focus the Romans applied to the proper observance of festivals throughout the year. For example, Robigus was the spirit of mildew or grain rust, and it was imperative to keep him on side if you wanted a decent harvest. The festival took place on 25 April, and included games (*ludi*) and a sacrifice of the blood and entrails of an unweaned puppy (*catulus*). For our purposes, though, they provide yet more versions of various war-related Roman myths, as well as cementing Augustus' connection to the Trojan exiles. Ovid will leave it to others to celebrate *Caesaris arma*, Caesar's arms; he will focus on *Caesaris aras*, Caesar's altars, and the days he has added to the sacred festival calendar.[14] In fact, it only takes Ovid nine lines to connect Augustus and his kin to many a Roman festival: Germanicus, to whom the poem is dedicated, will find 'festivals pertaining to your house; often the names of your father and grandfather will meet you on the page' (*Fasti* 1.9–10).[15]

Germanicus Julius Caesar (15 BCE–19 CE) may well have been Ovid's second choice as dedicatee. This proem was written after the death of Augustus, who was probably the first choice (*Tristia* 2.551–52), and while Tiberius was emperor. Unalloyed praise for Augustus would not have been entirely wasted on Germanicus – he was Augustus'great nephew, after all. Ovid is more explicit in his pleas for help in his *Epistulae ex Ponto* (4.8.31ff), written in 16 CE. However, it all proved to be in vain in the end, as Ovid died in exile two years later.

Unpromising as the subject matter may have seemed, the *Fasti* provide Ovid with a platform from which to endorse and support Augustus' programme of religious reform and, who knows, maybe win for himself a reprieve and a return to Rome.

Book 1 (January)

There are numerous sections of Book 1 which particularly interest us.

The reference to Quirinus at 1.37 is a nod, of course, to Romulus, who, as we have seen in the *Metamorphoses*, assumed this name upon his apotheosis.[16] Ovid, through Janus, decribes the attack on and siege of Rome by Titus Tatius, and Tarpeia's betrayal of Rome for gold (260ff); she is referred to as '*levis custos*' – 'lightweight guardian'. Janus then describes his clever thwarting of Tatius' advance. Later, we hear of the prophecy of Carmenta, the mother of Evander, who, as we know, along with other Trojan exiles, founded the town of Pallantium, one of the early contenders for the site of Rome. Carmenta repeats and reinforces what Ovid had said in Book 15 of the *Metamorphoses* regarding the destiny of Rome (*Fasti* 1.505–42, 587–616):

'Am I deceived? or shall yon hills by stately walls be hid, and from this spot of earth, shall all the earth take law? The promise runs that the whole world shall one day belong to yonder mountains … here, too, a woman [Lavinia] shall be the source of a new war … conquered Troy, thou shalt yet conquer and from thy fall shalt rise again … In the line of Augustus the guardianship of the fatherland shall abide: it is decreed that his house shall hold the reins of empire … Augustus alone bears a name that ranks with Jove supreme. Holy things are by the fathers called august: the epithet august is applied to temples that have been duly dedicated by priestly hands: from the same root come augury and all such augmentation as Jupiter grants by his power. May he augment our prince's empire and augment his years, and may an oaken crown protect your doors. Under the auspices of the gods may the same omens, which attended the sire, wait upon the heir of so great a surname, when he takes upon himself the burden of the world.'

Augustus is *ipso deo*, on a par with Jupiter. His very name makes him synonymous with all things august, with august temples and with augury. Just as Jupiter augments his power, may he augment Augustus' *imperium* and his years.

Book 1 reinforces Ovid's insistence that Augustus has a backstory which links him unequivocally with Aeneas and the battles Aeneas fought to win the foundation of Rome. Indeed, Ovid's gushing praise here surpasses anything in the *Metamorphoses*; while it supports his take on the Aeneas foundation myth, his own protracted exile was clearly forcing the poet into increasingly desperate efforts to win a reprieve. The book ends with Ovid expatiating on the *Ara Pacis* – one of the most visible and eloquent symbols of Augustus' brave new world and the *Pax Romana* he was determined to usher in.

Book 2 (February)

Ovid opens Book 2 with a proem dedicated to Augustus, celebrating again his military prowess and seeking his forgiveness for not writing warlike poetry – *militia* and *arma*. Ovid reiterates Augustus' achievement in restoring religious architecture (59–66), and at 133 launches into his synkrisis in which Ovid tells of the emperor's assumption of the title *pater patriae*. Oddly, Augustus is praised fulsomely at the expense of Romulus. Augustus is '*sancte pater patriae*', holy father of the fatherland; '*iam pridem tu pater orbis eras*' – 'you were long since father of the world; you [Augustus] are father of men, Jupiter of gods'. Romulus, on the other hand, is diminished and demonized in every way: Romulus is ordered to concede to Augustus, and while Augustus now reinforces the walls of Romulus, Remus could leap over the walls with ease when they were first built by Romulus. Subduing Titus Tatius is minimized by describing his city, Cures, as insignificant, while, on the other hand, Augustus has extended and delivered 'Romanitas' as far as the sun. Romulus' territory is tiny, but Augustus rules everything beneath the sun. Ovid accuses Romulus of wholesale rape, with reference to the abduction of the Sabine's women – the juxtaposition of the charged words '*castas*' and '*maritas*' would suggest that a critical (and hypocritical) Ovid, of all people, was intending his readers to read '*tu rapis* as *rapis cum vi*' – rape with sexual violence, as opposed to abduction. Augustus, on the other hand, is apparently busy restoring chastity to the institution of marriage and the family. Romulus harbours that which is wrong, while Augustus repels it. Violence pleases Romulus, but the rule of law flourishes under Augustus … and so on. Here, Ovid's Romulus is defined by paucity, diminishment, violence and barbarism, while his descendant is all power, growth, lawfulness and magnitude.

How would Augustus have received this? Flattered he may have been initially, even if he was oblivious to any irony which Ovid intended. But for Augustus, Ovid, in destroying Romulus, had come close to destroying the powerful brand that was Augustus. The myth of Romulus and the link the *princeps* enjoyed with his ancestor were seriously compromised by this piece. Romulus was central to Augustan politics and propaganda – desecrating him like this was tantamount to desecrating Augustus himself. Whether architecturally – statues of Romulus and Aeneas in the Forum Augustum; domestically – Augustus lived on the Palatine in a house within the original walls of Romulus' city; in literature – Virgil's *Aeneid*, Horace and Ovid himself all lionized Augustus and his lineage; or morally – Dionysius attributed Augustus' four prime virtues to Romulus (2.18), in every way Romulus was Augustus and Augustus was Romulus. If this was not *the* cardinal *error* which booked Ovid's passage to Tomis, then it surely came close. Augustus and his image people must have been horrified.

The problem would have been exacerbated by two further seemingly wilful Ovidian swerves from the traditional and canonic. First, Romulus is absolved of any charge of fratricide by the intercession of the spade-wielding Celer, the works foreman overseeing the erection of the walls. In rejecting the accepted account (as endorsed by Ennius, *Annales* 95, Skutch) and implicating Celer, Ovid robs Romulus of his kudos for building a strong and mighty Rome with whom no foe, kin included, should ever mess. Second, Aeneas – another ancestor of Augustus' – is relegated by the promotion of Evander as the major player in the foundation of Rome. In six episodes, Evander becomes the proto-Roman and quasi founder at the expense of Aeneas. Ovid's Evander exhibits *pietas*, he is pacifying and civilizing – everything a benign founder should be. Nevertheless, Romans could not have failed to notice that the one vital thing that Evander lacks, and that Aeneas had in spades, is that all-important genealogical link with their *princeps*.

Ovid mentions in passing the troubled circumstances surrounding the births and infancy of Romulus and Remus and their roles in the foundation myth of Rome (383–84; 411–22). The transformation of Romulus into Quirinus and his apotheosis are covered in detail (475–532). The section featuring Proculus Julius (499–510) is important because it provides an overt link between Romulus and the Julio-Claudians, with the inclusion of the myth of Romulus' miraculous appearance to Proculus Julius.

The Quirites are urged to gird themselves for new wars under the new Quirinus, namely Augustus, who will lead them in the ways of war: *patrias artes militiamque*.

The final section describing the Regifugium gives Ovid's versions of the legends relating to the fall of the Tarquins, Lucretia's rape and suicide, and Brutus' revenge (685–855). The Regifugium ('Flight of the King') or Fugalia ('Festival of the Flight') was an annual religious festival that took place on 24 February; Varro and Ovid traced the observance to the flight of the last king of Rome, Tarquinius Superbus, in 510 BCE. Ovid gives the oldest surviving account (685–88):

> 'Now I must tell of the flight of the King, six days from the end of the month. The last of the Tarquins possessed the Roman nation, an unjust man, but nevertheless strong in war.'

The sight of a snake prompts a consultation of the oracle of Apollo, which declares that he who kisses his mother will be *princeps*: '*matri qui dederit princeps oscula, victor erit.*' Brutus, pretending to be a dullard (that's what his name means), falls to the ground and kisses Mother Earth – the rest of the delegation, taking the oracle too literally, rush to kiss their mothers. As it happens, Brutus goes on to play a leading role in the avenging of Lucretia and ridding Rome of the monarchy. As we know from Livy, the siege of Ardea reached a tedious stalemate and the Roman commanders, fuelled by drink, ride back to Rome to discover which of their wives are the most faithful and matronly. The royal wives are enjoying a late-night party, while Lucretia is up working the wool by lamplight with her maids – a paragon of feminine virtue. It was no contest as to who was the most virtuous, and good news for Lucretia and her husband, Lucius Tarquinius Collatinus – but it was not to last. Sextus Tarquinius is on fire with love for her, smouldering with desire over everything he has seen in this virtuous woman: rape is the only answer. Rape is consummated, and Lucretia is left violated, shamed and distraught with all the guilt and the tragic consequences we heard of from Livy's version (1.53–60). Brutus shrugs off his pretence at idiocy: it was he who pulled the dagger from Lucretia's breast and sets in train the vengeance owed to the *matrona* of male valour – *animi matrona virilis* and the beginning of the end of the Roman monarchy: *dies regnis illa suprema fuit* – the last days of the kings.

Book 3 (March)

In Book 3, dedicated by Ovid to war god (*bellice*) Mars, there is more rape
– this time the violation of Rhea Silvia by Mars, the birth and discovery of
their twins, Romulus and Remus, and the story of the 'rape' of the Sabine
women.

As we know, Amulius and Numitor were the sons of Procas – king of Alba
Longa. Amulius deposed his brother and assumed the kingship, throwing
Rhea Silva into prison and forcing her into Vestal virginity to prevent her
producing sons who might pose a threat to him in the future. But when
Mars came, saw and conquered, Amulius' plan was derailed by the birth of
Romulus and Remus, whom he immediately threw into the Tiber to die; but
they survived, of course.

Mars then explains the circumstances surrounding the rape of the Sabine
women, how Rome at the time was mainly comprised of men of dubious
reputation, how they were needy and made unsuitable matches for the girls
of surrounding tribes, and how the abduction of Sabine women was the *casus
belli* of Rome's first war. No one wanted to wed a Roman – *at quae Romano
vellet nubere, nulla fuit*. There would be no more prayers; war was the answer
(195–98). Eventually, the Sabine women – now wives and mothers – have
had enough and famously throw themselves into the battle lines with their
children to stop the war. Thereafter, Tatius rules with Romulus.

In the context of Rome's most precious and vital accoutrements (422ff) –
the Vestal flame, the Palladium and the Penates which Aeneas salvaged from
flaming Troy – Augustus, as Pontifex Maximus, is referred to as a priest born
of Aeneas.

Book 4 (April)

At line 19, Ovid reminds us of Augustus' Trojan lineage through Aeneas to
Venus, and gives us here the genealogy of the Roman kings. We also learn
more about the festival of the Magna Mater (189ff), the Ludi Megalenses,
the goddess' transfer to Rome and the story of Claudia Quinta (179–375). At
835ff, Ovid tells us the story of the falling out between Romulus and Remus,
resulting in the murder of Remus by Celer, who was in charge of the city
walls. Remus' ridiculing of the defences prompts Celer to fell him fatally
with a spade; Romulus is bereft and buries his brother. The final sections tell
the story of Mezentius in relation to the Vinalia (863–900).

Book 5 (May)

Book 5 includes the funeral of Remus. The ghost of Remus appears at 451ff and gives a partial retelling of the myth of Romulus and Remus, including the assertion by Remus that Romulus was innocent of any blame and Celer is the villain and murderer (472): 'my brother did not want this, his piety is equal to mine' – '*noluit hoc frater, pietas aequatis in illo est*'. The origin of the Temple of Mars Ultor is described (545–98), and a description of the death of Castor and Pollux (693–720).

The temple was dedicated in 2 BCE, some years after Augustus (at that time Octavian) vowed he would do so if he was victorious at Philippi, fought in a bid to avenge the murder of Julius Caesar, his adopted uncle. In Octavian's words here, 'Mars, come here and soak this sword with guilty blood' ('*Mars, ades et satia scelerato sanguine ferrum*') Ovid echoes the words of Virgil when he says that Aeneas, as he slays Turnus in revenge for the death of Pallas, 'exacts payment with guilty blood'.[17]

Book 6 (June)

Ovid refers to Tullia (at 587–96), the pushy daughter of Servius Tullius and married to the equally ambitious Tarquinius Superbus, who was son of the first Tarquin king, Tarquinius Priscus (Servius' predecessor).

Tullia, the last queen of monarchical Rome (r. *c.* 535–509 BCE), set an extreme precedent for ambitious women who would do anything to achieve their objectives. Livy tells us how Tullia and her elder sister (also Tullia) were married off by their father, Servius Tullius, to the two sons of his predecessor, Lucius Tarquinius Priscus.[18] The sons were Lucius and Arruns. Unfortunately, the marriages were both terrible mismatches; Tullia the Younger had the more fiery temperament, but she was married to Arruns, the calmer of the two sons. Fierce (*ferox*) Tullia resented her new husband's timidity, and inevitably the younger Tullia and Lucius, the other brother, were attracted to each other – 'evil fits best with evil' ('*malum malo aptissimum*').[19]

The infatuated Tullia repeatedly slurred her younger sister and Arruns, conspiring with her brother-in-law to murder their siblings and marry. She then relentlessly urged Lucius to prove his worth and overthrow Servius – which he set about doing, drumming up support in the Senate. Tullia was desperate to be seen as a kingmaker. Lucius was inspired by her womanly frenzy (*his muliebribus instinctus furiis*) and eventually took his seat on the throne of Tullia's father, King Servius Tullius. Servius naturally protested, but Lucius flung him into the street for his troubles, where he was murdered by Lucius' thugs – they were goaded by Tullia, the enormity of her crime consistent with her evil character. After hailing her husband as king in the Senate, she returned home in her carriage; on the way she came across her father's corpse lying in the road, and she callously drove over it. Livy called it a crime of ineffable inhumanity (*'foedum inhumanumque scelus'*).[20] Tullia was possessed and driven to frenzy by the avenging ghosts of her murdered sister and husband, returning home spattered by the blood of her mutilated father. The street where this shocking event took place was forever called 'Evil Street' ('Vicus Sceleratus').

When the revolution led by Lucius Junius Brutus ended the Roman monarchy after the rape of Lucretia, and King Tarquinius and his family were exiled from Rome, Tullia in particular was cursed by the Roman people as she fled – due to her role in the murder of her own father.[21]

The passage serves to remind Ovid's audience of the ending of monarchism in Rome that was given impetus by the violation of Lucretia; the abuse of marriage and of spouses, and of unbridled ambition, also provided a stark comparison with the programme of moral and marital reform Augustus was attempting to impose on Rome and the Romans.

Chapter 12

The Theban Legion Massacre 286 CE:
Myth or History?

In 286 CE, a legion of soldiers, made up of 6,666 men, was massacred in its entirety. Two significant factors set this legion apart from other Roman legions of the time: the high number of legionaires and the special number of soldiers, and the fact that it was made up exclusively of Christians.[1] It was called the Theban Legion (*Alkateeba al Teebia*) because the men were Egyptian Christian Copts recruited from and stationed in Thebes in Upper Egypt. They stayed there until the emperor Maximian posted them to Gaul to fight against a rebellious Gallic tribe, the Bagaude, around modern Burgundy. This was in line with standard Roman policy of not having Roman armies fight in their own recruiting grounds for fear of uprisings aimed at liberating their homelands. The Theban Legion served at a time when Christianity was very popular amongst Copts, and just as unpopular amongst the Roman authorities; so much so that there were a number of persecutory measures to suppress Christianity. The edict of 202 CE decreed that an end should be put to all conversions; the edict of 250 CE decreed that all citizens were required, by means of an official certificate, to show evidence that he or she had offered sacrifice to the pagan gods.

Thebaei is the name of the Legio I *Maximiana*, or the *Maximiana Thebaeorum*, as recorded in the *Notitia Dignitatum*. There were two legions with the name 'Theban', both formed by Diocletian and stationed at Alexandria.[2]

Dissenters, regardless of age or sex, were cruelly tortured: some were decapitated, others were thrown to the lions or burnt alive. The Catechetical School of Alexandria was shut down, though this led to clandestine meetings elsewhere, and the number of bishops was restricted to three. The persecutions reached their high point during the reign of Diocletian (284–305 CE). Such was the ferocity of the programme of mass executions and torture that the Copts took the day of Diocletian's election as emperor to mark the beginning of the era of the Coptic martyrs. This became the start of the Coptic Calendar known as *Anno Martyrum* (AM), the year of the martyrs. Eusebius describes some of the torture in a campaign of breathtaking atrocity which, it is estimated, claimed 20,000 lives:

'They were torn to bits from head to foot with broken pottery like claws till death released them. Women were tied by one foot and hoisted in the air, head downwards, their bodies completely nude ... the most shameful, brutal and inhuman of all spectacles to anyone watching. Others again were tied to trees and stumps and died horribly; for with the aid of machines they drew together the very stoutest of boughs, fastened one of the martyr's legs to each and let the boughs fly back to their normal position ... in this they continued not for a few days or weeks but year after year.'[3]

Thebes was a hotbed of Christianity. Some of the first Chrisitian 'monks', the Desert Fathers, were largely made up of Thebans. Historically, Theban Christians honoured a number of martyrs who defied the authorities during the persecutions. The purge of Christians from the military between 284 and 299 CE under Diocletian suggests that noncompliance with emperor worship was a common way of revealing Christian soldiers and effecting their eventual execution.

The Theban Legion reached Maximian in Gaul by way of the St Bernard's Pass in the Alps, led by Mauritius (St Maurice or St Moritz), Candidus and Exupernis (Exuperantius), and the revolt was quashed. The legion camped at Agaunum (what is now St Maurice), where Maximian organized a universal sacrifice in which the whole army was required to participate and swear an oath of allegiance, as well as promise to help in the extermination of Christianity from Gaul. This of course presented insoluble problems for the Christians of the Theban Legion. They all refused point-blank to sacrifice or take the oaths, incensing Maximian, who immediately ordered the decimation of the legion. But it was not to be an ordinary decimation. When every tenth man had been butchered, the survivors enthusiastically reasserted their Christian faith, further enraging Maximian; 666 more soldiers then met their deaths, their blood turning the River Rhone crimson. Mauritius fired the survivors' enthusiasm for martyrdom, urging them to join their newly murdered comrades in death and reminding them of their their baptismal vow: to renounce satan and to worship only God. The Christians compromised when they agreed to swear loyalty to Maximian, but he remained implacable and slew them all. The Maximian atrocity is what is known as the Sixth Primitive Persecution in *Fox's Book of Martyrs*. Thousands of Christians were slaughtered without trial and buried unceremoniously in unmarked mass graves:

'The principal persons who perished under this reign were Pontianus, bishop of Rome; Anteros, a Grecian, his successor, who gave offence to the government by collecting the acts of the martyrs, Pammachius and Quiritus, Roman senators, with all their families, and many other Christians; Simplicius, senator; Calepodius, a Christian minister, thrown into the Tyber; Martina, a noble and beautiful virgin; and Hippolitus, a Christian prelate, tied to a wild horse, and dragged until he expired. During this persecution, raised by Maximinus, numberless Christians were slain without trial, and buried indiscriminately in heaps, sometimes fifty or sixty being cast into a pit together, without the least decency.'

Eucherius of Lyon (d. 494 CE)[4] records that during the massacre and martyrdom, there were a series of miracles. In Zurich, the three decapitated saints Felix, Regula and Exuperantius rose from the dead and carried their heads to the top of a hill, where they knelt, prayed and lay down. A cathedral was later built here. The three saints, their heads in their hands, feature on the modern coat of arms and seal of Zurich. When saints Victor, Orsus and their comrades were tortured by Hirtacus, the Roman governor of Solothurn, their shackles snapped and the fire was extinguished. The bodies of the saints which were thrown in the River Aar stepped out of the waters, and knelt and prayed at the spot where the Basilica of St Peter was later built. The bodies of the martyrs of Aguanum were discovered and identified by Saint Theodore, the Bishop of Octudurm, around 350 CE.

There is much controversy surrounding the historicity of the the Theban Legion. Some scholars believe it to be a myth, as seems likely, born out of Christian hagiography; others argue that it was an actual event[5]. Either way, it was a catastrophe of the first order for the legion, although it seems that many would not have seen it that way, delighting as they did in their martyrdom.

Chapter 13

The View from the Bridge:
The Vision of Constantine

Constantine the Great, also known as Constantine I, ruled between 306 and 337 CE. His reign and conversion to Christianity is, of course, well attested in the literature, but there are elements of his epiphany that are to some extent contrived and border on the mythological at the expense of historicity to suit historians of Christianity. In 305, the two reigning emperors, Diocletian and Maximian, abdicated, to be succeeded by their respective deputy emperors, Galerius and Constantius. These in turn were replaced by Galerius Valerius Maximinus in the Eastern empire and Flavius Valerius Severus in the West; Constantine, son of Constantius, had been passed over. Constantine made his way through the territories of the hostile Severus to join his father at Gesoriacum (modern Boulogne). They crossed together over to Britain and fought a campaign in the north before Constantius's death at Eboracum (modern York) in 306. Constantine was then proclaimed emperor by the army, leading to a series of civil wars with Maxentius, the son of Maximian. With his father's help, Maxentius defeated Severus, who had been proclaimed Western emperor by Galerius and who was then replaced by Licinius. When Maximian was rejected by his son, he allied with Constantine in Gaul; when he subsequently betrayed Constantine, he was either murdered or forced to commit suicide in 310. Constantine, who in 307 had married Maximian's daughter, Fausta, as his second wife, invaded Italy in 312, and after a lightning campaign defeated his brother-in-law, Maxentius, at the Milvian Bridge near Rome. He then confirmed an alliance that he had already entered into with Licinius (Galerius having died in 311): Constantine became Western emperor and Licinius shared the East with his rival Maximinus. Licinius defeated Maximinus and became the sole Eastern emperor, but lost territory in the Balkans to Constantine in 316. After a further period of tension, Constantine attacked Licinius in 324, routing him at Adrianople and Chrysopolis (modern Edirne and Üsküdar in Turkey) and becoming sole emperor of East and West.

The decisive Battle of the Milvian Bridge took place between Constantine I and Maxentius on 28 October 312 CE. It takes its name from an important strategic crossing over the Tiber north of Rome. Constantine's victory enabled him to end the Tetrarchy and become the sole ruler of the Roman Empire. Maxentius drowned in the Tiber during the battle; his body was later fished from it and decapitated, and his head was paraded through the streets of Rome the day after the battle.

Maxentius' forces were twice the size of those of Constantine, and he positioned them facing the plain with their backs to the river. Constantine's army is recorded to have come to the battle with strange symbols on their standards and their shields. Lactantius states that, on the eve of the battle, Constantine was told in a dream to 'depict the heavenly sign on the shields of his soldiers ... he marked on their shields the letter X, with a perpendicular line drawn through it and turned round thus at the top, being the cipher of Christ'. This was known as the 'heavenly divine symbol' (*coeleste signum dei*).

Eusebius of Caesarea (d. 339) gives two different accounts of events. In his *Ecclesiatical History*, written shortly after the battle, he does not mention any dream or vision, but leaves no doubt that God helped Constantine achieve victory. In his later *Life of Constantine* (*c*. 337–339), Eusebius provides a detailed account of a vision and stresses that he had heard the story from the emperor himself. According to this version, Constantine was marching somewhere (Eusebius does not specify the actual location, but it clearly is not in the camp at Rome) when he looked up to the sun and saw a cross of light above it, and with it the Greek words Ἐν Τούτῳ Νίκα. The traditional Latin translation of the Greek is '*in hoc signo vinces*' – literally 'In this sign, you will conquer' or 'By this, conquer!' (1.28–32).

At first Constantine was baffled, unsure of the meaning of the apparition, but the following night he had a dream in which Christ explained to him that he should use the sign against his enemies. Eusebius then describes the *labarum*, the military standard used by Constantine in his later wars against Licinius, showing the 'Chi-Rho' sign. The *labarum* (λάβαρον) was a *vexillum* or military standard that displayed the 'Chi-Rho' symbol ☧, a christogram formed from the first two Greek letters of the word 'Christ' (ΧΡΙΣΤΟΣ, or Χριστός) – Chi (χ) and Rho (ρ). Since the *vexillum* consisted of a flag suspended from the crossbar of a cross, it was ideally suited to symbolize the crucifixion of Christ.[1]

The two accounts have been conflated into Constantine seeing the Chi-Rho sign on the evening before the battle. Both Eusebius and Lactantius concur that the sign was not immediately understandable as denoting Christ, which corresponds with the fact that there is no certain evidence of the use of the letters 'Chi' and 'Rho' as a Christian sign before Constantine.

Its first appearance is on coins issued at Siscia in 317/318 CE, proving that Constantine did use the sign at that time. A medallion was minted at Ticinum in 315 showing Constantine wearing a helmet emblazoned with the Chi Rho. Otherwise, the *labarum* was rare, and is uncommon in imperial iconography before the 320s. Constantine made extensive use of the 'Chi-Rho' and the *labarum* in the later conflict with Licinius.

In Eusebius' *Life of Constantine*, Constantine is said to have witnessed a miraculous appearance in Gaul long before the Battle of the Milvian Bridge. In this later version, the Roman emperor had been contemplating the misfortunes that befell commanders who invoked the help of various different gods, and decided to seek divine aid in a forthcoming battle from the 'One God'. At noon, Constantine saw a cross of light imposed over the sun. Attached to it, in Greek characters, was the saying 'Τούτῳ Νίκα!' ('In this sign you will conquer!'). Constantine was not the only one to see the miracle; the whole army did too. That night, Christ appeared to the Roman emperor in a dream and told him to make a replica of the sign he had seen in the sky, which would be a talisman in battle. In another version, Eusebius describes a vision that Constantine had while marching at midday, in which 'he saw with his own eyes in the heavens and a trophy of the cross arising from the light of the sun, carrying the message, *In Hoc Signo Vinces* ['with this sign, you will conquer']'. In Eusebius' account, on the next night, Constantine had a dream in which Christ appeared with the same heavenly sign and told him to make an army standard in the form of the *labarum*.

Constantine dealt with Maxentius in a brief battle: he ordered his cavalry to charge, and they easily broke Maxentius' cavalry. He then deployed his infantry against Maxentius' foot soldiers, forcing many into the Tiber, where they were slaughtered or drowned. Maxentius attempted to cross the bridge of boats, but he was pushed into the Tiber and drowned in the turbulence caused by his fleeing soldiers.

Constantine triumphantly entered Rome on 29 October 312 CE in a grand *adventus* ('arrival'), met with jubilation by the Roman citizens. As noted, Maxentius' body was retrieved from the Tiber; his head was cut off and paraded through the streets. After the ceremonies, the disembodied head was sent to Carthage as proof of his downfall, with the result that Carthage offered no further resistance. Significantly, unlike his predecessors, Constantine did not make the trip to the Capitoline Hill and perform customary sacrifices at the Temple of Jupiter.

Throughout his later life, Constantine ascribed his success to his new religious allegiance, his conversion to Christianity and the support of the Christian God. The famous triumphal arch erected in his honour at Rome after the defeat of Maxentius ascribed the victory to the 'inspiration of the Divinity', as well as to Constantine's own genius (although it does not feature the powerful 'chi rho' symbol). A contemporary statue showed Constantine himself holding aloft a cross and the legend 'By this saving sign I have delivered your city from the tyrant and restored liberty to the Senate and people of Rome'. After his victory over Licinius in 324 CE, Constantine wrote that he had come from the farthest shores of Britannia as God's chosen instrument for the suppression of impiety, and in a letter to the Persian king Shāpūr II he proclaimed that, aided by the divine power of God, he had come to bring peace and prosperity to all lands.

Constantine's victory gave him total control of the Western Roman Empire, paving the way for Christianity to become the dominant religion for the Roman Empire and ultimately for Europe. The following year, 313 CE, Constantine and Licinius issued the Edict of Milan, which made Christianity an officially recognized and tolerated religion in the Roman Empire.

At the time, only around 10 per cent of the Roman Empire's population was Christian. The majority of the ruling elite worshipped the old gods of Rome. Constantine was the first emperor to allow Christians to worship freely, helping to unite and promote the faith. He went on to instigate the celebration of the birth of Christ that we call Christmas.

Epilogue

War, then, is clearly an ever-present and salient feature of Roman mythology and legend; it courses through and characterizes what are arguably the most important and existentialist Roman legends and myths – those twin foundation myths of Aeneas and of Romulus and Remus. This should hardly surprise us, given that war was a constant in Roman life from the legendary foundation of Rome in 753 BC to the final, historical sacking in the early fifth century. Without serial war there would have been no Rome and no Roman Empire: Rome was built by war, it thrived on war and it died in war. It should not surprise us because myth and legends are often described as reflections of life; they are a mirror to the reality of the actual world, and because war and conflict defines Rome – and Roman history is freighted with constant warfare – it follows that war will emerge as a constant theme, a vital and vibrant *topos* in much of Roman mythology and legend.

Once we established that the Romans did not just lazily recycle Greek myths into a second-hand Roman mythology (which some have argued is the case) but worked and refashioned ancient mythologies to create their own decidedly and emphatically Roman political and historical narratives, we find a distinctly Roman pantheon made up of numerous Roman deities and semi-divine heroes with a militaristic portfolio. These, of course, service and sustain the Roman tradition of war and the Roman ways of war; they culminate in the foundation myths, which were construed in the early Empire to propagandize Augustus' ambition to trace a direct lineage back to Troy and Aeneas, and through Romulus, in order to facilitate the apotheosis of Julius Caesar and thus his own elevation to Olympus. Rome itself would bathe in the reflected glory of such a marvellous event. The *tour de force* of the showpiece for this nationalism, the commissioned nationalist poem, was, of course, the *Aeneid* of Virgil, but Virgil was joined by a number of other poets: Horace, Propertius and Ovid, who largely sang the same praises, and joined in the eulogies – to a greater or lesser extent. Mythology now had a defining role – to exalt the new Augustan Age, which ironically espoused peace and stability over expansionist warfare – and it was enthusiastically supported by mythologically themed architecture, wall paintings and mosaics.

The ancient origins of traditional Roman *mores*, laws and social values are likewise adumbrated – through Roman pre-history in the work of historians such as Livy, who deployed legend as a prelude to real Roman historiography. The dubious historicity of the Theban Legion Massacre and the equally suspect Constantine Christian epiphany conclude the book as probable mythologies based in battle and war.

Appendix I

The Seven Kings of Rome

Romulus (753–715 BCE), the fabled founder of Rome.

Numa Pompilius (715–673 BCE), untypically peaceful Roman king.

Tullius Hostilius (673–642 BCE), responsible for the destruction of Alba Longa and the migration of its inhabitants to Rome.

Ancus Marcius (642–617 BCE), extended the city, built the first bridge across the Tiber, and founded Ostia to give Rome a seaport.

Tarquinius Priscus (617–579 BCE), was an Etruscan who built Rome's first sewer, the Cloaca Maxima, laid out the Circus Maximus and started work on a temple to Jupiter on the Capitoline Hill.

Servius Tullius (579–535 BCE), divided the Romans into tribes and classes, and so established a constitution in which wealth was the main factor. Built the city walls: 5 miles in circumference, with nineteen gates, embracing all the Seven Hills of Rome. He transferred the regional festival of Diana from Aricia to the Aventine Hill.

Tarquinius Superbus (534–510 BCE), Rome's last king. His son, Sextus, raped Lucretia, a virtuous *matrona*, with the consequence that Tarquinius was exiled and the monarchy gave way to the Roman Republic.

Timeline 1 – The Mythical Age

1260 BCE (*c.*)	Trojan war begins.
1160 BCE	The fall of Troy and Aeneas' flight.
1215–753 BCE	The Alban kings(see Appendix 3).
753 BCE	The foundation of Rome.
753 BCE	Romulus, founder and first king of Rome (r. 753–715 BCE).
715 BCE	Numa Pompilius, second king of Rome (715–673 BCE).
673 BCE	Tullius Hostilius (673–642 BCE).
642 BCE	Ancus Marcius (642–617 BCE).
617 BCE	Tarquinius Priscus (617–579 BCE).
579 BCE	Servius Tullius (579–535 BCE).
534 BCE	Tarquinius Superbus (534–510 BCE).
509 BCE	Battle of Silvia Arsia: The Romans defeat the Tarquinii and Veii under deposed king Lucius Tarquinius Superbus.
506 BCE	Battle of Aricia: Latins defeat the Etruscans under Lars Porsena.
501 BCE	The Bloodless War.
497 BCE	Battle of Lake Regillus: Aulus Postumius Albus Regillensis defeats the Tarquinii, commanded by Tarquinius Superbus.
495 BCE	Battle of Aricia: Romans defeat the Aurunci. The inconclusive One-Day War.
480 BCE	Battle of Veii: Romans win against the Veii and their Etruscan allies.

Appendix III

The Alban Kings

There are at least fifteen different lists from ancient sources – and much controversy and confusion. The following is from http://self.gutenberg.org/articles/eng/Latin_kings_of_Alba_Longa? and uses information from Livy and Dionysius of Halicarnassus, who is the source for the length of each reign.

Latinus, reigned 1215–1180 BCE: King of the 'Aborigines', who gave his name to the new state of the Latins to be ruled from Laurentum by Aeneas and his own daughter Lavinia, given in marriage to Aeneas. Reigned for thirty-six years.

Aeneas, 1180–1177 BCE: A noble Trojan leading a force fleeing from the collapse of Troy. Listed as the first Latin king by both Livy and Dionysius. He founded Lavinium in 1181 BCE, where he would rule the Latins until his death.

Ascanius (in Dionysius) or Iulus, 1177–1139 BCE: The son of Aeneas and his Trojan wife Creusa, also known as Iulus, from which the gens Iulia was said to derive. Founder of Alba Longa (1151 BCE, thirty years after the founding of Lavinium). Reigned for thirty-eight years.

Silvius, 1139–1110 BCE: A son of Aeneas and Lavinia, younger half-brother of Ascanius. Reigned for twenty-nine years.

Aeneas Silvius, 1110–1079 BCE: A son of Silvius. Reigned for thirty-one years.

Latinus Silvius, 1079–1028 BCE: Possibly a son of Aeneas Silvius. Reigned for fifty-one years.

Alba Silvius, 1028–989 BCE: Possibly a son of Latinus Silvius. Reigned for thirty-nine years.

Atys (in Livy) or Capetus (in Dionysius), 989–963 BCE: Possibly a son of Alba. Reigned for twenty-six years.

Capys, 963–935 BCE: Possibly a son of Capetus. Reigned for twenty-eight years.

Capetus Silvius or Calpetus, 935–922 BCE: Possibly a son of Capys. Reigned for thirteen years.

Tiberinus Silvius, 922–914 BCE: Possibly a son of Capetus II. Reigned for eight years. Reportedly slain in battle near the Albula River and his body was carried away by it. The river was renamed the Tiber.

Agrippa, 914–873 BCE: Possibly a son of Tiberinus. Reigned for forty-one years.

Romulus Silvius (in Livy) or Alladius (in Dionysius), 873–854 BCE: Possibly a son of Agrippa. Reigned for nineteen years. Reportedly a tyrant and contemptuous of the gods. He frightened the people by throwing thunderbolts at them, until he himself was murdered by one and his house was submerged in the Alban Lake.

Aventinus, 854–817 BCE: Possibly a son of Alladius. Reigned for thirty-seven years. The Aventine Hill was reportedly named after him.

Procas or Proca, 817–794 BCE: Possibly a son of Aventinus. Reigned for twenty-three years.

Amulius, 794–752 BC: A younger son of Procas who reportedly usurped the throne. Reigned for forty-two years. Slain by his grand-nephews Romulus and Remus.

Numitor, 752–(?) BCE: The older brother of Amulius. Reportedly succeeded him a year before the foundation of Rome.

Gaius Cluilius, (?)–(?) BCE: Last king of Alba Longa, who died of natural causes while in camp during the siege of Rome under the kingship of Tullus Hostilius. Cluilius may have held the title of praetor at the time of the war with Rome.

Mettius Fufetius, (?)–(?) BCE: Elected dictator of Alba Longa by Cluilius' forces following his death. Mettius agreed to become vassal to the Romans for fear of the Fidenates and Veienates. Was executed by Tullus Hostilius for committing perfidy (mid-seventh century BCE).

Kings of Alba Longa would have claimed to be descendents of Jupiter, as Virgil shows in the *Aeneid*.

Timeline 2: Octavian (Augustus), 133–27 BCE

133 BCE	Tiberius Gracchus tribune
123–122 BCE	Gaius Gracchus tribune
91–89 BCE	Social War between Rome and its Italian allies. Italians demand Roman citizenship and equal share in power.
88–87 BCE	First Civil War between Marius and Sulla. First march on Rome by Sulla.
86 BCE	Death of Marius.
83 BCE	Pompey fights under the Roman dictator Sulla.
83 BCE	Sulla's second march on Rome. Proscriptions.
70 BCE	Pompey and Crassus are consuls. Virgil born.
65 BCE	Horace born.
63 BCE	Cicero consul. Catiline conspiracy.
62 BCE	Pompey returns to Italy and disbands his army.
60–53 BCE	First Triumvirate between Caesar, Pompey and Crassus.
58–51 BCE	Julius Caesar's conquest of Gaul.
58–57 BCE	Cicero exiled from Rome.
55 BCE	Caesar invades Britain.
54 BCE	Caesar invades Britain for a second time.
53 BCE	Battle of Carrhae. Crassus is captured and executed by the Parthians. Standards lost.
52 BCE	Pompey consul.
51 BCE	Caesar's siege and capture of Uxellodunum ends the Gallic War.
43 BCE	Ovid born.
49 BCE	Caesar crosses the Rubicon. Civil war between Caesar and Pompey begins.
48 BCE	Caesar defeats Pompey at Battle of Pharsalus.
c. 45 BCE	Propertius born.
44 BCE	Caesar becomes dictator for life. On the 'Ides of March' (the 15th) he is killed by conspirators, including Brutus and Cassius. Octavian, son of Caesar's niece Atia, is adopted as his heir. Mark Antony consul. Antony attacks Brutus.

43 BCE	Octavian marches on Rome. Octavian consul.
43–36 BCE	Second Roman Triumvirate: Antony, Octavian and Lepidus. Mass proscriptions, including Cicero.
42 BCE	Octavian and Antony defeat Republicans under Brutus and Cassius at the Battle of Philippi. Death of Cassius. Death of Brutus. Lucius Antonius consul.
41 BCE	Antony meets Cleopatra. Perusine War. Peace of Brundisium.
39 BCE	Octavian marries Livia.
38 BCE	Octavian makes war with Sextus Pompeius.
36 BCE	Octavian strips Lepidus of all power except Pontifex Maximus.
32 BCE	War between Antony and Octavian.
31 BCE	Octavian defeats Antony and Cleopatra at the Battle of Actium. Antony and Cleopatra commit suicide.
29–19 BCE	Virgil composing the *Aeneid*.
27 BCE	Octavian granted extraordinary powers by the Senate and assumes the name Augustus.
19 BCE	Virgil dies.
18 BCE	Augustus begins his moral recovery legislation.
18 BCE	Ovid dies.
c. 15 BCE	Propertius dies.
8 BCE	Horace dies.

Appendix V

The Archaeology of Early Rome

Archaeological evidence of human occupation of the area around Rome goes back about 14,000 years. Several excavations support the view that Rome grew from pastoral settlements on the Palatine Hill, built above the area of what was to be the Roman Forum. Between the end of the Bronze Age and the beginning of the Iron Age, each hill between the sea and the Capitol was surmounted by a village.

The area that became the city of Rome was inhabited by Latin farming settlers from various surrounding regions, as evidenced by differences in pottery and burial techniques. The historical Latins were originally an Italic tribe who inhabited the Alban Hills. They later moved down into the valleys, which provided less challenging land for agriculture. The Isola Tiberina island was the site of an important ancient ford. The area around the Tiber was particularly advantageous and offered significant strategic benefits: the river was a natural border on one side, and the hills could provide a safe defensive position on the other. This would also have enabled the Latins to control the river and the commercial and military traffic on it from the natural observation point at Isola Tiberina. Moreover, road traffic could be controlled, since Rome was at the intersection of the principal roads to the sea coming from Sabinum (in the north-east) and Etruria (to the north-west).

On this matter, F. Coarelli has written:

'There is a wide consensus that the city developed gradually through the aggregation ('synoecism') of several villages around the largest one on the Palatine. This aggregation, signalling the transition from a proto-urban to an urban settlement, was made possible by the increase in agricultural productivity above the subsistence level ... in turn, these boosted the development of trade with the Greek colonies of southern Italy – mainly Ischia and Cumae. All these events, which according to the archeological excavations occurred around the mid 8th century BCE, may be considered as the origin of the city.'[1]

The Germalus on the northern part of the Palatine was the site of a village (dated to the ninth century BCE) with circular or elliptical dwellings. It was protected by a clay wall (perhaps reinforced with wood), and it is likely that this is the exact place on the Palatine Hill where Rome was actually founded. The neighbouring territory was surrounded by a sacred border called the *pomerium*.

Appendix VI

Dating the Foundation

The Romans had no doubts about the day on which Rome was founded: 21 April, the day of the festival sacred to Pales, goddess of shepherds, on which date they celebrated the Parilia (or Palilia). Plutarch wrote (*Romulus* 12; trans. Bernadotte Perrin):

'Now it is agreed that the city was founded on the twenty-first of April, and this day the Romans celebrate with a festival, calling it the birthday of their country. And at first, as it is said, they sacrificed no living creature at that festival, but thought they ought to keep it pure and without stain of blood, since it commemorated the birth of their country. However, even before the founding of the city, they had a pastoral festival on that day, and called it Parilia.'

However, the exact year of the foundation was more problematic and was one of the reasons why they originally dated their years by the presiding consuls rather than using A.U.C., or Ab Urbe Condita. Dionysius of Halicarnassus records the several dates proposed by ancient authorities (1.74–75):

'The Greek historian Timaeus, one of the first to write a history to include the Romans, stated that Rome was founded in the 38th year prior to the first Olympiad, or 814/3 BCE; Quintus Fabius Pictor, the first Roman to write the history of his people, in Greek, records that Rome was founded in the first year of the eighth Olympiad, or 748/7 BCE; Lucius Cincius Alimentus goes for the fourth year of the twelfth Olympiad, or 729/8 BCE; and Cato the Elder calculated that Rome was founded 432 years after the Trojan War, which Dionysius states was equivalent to the first year of the seventh Olympiad, or 752/1 BCE. Dionysius himself showed, rather tortuously, that Rome was founded in 751 BCE, starting with the Battle of the Allia, which he dated to the first year of the ninety-eighth Olympiad, 388/7 BCE, then added 120 years to reach the date of the first consuls, Junius Brutus and Tarquinius Collatinus, 508/7 BCE, then added the combined total of the reigns of the Kings of Rome (244 years) to arrive at his date of 751 BCE. The official *Fasti* Capitolini has 752 BCE.'

The accepted date today, 753 BCE, was arrived at by the Roman antiquarian Titus Pomponius Atticus, and adopted by Marcus Terentius Varro, as part of what has come to be known as the Varronian chronology.

Some Latin Terms

aedile	public officer responsible for public works, entertainment and the distribution of grain, markets etc.
aerarium	the public treasury
ager publicus	Roman land in Italy; public land belonging to the Roman people
aristeia	epic poetry convention in which a hero in battle has his or her finest hour. An *aristeia* can result in the death of the hero
auctoritas	influence, prestige
auxilia	troops provided by Rome's allies (*socii*)
capite censi	the head–count of *proletarii* of Roman citizens who did not have sufficient property to qualify for military service and featured as numbers in the census. Marius changed all that and included the *proletarii* in his armies
Capitol	one of the seven hills – the religious and symbolic centre of Rome
civitas sine suffragio	citizenship without suffrage – a form of citizenship granted to towns (eg Capua in 338 BCE) who were subject to Roman taxation and military service, but were denied the right to vote or hold political office
cognomen	a man's third name; a woman's second. The name of a legion
colonia	a town founded at a strategic place (eg a river crossing), populated with Romans and/or Latins
Comitia Centuriata	the assembly of citizens which legislated, elected magistrates, declared war, ratified treaties and judged capital offences
consul	the highest political office on the *cursus honorum*; two elected annually (usually). Consuls held *imperium*
cursus honorum	the sequence of public offices held by men of senatorial class

damnatio memoriae	the erasing of records, statuary and the memory of *persona non grata* after their death
decimation	the execution of every tenth man, chosen by lot from the ranks
deditio	surrender, with the assumption that the victor would extend *fides* and spare the lives of the defeated
devotio	an extreme act of bravery, in which a Roman gave himself up in battle in a suicidal attack against the enemy
dictator	temporary absolute leader, appointed for a limited period to resolve a crisis
dies nefasti	inauspicious days
dignitas	political dignity, related to tenure of offices in the *cursus honorum*
dilectus	the annual military levy
dona militaria	military decorations
dux	leader
equites	the equestrian order ranked below senators; the *equites* were middle-class businessmen and farmers; also cavalry
exercitus	army
Fetialis	war priest responsible for ensuring that Rome's wars were just in the eyes of the gods. Responsible for the rites performed for declaring war and concluding peace
fides	trustworthiness, good faith, loyalty – a quality the Romans were anxious to be seen to uphold, including respect for the law and *fides* in foreign relations
foederati	nations to which Rome provided benefits in exchange for military assistance
foedus	originally a sacred oath made by a Fetial priest on behalf of the Roman people; a treaty
gens	family; clan, e.g. Claudii
haruspex	soothsayer
hastati	soldiers of the second class, who stood in the front line; green, raw recruits
Hellenism	a culture of classical Greece, which percolated into Rome in the second century BCE

imagines	portraits of ancestors
imperium	power, command, empire; particularly that power bestowed on consuls, generals and praetors
incestum	unchastity, particularly in Vestal Virgins; incest
latifundia	large estates in Italy
Latin League	an association of communities in Latium, who were allied militarily
laudatio	eulogy
legio	legion; a levy of troops
lex	law
magister equitum	second-in-command to the dictator; the master of the horse usually commanded the cavalry, as the dictator was forbidden to ride a horse
maiestas	power; authority; treason
manipulus	maniple; sub-unit of the legion, comprising two centuries
miles	soldier
novus homo	a 'new man'; a man not of the aristocracy; a self-made man
otium	a lifestyle of ease and commercial, political or military inactivity
patricius	patrician; the dominant political class; aristocratic families
pax	peace
phalanx	close-knit body of heavily armed infantry
pietas	dutifulness – in all aspects of life
plebeian	non-patricians
polis	a Greek city-state
pontifex maximus	chief priest
praefectus	prefect, commander of an auxiliary force
preafectus urbi	prefect of the city
praetexta	white robe with a purple border, worn by a Roman boy before he was entitled to wear the *toga virilis*, and by girls until their marriage. Also worn by magistrates and priests
praetor	public office, responsible for justice. Second-highest political and military office
Principate	the period of the emperors, from 27 BCE onwards
principes	troops in their 20s and 30s

proconsul	acting consul
proletarii	volunteer soldiers of the poorer orders, first recruited by Marius
raptus	seized, abducted, raped
Republic	the period of Republican government from 509–43 BCE
res gestae	political and military achievements
rex	king
secessio plebis	a general strike in which the plebeians downed tools, shut up shop and deserted Rome, leaving the patricians to get on with running the city on their own. All business and services ground to a halt; there were five between 494 and 287 BCE
Sibylline Books	three sacred scrolls, kept under guard. Only consulted when decreed by the Senate to give oracular advice in times of crisis, or to interpret portents and omens
signifier	standard-bearer
societas	synonymous with *amicitia*. Peace and neutrality, with an obligation to military support
socius (pl. *socii*)	ally
spolia opima	the highest award for gallantry – won when a commander defeated an enemy leader in single combat
toga virilis	the plain white toga worn on formal occasions by Roman men between 14 and 18 years of age; also worn by senators. The first wearing of the *toga virilis* was one of the rites of passage of reaching maturity. See *praetexta*
triarii	veteran troops
tribuni plebei	officials responsible for protecting their fellow plebeians against injustices from the patricians; had a veto and sacrosanctity
tribunus militum	military tribune
triumphator	a general who had been awarded a triumph
triumphus	triumph: the military procession along the Via Sacra, in Rome, for victorious generals. Spoils of war, prisoners and captured chieftains were paraded. The enemy chieftains were sometimes

	executed; the *triumphator* rode in a chariot, and was dressed as Jupiter
tumultus	crisis
vates	soothsayer; prophetess; priestess
velites	lightly armed skirmishing troops, 1,200 or so in a legion
via	road, as in Via Appia
virtus	manliness; courage; virtue
vis	force; rape; military strength

Appendix VIII

Typical *Cursus Honorum* in the First Century BCE

Ten years' military service in cavalry or on the political staff of a relative or friend.

Minimum Age

30   *quaestor* (eight to twelve in number): financial admin in Rome, or in a province, as second-in-command to the Governor.

    'tribune of the plebs' (ten): preside over the *concilium plebis*.

36   *aedile* (four;, two curule and two plebeian): admin role in Rome; responsible for the corn supply, festivals etc.; optional.

39   *praetor* (six): judicial role in Rome; in charge of provinces not allocated to consuls; commanded one legion and allies.

40   *consul* (two): governed larger provinces and held major commands in all wars; led two legions and two allied *alae*. Other roles: to preside over the Senate and assemblies.

    censor: magistracy held by most distinguished ex-consuls. Two in office for five years. Function: to carry out the census.

Appendix IX

Roman Assemblies

Senate
Three hundred members regulated by the censors; members were from the eighteen senior centuries, i.e. they had property worth more than 400,000 sestertii; role was to advise magistrates, especially the consuls.

Concilium Plebis
Made up of plebeians; divided into thirty-five tribes; membership based on ancestry; role was to elect the tribune and the *aedile*; passed laws.

Comitia Tributa
Made up of citizens, including patricians; role as above, but elected *curule aediles* and *quaestors*.

Comitia Centuriata
Comprised citizens divided into 193 voting centuries; originally formed from citizen militia, with membership based on possession of military equipment; presided over by a consul or praetor; function: election of consuls, praetors and censors, declarations of war and ratification of peace treaties.

Appendix X

The *Mos Maiorum*

The *mos maiorum* – 'ancestral custom' or 'the way the ancestors did things' – was the hallowed unwritten code from which the ancient Romans derived their social norms. It represented the core concept of Roman traditionalism, distinguished from but complementary to written law. The *mos maiorum* developed over time and constituted the time-honoured principles, behavioural models and social practices that affected private, political and military life in ancient Rome. The following are some of the values embraced in the *mos maiorum*:

Fides

Embodied trust/trustworthiness, good faith/faithfulness, confidence, reliability and credibility. It was a vital concept in Roman law, as oral contracts were common. The concept of *fides* was personified by the goddess Fides, whose role in the *mos maiorum* was indicated by the antiquity of her cult.

Pietas

Pietas was the Roman attitude of dutiful respect towards the gods, homeland, parents and family, which required the maintenance of relationships in a moral and dutiful manner. Cicero defined pietas as 'justice towards the gods'. It went beyond routine sacrifice and proper ritual to inner devotion and righteousness of the individual, and, as we have seen, it was the cardinal virtue of the Roman hero Aeneas in Virgil's *Aeneid*. Like Fides, Pietas was cultivated as a goddess, with a temple vowed to her in 191 BCE and dedicated ten years later.

Religio and cultus

Religio is related to the Latin verb *religare*, 'to bind'. It was was the bond between gods and mortals, as carried out in traditional religious practices for preserving the *pax deorum* ('peace of the gods'). *Cultus* was the active observance and correct performance of rituals.

Disciplina

Given the importance of all things military, *disciplina* ('discipline') was very important in civic and military life, and extended to education, training, discipline and self-control.

Gravitas and constantia

Gravitas was dignified self-control. *Constantia* was steadiness or perseverance. Faced with a problem or adversity, a good Roman should put on an inscrutable, unperturbed face. Roman myth and history reinforced this value by recounting tales of figures such as Gaius Mucius Scaevola, who in a founding legend of the Republic demonstrated his determination to the Etruscan king Lars Porsena by holding his right hand in a fire and ignoring the obvious pain.

Virtus

Derived from the Latin word *vir* ('man'), *virtus* constituted the ideal of the true Roman male. Gaius Lucilius discusses *virtus*, and says that it is *virtus* for a man to know what is good, evil, useless, shameful or dishonourable. Women, too, could exhibit *virtus*.

Dignitas and auctoritas

Dignitas and *auctoritas* are what you got when you exhibited the values of the ideal Roman and paid service to the state, in the form of priesthoods, military rank and magistracies. *Dignitas* was a reputation for worth, honour and esteem. Thus, a Roman who displayed their *gravitas*, *constantia*, *fides*, *pietas* and other values would possess *dignitas* among their peers. A Roman could earn *auctoritas* ('prestige and respect') in much the same way.

Notes

Introduction
1. Scott, K. (1930), 'Emperor Worship in Ovid', in *TAPhA* 61, pp.43–69

Chapter 1
1. Morford, M.P.O., *Classical Mythology*, p.431
2. https://www.cs.mcgill.ca/~rwest/wikispeedia/wpcd/wp/r/Roman_mythology.htm
3. Cicero, *De Oratore* 2.2.52, trans. E.W. Sutton
4. Plutarch, *Cato the Elder* 8.1; 18; Polybius, 31
5. See Colin, G., *Rome et la Grece*; Griffin, J., *Augustan Poetry*, p.88ff and the Appendix, *Some Imperial Servants*. Various suggestions for the start and/or cause of the decline have been made: Polybius 31.25 ascribes it to the victory over Macedonia; L. Calpurnius Piso (Pliny, *NH* 17.38.244) goes with 154 bce; Appian, *Bellum Civili* 1.7 for the end of the war in Italy; Livy 39.6.7 prefers 186 bce; Velleius Paterculus, *Historiae Romanae*, and Sallust, *Catilina*, go for the end of the Third Punic War. See also Putnam, *The Roman Lady*; Reinhold, *The Generation Gap*, p.52ff
6. Isidore of Seville (*c.* 560–636 ce), *Etymologies* 6.17
7. Cornelius Nepos, *Life of Cato, §3*
8. Hanson-Heath, V.D., *Who Killed Homer?*, p.37
9. See Ogilvie, *Livy: The Early History of Rome*, pp.12–13.

Chapter 2
1. Virgil describes her as armed with a bloody scourge. Virgil, *Aeneid* 8.703; Lucan, *Pharsalia* 7.569; Horace, *Satires* 2.3.223.
2. Livy, 10.19; Ovid, *Fasti* 6.201
3. Varro, *On the Latin Language* 8.49
4. Hesiod, *Theogeny* 934
5. Apollodorus, 2.5.11; 2.7.7. Pausanias, *Description of Greece* 3.19.7–8
6. *Iliad* 5, 798–891, 895–898
7. Homer, *Odyssey* 8, 361; for Ares/Mars and Thrace, see Ovid, *Ars Amatoria* 2.11.585, which tells the same tale: 'Their captive bodies are, with difficulty, freed, at your plea, Neptune: Venus runs to Paphos: Mars heads for Thrace.' See also Statius, *Thebaid* 7.42; Herodotus 4.59.62
8. Ovid, *Fasti* 6.205

9. Plutarch, *Sulla* 3.57–58
10. Livy, 2.19–22; Dionysius of Halicarnassus, *Roman Antiquities* 6.4–12; Florus, 1.5.1–4
11. See Cicero, *De Natura Deorum* 2.6; Dionysius of Halicarnassus, *Roman Antiquities* 6.13; Plutarch, *Life of Coriolanus* 3.4; cf Livy, 2.20.12
12. *De Nupt. Merc. et Philol.* II 149.
13. The official website of the Musei Capitolini, Comune di Roma, gives details on the location and architectural features of the temple. Cf Livy, 5.54.7 on the annual procession commemorating her role of saviour: in it, the image of the goddess represented as a goose was taken from her sanctuary on the Arx to the Capitoline temple, where she was placed in the sacellum of Iuventas, in the space between the cellae of Jupiter and Minerva
14. Livy, 5.47; Plutarch, *Life of Camillus* 27
15. Livy, 34.53.3
16. Livy, 6.33; 8.27; 28.11. Satricum (modern Le Ferriere) was an ancient town of Latium on the right bank of the Astura River some 37 miles south-east of Rome
17. Julius Obsequens, 55.
18. Livy, 6.5.7
19. Livy, 22.1.12; 10.27
20. Pliny, *Natural History* 26.36
21. Aulus Gellius, *Attic Nights* 4.6.1; Cassius Dio, 44.17.2
22. Livy, 2.45
23. Statius, *Thebaid* 9.4. See also 7.695
24. Valerius Maximus, 2.131.1, *auctor ac stator Romani nominis*
25. *Mars enim cum saevit Gradivus dicitur, cum tranquillus est Quirinus*: Servius, note to *Aeneid* 1.292. At *Aeneid* 6.860, Servius further notes: 'Quirinus is the Mars who presides over peace and whose cult is maintained within the civilian realm, for the Mars of war has his temple outside that realm.'
26. Ovid, *Fasti* 3.809ff
27. Cicero, *De Legibus* 2.28
28. Ambrose, *Epistles* 17–18; Symmachus, *Relationes* 1–3

Chapter 3
1. G. Williamson (tr.), Josephus, *The Jewish War* (1959), p.378. Adcock, *The Roman Art of War*, pp.4–5
2. Ovid, *Metamorphoses* 1.89–100
3. See Cornell, *The Beginnings of Rome*, pp.179–97; Ogilvie, *Early Rome and the Etruscans*, p.45ff. Livy, 1.43; Dionysius of Halicarnassus, 4.16; Cicero, *De Re Publica* 1.39
4. Cicero, *De Officiis* 1.34–36, trans. W. Miller, Loeb Classical Edition (Harvard, 1913). Virgil, *Aeneid* 6.850–53. Horace, *Carmen Saeculare* 49ff

5. Polybius, 18.37; trans. E.S. Shuckburgh (London, 1889). See also Livy, 9.1.10, 30.42.17 and 37.45.8ff. Cicero, *Divinatio in Caecilium* 63; *De provinciis consularibus* 4; *Ad Atticum* 7.14.3; 9.19.1; *Pro Rege Deiotauro* 13; *Philippicae* 11.37; 13.35
6. Lewis & Short, *ad loc.* See Chrystal, *Women in Ancient Rome*, pp.20, 22: 'Women also exhibit *virtus*, with its connotations of manliness (*vir*) and traditional male attributes of strength and bravery, as well as of virtue. Seneca describes the conspicuous valour of Cornelia and Rutilia as *conspecta virtus*. In the *Ad Marciam* he spells out his belief that women are just as capable of displaying virtutes as men. The elderly Ummidia Quadratilla shows vitality (*viridis*) and a physique unusual in an octogenarian woman.' See also Cicero: *Fam* 14.11 and *Att.* 10.8; *Fam* 14.1. Also McDonnell, *Roman Manliness* (Cambridge, 2006)
7. For a litany of anti-Carthaginian and anti-Greek vitriol, see Sidebottom, *Ancient Warfare*, pp.8–14
8. Tacitus, *Histories* 3.47; Lucan, *De Bello Civile* 7.400–10
9. See Ogilvie, *The Etruscans*; Cornell, *The Beginnings of Rome* for details of these early days
10. Livy, 1.2–3
11. Livy, 1.14–15
12. Livy, 1.27
13. Livy, 1.22–23. Peddling misinformation to one's troops to instil confidence was an old device well established by Tullus' day; see Polyaenus, *Stratagems in War* 1.33.1; 1.35.1
14. Livy, 1.23–28
15. Livy, 1.30–31
16. Livy, 1.42
17. Livy, 2.6–7; *Fasti Triumphales*; Plutarch, *Life of Poplicola*
18. Livy, 2.10. Pliny, *Natural History* 24.11. Dionysius of Halicarnassus, 5.25

Chapter 4
1. Suetonius, *Augustus* 28.3; cf Virgil, *Aeneid* 8.98–100. Only Sallust (*Cat.* 6.1.2) refers to Aeneas as the founder of Rome
2. Aulus Gellius, *Noctes Atticae* 1.6.2; 1.17.4
3. Malcovati fr. 6
4. Tacitus, *Annals* 3.25

Chapter 5
1. See Aeneid, 8.478ff
2. The practice is referred to in a fragment of Cicero's *Hortensius* (95M) preserved by Augustine (*contra Pel.* 4)
3. *P. Vergili Maronis liber quartus*, Oxford, 1955, Introduction, XVI

Chapter 7

1. Lewis & Short, *ad loc*; Liddell & Scott, *ad loc*. See also Chrystal, *In Bed with the Romans*, chapters 9 on rape and 12 on sexual vocabulary. See also Cicero, *Ad Familiares* 14.11 and *Ad Atticus* 10.8. Also McDonnell, *Roman Manliness* (2006)
2. See Ziolkowski, *Urbs Direpta*, for an analysis of rape and plunder, and 'how the Romans sacked cities'.
3. 'A festival, with games, celebrated by the Romans, according to Festus, Ovid (Fast. III.199), and others, in honour of Consus, the god of secret deliberations, or, according to Livy (I.9), of Neptunus Equestris. Plutarch (Quaest. Rom. 48), Dionysius of Halicarnassus (II.31), and the Pseudo Asconius, however (ad Cic. in Verr. p142, ed. Orelli), say that Neptunus Equestris and Consus were only different names for one and the same deity. It was solemnised every year in the circus, by the symbolical ceremony of uncovering an altar dedicated to the god, which was buried in the earth. For Romulus, who was considered as the founder of the festival, was said to have discovered an altar in the earth on that spot (cf. Niebuhr, Hist. Rom. vol. I notes 629 and 630). The solemnity took place on 21 August with horse and chariot races, and libations were poured into the flames which consumed the sacrifices. During these festive games, horses and mules were not allowed to do any work, and were adorned with garlands of flowers. It was at their first celebration that, according to the ancient legend, the Sabine maidens were carried off (Varro, De Ling. Lat. VI.20; Dionys. I.33.2; Cic. De Rep. II.7). Virgil (Aen. VIII.636), in speaking of the rape of the Sabines, describes it as having occurred during the celebration of the Circensian games, which can only be accounted for by supposing that the great Circensian games, in subsequent times, superseded the ancient Consualia; and that thus the poet substituted games of his own time for ancient ones – a favourite practice with Virgil; or that he only meant to say the rape took place at the well-known festival in the circus (the Consualia), without thinking of the ludi Circenses, properly so called.' William Smith, D.C.L., LL.D., *A Dictionary of Greek and Roman Antiquities* (John Murray, London, 1875)
4. Ovid, *Fasti* 2
5. Livy, 1.57–60. See also Juvenal, 10.293. For the controversies surrounding this episode, and the dates, see Cornell, *The Beginnings of Rome*, pp.215–18
6. Cicero, *De Legibus* 2.5; *de Republica* 2.25.46. See also *de Finibus* 2.20.66
7. Martial, 11.104.21. See also Petronius, 9.5
8. Ovid, *Fasti* 2.721–852
9. Valerius Maximus, *Factorum et Dictorum Memorabilium* 6.1.1. Livy, 1.11
10. Virgil, *Aeneid* 1.464; Tacitus, *Agricola* 16.1; 31.4. Tacitus calls the militarily minded Agrippina the Elder *dux* at Annals 1.69.2: '*sed femina ingens animi munia ducis per eos dies induit*' – 'but that determined woman took on the

duties of a leader during those times'. See below, Cloelia is described by Livy as *dux* in her brave escapade; see page xxx

11. Livy, 3.44–48; Dionysius of Halicarnassus, 11.35.4
12. Livy, 2.10
13. Livy, 2.10.2ff.; Cic. *Off.* 1.18.61; *id. Leg.* 2.4.10; Verg. *A.* 8.650; Plin. 34.5.11.22; 36.15.23.100 al.; Prop. 3 (4).11.63; Sen. *Ep.* 120.7
14. Dionysius, 5.23
15. Livy, 2.10
16. Dionysius, 5.24
17. Livy, 2.10; Pliny, *Natural History* 34.11
18. Polybius, 6.55
19. Livy, 2.12
20. 'Just a myth or possibly a case of Congenital Insensitivity to Pain (also known as Congenital Analgesia) – a condition that inhibits the ability to perceive physical pain. From birth, affected individuals never feel pain in any part of their body when injured. People with this condition can feel the difference between sharp and dull, and hot and cold, but cannot sense, for example, that a drink is burning their tongue. This lack of pain awareness often leads to an accumulation of wounds, bruises, broken bones and other health issues that may go undetected … These repeated injuries often lead to a reduced life expectancy in people with congenital insensitivity to pain. Many people with congenital insensitivity to pain also have a complete loss of the sense of smell (anosmia).' (https://ghr.nlm.nih.gov/condition/congenital-insensitivity-to-pain)
21. Varro, *Ling.* 5.150; Livy, 7.6

Chapter 8

1. Virgil, *Aeneid* 11.648
2. *Op. cit.* 7.803ff
3. *Op. cit.* 11.603–07
4. *Op. cit.* 11.552–66
5. *Op. cit.* 11.581–82
6. *Op. cit* 11.651–63
7. *Op. cit.* 4.300–01; 4.384–87; 4.450–73; 4.483ff
8. *Op.cit.* 12.593–613
9. *Op. cit.* 12.139–60; 12.222ff; 12.460–500
10. *Op.cit.* 7.546ff
11. Ovid, *Metamorphoses* 2.411ff
12. *Op.cit.* 8.318ff; Apollonius of Rhodes, *Argonautica* 1.769–73
13. Statius, *Thebaid* 4.2.48; see also 4.267; 6.563
14. *Ibid.* 4.337–40
15. *Lucan, De Bello Civili* 6.508ff

16. Silius Italicus, *Punica* 2.56ff
17. Statius, *op. cit.* 12.177–86
18. Seneca, *Consolatio Ad Helviam* 16.5. *Consolatio Ad Marciam* 16.1
19. *Ibid*, 12.312–13
20. Valerius Flaccus, *Argonautica* 2.107ff
21. *Ibid*, 191–95
22. Statius, *Thebaid* 5.129ff
23. Apollonius of Rhodes, *Argonautica* 1.625ff
24. See Valerius Flaccus, 2.316ff
25. Aeschylus, *Libation Bearers* 594ff
26. Apollodorus, *Library* 1.9.17

Chapter 9

1. Achates appears in Book 1, lines 120, 174, 188, 312, 459, 513, 579, 581, 644 and 656; Book 3, line 523; Book 6, lines 34 and 158; Book 8, lines 466, 521 and 586; Book 10, lines 332 and 344; and and Book 12, lines 384 and 459.

Chapter 10

1. Michie, J., *The Odes of Horace*, p.14
2. From John Dryden's 'Discourse Concerning the Original and Progress of Satire', taken from W.P. Ker's edition of Dryden's essays (Oxford, 1926), vol. 2, pp.86–87
3. *Epistles* 2.2.51–52
4. Probably near Licenza, 22 miles north-east of Rome
5. https://www.britannica.com/biography/Horace-Roman-poet/ Influences-personality-and-impact
6. *Odes* 4.4; 4.19
7. ie *parcere subiectis*, Virgil, *Aeneid* 6.853
8. See *Odes* 1.3; 1.12; 4.5; 3.3; 3. 29.
9. West, D., *Horace Odes I: Carpe Diem* (Oxford, 1995), p.61
10. McCune, B.C., ' Mythological Lexicon: Repeated Myths and Meaning in *Odes* 1–3', p.177
11. Propertius, 2.7.13f
12. Varro, *De Lingua Latina* 5,.41: *hic mons ante Tarpeius dictus a virgine Vestali Tarpeia.*
13. Watts, A.E., *The Poems of Propertius* (Harmondsworth, 1966)
14. Tacitus, *Annals* 2.86.2
15. Aulus Gellius, *Attic Nights* 1.12
16. Tacitus, *Annals* 2.86.1; 3.69.9; *ILS* 4923. For details, see Ryberg, *Rites of the State Religion*, p.41
17. See Ovid, *Fasti*
18. Suetonius, *Caesar* 83; Dio, 61.30
19. *Roman Questions* 96; *Moralia* 286–87

20. Plutarch, *Numa* 10
21. On the Trojan origin of Vesta's flame, see Ovid, *Fasti* 3.417–18, 6.365, 6.455–56. Aeneas, according to legend, was responsible for carrying Vesta's fire from Troy to Rome, *Aeneid* 2.296–97

Chapter 11

1. The *Metamorphoses* features 250 stories in fifteen books
2. Ovid, *Amores* 1.1.1–4
3. Suetonius, *Augustus* 64–65
4. Velleius Paterculus, *op. cit.* 2.100
5. Seneca, *De Beneficiis* 6.32. Pliny, *NH* 21.8–9
6. Ovid, *Metamorphoses: A New Verse Translation*. Introduction, p.xx
7. Stephen M. Wheeler notes that 'metamorphosis, mutability, love, violence, artistry, and power are just some of the unifying themes that critics have proposed over the years'. Wheeler, Stephen M., *A Discourse of Wonders: Audience and Performance in Ovid's Metamorphoses* (Philadelphia: University of Pennsylvania Press, 1999)
8. 4.223ff
9. Livy, 29.10; 29.14.10–14
10. Varro, *de Lingua Latina* 6.15
11. Lucretius, 2.594–601; 606–14; 618–32
12. Ovid does not include Aeneas Silvius, who assumed his father's name as a cognomen; henceforth all of his descendants bore the name 'Silvius' in addition to their personal names. This was the same process by which the *nomen gentilicium* later developed throughout Italy. Aeneas reigned for thirty-one years. Also absent is the next king, the fourth, Latinus Silvius, who reigned for fifty-one years according to Dionysius (1.71). Ovid also elected not to ingratiate himself with Augustus by omitting to include Agrippa, who ruled for forty-one years (914–873 bce) and would have been instantly recognizable as an ancestor of Augustus' friend and son-in-law, Marcus Vipsanius Agrippa (63–12 bce)
13. Some scholars reject this, seeing the episode as something of a parody and an example of Ovid's anti-Augustanism. See in particular Galinsky, G., 'The Cipus Episode in Ovid's Metamorphoses (15.565–621)', *Transactions and Proceedings of the American Philological Association*, 98 (1967), pp.181–91; and Otis, B., *Ovid as an Epic Poet* (Cambridge, 1966), pp.303–05, who sees Ovid as anti-Augustan
14. Augustus himself tells us in his *Res Gestae* 20.4 that he restored eighty-two temples in Rome in 28 bce alone, neglecting none that required restoration. See also *Fasti* 2.59–60
15. Germanicus Julius Caesar (15 bce – 19 ce), the great-nephew of Augustus, nephew of Tiberius, father of Caligula and maternal grandfather of Nero
16. See also *Fasti* 2.481–86

17. Virgil, *Aeneid* 12.950
18. See Livy, 1.42.1; 1.46; Dionysius, 4.28–30
19. Cicero, *Pro Milone* 28; 55
20. Asconius, *Pro Milone* 31–32
21. Livy, 1.59

Chapter 12

1. Note the similarity with 666 – a number with a very different significance when it appears as the 'Number of the Beast' in the *Book of Revelations*
2. Girgis, S.F., 'Theban Legion', *The Coptic Encyclopedia*, Vol. 7 (Macmillan, 1991)
3. Eusebius, *Historia Ecclesia* 8, 19
4. *Codex Parisiensis*, Bibliothèque National, 9550, reproduced in Louis Dupraz, *Les passions de St Maurice d'Agaune: Essai sur l'historicité de la tradition et contribution à l'étude de l'armée pré-Dioclétienne (260–286) et des canonisations tardives de la fin du IVe siècle* (Fribourg, 1961), Appendix I. Dupraz confirms what he believes to be the historicity of the Theban Legion
5. See Van Berchem, *The Martyrdom of the Theban Legion;* Woods, *The Origin of the Legend of Maurice and the Theban Legion* (1994); O'Reilly, *Lost Legion Rediscovered* (2011)

Chapter 13

1. Eusebius' description of the *labarum*: 'A Description of the Standard of the Cross, which the Romans now call the Labarum ... Now it was made in the following manner. A long spear, overlaid with gold, formed the figure of the cross by means of a transverse bar laid over it. On the top of the whole was fixed a wreath of gold and precious stones; and within this, the symbol of the Saviour's name, two letters indicating the name of Christ by means of its initial characters, the letter P being intersected by X in its centre: and these letters the emperor was in the habit of wearing on his helmet at a later period. From the cross-bar of the spear was suspended a cloth, a royal piece, covered with a profuse embroidery of most brilliant precious stones; and which, being also richly interlaced with gold, presented an indescribable degree of beauty to the beholder. This banner was of a square form, and the upright staff, whose lower section was of great length, of the pious emperor and his children on its upper part, beneath the trophy of the cross, and immediately above the embroidered banner. The emperor constantly made use of this sign of salvation as a safeguard against every adverse and hostile power, and commanded that others similar to it should be carried at the head of all his armies.'

Appendix V

1. Coarelli, F., *Guida archeologica di Roma. 1. ed. Varia Grandi opere* (Milano, 1974), A. Mondadori, p.19

Further Reading

Achaud, G. (1994), *Bellum iustum, bellum sceleratum Sous les Rois et Sous la Republique* (B Stud Lat 24), pp.474–86

Adcock, F.E. (1940), *The Roman Art of War Under the Republic* (Cambridge MA)

Adie, K. (2003), *Corsets to Camouflage: Women and War* (London)

Alfoldi, A.A. (1965), *Early Rome and the Latins* (Ann Arbor)

Allen, K. (1922), 'The Fasti of Ovid and the Augustan Propaganda', *The American Journal of Philology*, 43(3), pp.250–66

Allen, R.A.(2001), 'Romulus and Quirinus: An Etruscan Deity in Ancient Rome', *Studia Antiqua* 1

Alonso-Nunez, J.M. (1987), 'An Augustan World History: the *Historiae Philippicae* of Pompeius Trogae', *Greece & Rome* 34, pp.56–72

Ando, C. (2005), 'Interpretatio Romana', *Classical Philology* 100(1), pp.41–51

Andrews, T. (2000), *Dictionary of Nature Myths: Legends of the Earth, Sea and Sky* (Oxford)

Arieti, J.A. (1980), 'Empedocles in Rome: Rape and the Roman Ethos', *Clio* 10, pp.1–20

Arieti, J.A. (1997), 'Rape and Livy´s View of Roman History', in Deacy, *Rape in Antiquity*, pp.209–29

Austin, R.G. (1959), 'Vergil and the Wooden Horse', *Journal of Roman Studies* 49, pp.16–25

Badian, E. (1958), *Foreign Clientelae* (London)

Badian, E. (1966), 'The Early Historians', in Dorey, *Latin Historians*, pp.1–38

Baker, R. (1968), '*Miles annosus*: The Military Motif in Propertius', *Latomus* 27, pp.322–49

Balsdon, J.P.V.D. (1979), *Romans and Aliens* (London)

Barber, E.W. (1994), *Women's Work: The First 20,000 Years – Women, Cloth and Society in Early Times* (New York)

Barnes, J. (1986), 'Ciceron et la Guerre Juste', *Bulletin de la Societe Francaise de Philosophie* 80, pp.41–81

Bartsch, S. (1988), 'Ars and the Man: The Politics of Art in Virgil's Aeneid', *Classical Philology* 93, pp.322–42

Basson, W.P. (1984), 'Virgil's Mezentius: A Pivotal Personality', *Acta Classica* 27, pp.57–70

Basson, W.P. (1988), 'Virgil's Camilla: A Paradoxical Character', *Acta Classica* 30

Bauman, R.A. (1993), 'The Rape of Lucretia: *quod metus causa* and the Criminal Law', *Latomus* 52, pp.550–66

Baynes, N.H. (1930), *Constantine the Great and the Christian Church* (London)

Beard, M. (1980), 'The Sexual Status of the Vestal Virgins', *Journal of Roman Studies*, pp.12–27

Beard, M. (1993), 'Looking (Harder) for Roman Myth: Dumézil, Declamation, and the Problems of Definition', in *Mythos in Mythenloser Gesellschaft: Das Paradigma Roms* (Stuttgart)

Beard, M.R. (1946), *Women as a Force in History: A Study in Tradition and Realities* (New York)

Becker, T.H. (1997), 'Ambiguity and the Female Warrior: Virgil's Camilla', *Electronic Antiquity* 4, www.scholar.lib.vt.edu/ejournals/ElAnt/V4N1/becker.html

Bell, Kimberly K. (2008), '"*Translatio*" and the Constructs of a Roman Nation in Virgil's "*Aeneid*"', *Rocky Mountain Review* 62 (1), pp.11–24

Bell, R.E. (1993), *Women of Classical Mythology: A Biographical Dictionary* (Oxford)

Bennett, F.M. (1912), *Religious Cults Associated with the Amazons*

Bergmann, F.G. (1853), *Les Amazones dans l'histoire et dans la fable*

Bisset, K.A. (1971), 'Who Were the Amazons?', *Greece & Rome* 18, pp.150–51

Block, E. (1984), *The Effects of Divine Manifestation on the Reader's Perspective in Vergil's Aeneid* (Salem, NH)

Blok, J.H. (tr. Peter Mason) (1995), *The Early Amazons: Modern and Ancient Perspectives on a Persistent Myth* (Leiden)

Bonfante, W.L. (1980), 'Roman Triumphs and Etruscan Kings', *Journal of Roman Studies* 60, pp.49–66

Bonfante, W.L. (1994), 'Etruscan Women', in Fantham, *Women in the Classical World*, pp.243–59

Boot, M. (2014), *Invisible Armies: An Epic History of Guerrilla Warfare from Ancient Times to the Present* (London)

Boyd, B.W. (1992), 'Virgil's Camilla and the Traditions of Catalogue and Ecphrasis', *AJPh* 113, pp.213–34

Bradshaw, A. (1978), 'Horace and the Therapeutic Myth: *Odes* 3.7; 3.11 and 3.27', *Hermes* 106 (1), pp.156–76.

Braund, David (ed.) (2003), *Myth, History, and Culture in Republican Rome: Studies in Honour of T.P. Wiseman* (Exeter)

Breed, B. (2010), 'Propertius on Not Writing about Civil Wars', in *Citizens of Discord: Rome and Its Civil Wars* (Oxford)

Bremmer, J.N. (1987), *Roman Myth and Mythography*, Bulletin Supplement (University of London, Institute of Classical Studies), No.52

Brown, R.D. (1995), 'Livy's Sabine Women and the Ideal of *concordia*', *Transactions of the American Philological Society* 125, pp.291–319

Brunt, P.A. (1962), 'The Army and the Land in the Roman Revolution', *Journal of Roman Studies* 52, pp.69–86

Brunt, P.A (1971), *Italian Manpower* Oxford

Bruun, P. (1975), *Studies in the Romanization of Etruria* (1975)

Bryson, N. (1986), 'Two Narratives of Rape in the Visual Arts: Lucretia and the Sabine Women', in S. Tomaselli, *Rape* (Oxford)

Bullock, A. (2004), 'Rape of Lucretia', in *Encyclopedia of Rape* (Westport), pp.193–94

Bullock, A. (2004), 'Rape of the Sabine Women', in *Encyclopedia of Rape* (Westport), pp.196–97

Burke, P.F. (1976), 'Virgil's Amata', *Vergilius* 22, pp.24–29

Burke, P. (1974), 'The Role of Mezentius in the "*Aeneid*"', *The Classical Journal* 69 (3), pp.202–09

Burckhardt, J. (1949), *The Age of Constantine the Great* (London)

Burkert, W. (1985), *Greek Religion* (Oxford)

Burkert, W. (1987), *Ancient Mystery Cults* (Cambridge, MA)

Burnell, P. (1987), 'The Death of Turnus and Roman Morality', *Greece & Rome* 34, pp.187–201

Cadotte, A. (2007), *La Romanisation Des Dieux: L'interpretatio Romana En Afrique Du Nord Sous Le Haut-Empire*

Cahoon, L. (1988), 'The Bed as Battlefield: Erotic Conquest and Military Metaphor in Ovid's *Amores*', Transactions of the American Philological Association 118, pp.293–307

Cairns, F. (1995), 'Horace, *Odes* 3.7: Elegy, Lyric, Myth, Learning, and Interpretation', in S.J. Harrison (ed.), Homage to Horace. A Bimillenary Celebration (Oxford), pp.65–99

Cameron, Alan (2004), *Greek Mythography in the Roman World* (Oxford)

Campbell, B. (2004), *Greek & Roman Military Writers* (London)

Campbell, B. (ed) (2013), *Oxford Handbook of Warfare in the Classical World* (Oxford)

Caradini, Andrea (2011), *Rome: Day One* (Princeton: Princeton University Press)

Carroll, Michael P. (1984), 'The Folkloric Origins of Modern "Animal-Parented Children" Stories', Journal of Folklore Research 21.1, pp.63–85

Cartledge, Paul (2020), *Thebes: The Forgotten City of Ancient Greece* (London)

Champanis, L.A. (2012), 'Female Changes: The Violation and Violence of Women in Ovid's *Metamorphoses*', MA thesis, Rhodes University

Chaplin, D. (2000), *Livy's Exemplary History* (Oxford)

Chaplin, D. (ed.) (2009), *Livy: Oxford Readings in Classical Studies* (Oxford)

Chiu, A. (2016), *Ovid's Women of the Year: Narratives of Roman Identity in the Fasti* (Ann Arbor)

Chrysanthou, Chrysanthos S. (2017), 'The Proems of Plutach's Lives and Historiography', Histos 11, pp.128–53

Chrystal, P. (2014), 'A Powerful Body of Women', Minerva, January–February 2014, pp.10–13

Chrystal, P. (2014), 'Roman Women Go to War', *Omnibus* 68, October 2014

Chrystal, P. (2014), *Women in Ancient Rome* (Stroud)

Chrystal, P. (2015), *Roman Women: The Women Who Influenced the History of Rome* (Stroud)

Chrystal, P. (2015), *Wars and Battles of the Roman Republic to 100 BCE* (Stroud)

Chrystal, P. (2016), *Roman Military Disasters: Dark Days and Lost Legions* (Barnsley)

Chrystal, P. (2017), *How to be a Roman* (Stroud)

Chrystal, P. (2017), *When in Rome ... A Sourcebook for Daily Life in Ancient Rome* (Stroud)

Chrystal, P. (2017), *Women at War in Ancient Greece & Rome* (Barnsley)

Chrystal. P. (2018), *Roman Record Keeping & Communications* (Stroud)

Chrystal, P. (2019), *Reportage from Ancient Greece & Rome* (Stroud)

Chrystal, P. (2019), *Republic into Empire: The Wars & Battles of the 1st Century BCE* (Barnsley)

Chrystal, P. (2019), 'Rome's Civil War: Julius Caesar vs the Senate', *All About History* 082, October 2019, pp.28–37

Chrystal. P. (2019), *The Romans in the North of England* (Darlington)

Chrystal, P. (2020), *War in Greek Myth*

Claassen, J.M. (1998), 'The Familiar Other: The Pivotal role of Women in Livy's Narrative of Political Development in Early Rome', *Acta Classica* 41, pp.71–104

Coleman, Robert (1982), 'The Gods in the *Aeneid*', *Greece and Rome* 29, pp.143–68

Cook, B.A. (ed.) (2006), *Women and War: A Historical Encyclopedia from Antiquity to the Present*, 2 Vols (Oxford)

Cooper, H.M. (ed.) (1989), *Arms and the Woman: War, Gender and Literary Representation* (Chapel Hill NC)

Cornell, T.J. (1995), *The Beginnings of Rome: Italy and Rome from the Bronze Age to the Punic Wars (c. 1000–264 BC)* (London)

Cornell, T.J. (1997), *Gender and Ethnicity in Ancient Italy* (London)

Courtney, E. (1988), 'Virgil's Military Catalogues and their Antecedents', *Vergilius* 34, pp.3–8

Cowan, R. (2009), *The Roman Conquests: Italy* (Barnsley)

Curran, L.C. (1972), 'Transformation and Anti-Augustanism in Ovid's "*Metamorphoses*"', *Arethusa* 5

Curran, L.C. (1978), 'Rape and Rape Victims in the *Metamorphoses*', *Arethusa* 11, pp.213–41

Curran, L.C. (1978), 'The Mythology of Rape', *CW* 72, pp.97–98

Darmon, J.P. (ed.) (1992), *The Powers of War: Athena and Ares in Greek Mythology* (trans. Danielle Beauvais)

David, J.M. (1997), *The Roman Conquest of Italy* (Oxford)

Dawson, D. (1997), *The Origins Of Western Warfare: Militarism and Morality In The Ancient World* (Boulder CO)

Deacy, S. (ed.) (2002), *Rape in Antiquity: Sexual Violence in the Greek and Roman Worlds* (London)

Deacy, S. (2013), 'From "flowery tales" to "heroic rapes": virginal subjectivity in the mythological meadow', *Arethusa* 46, pp.395–413

Delbrück, H. (1920), *Warfare in Antiquity: History of the Art of War*, Volume 1 (Lincoln NE)

Del Castillo, A. (1977), 'The Position of Women in the Augustan Age', LCM 2, pp.167–73

De Luce, J. (2005), 'Roman Myth', *The Classical World* 98(2), pp.202–05

DeRose Evans, J.(1992), *The Art of Persuasion: Political Propaganda from Aeneas to Brutus* (Princeton)

Dion, S. (1982), 'Women and Rape in Roman Law', in Christensen, E. (ed.), *Roman Law in Kønsroller, parforhold og samlivsformer. Rapport fra en seminarrækk* (Copenhagen)

Dixon, S. (1983), 'The Family Business: Women and Politics in the Late Republic', *C&M* 34, pp.91–112

Dixon, S. (2001), 'Rape in Roman Law and Myth', in S. Dixon (ed.), *Reading Roman Women* (London)

Dominik, W.J. (2009), 'Vergil's Geopolitics', in W.J. Dominik & J. Garthwaite (eds), *Writing Politics in Imperial Rome* (Leiden), pp.111–32

Donaldson, I. (1982), *The Rapes of Lucretia: A Myth and its Transformations* (Oxford)

Donlan, W. (1970), 'The Foundation Legends of Rome: An Example of Dynamic Process', *The Classical World* 64, pp.109–14

Doherty, L. (2001), *Gender and the Classicication of Classical Myth* (London)

Dougherty, C. (1988), 'Sowing the Seeds of Violence: Rape, Women and the Land', in Wyke, *Parchments of Gender*, pp.267–84

Dowden, K. (1997), 'The Amazons: Development and Function', *RhM* 140, pp.97–128

Downing, C. (1996), The Goddess: Mythological Images of the Feminine *(London)*

Du Bois, P. (1982), *Centaurs and Amazons: Women and the Pre-History of the Great Chain of Being* (Ann Arbor)

Duckworth, G. (1967), 'The Significance of Nisus and Euryalus for *Aeneid* IX–XII', The American Journal of Philology 88 (2), pp.129–50

Dumézil, G. (1968), 'Lua Mater' in Déesses latines et mythes védiques Bruxelles, pp.98–115

Dumézil, Georges (1996), *Archaic Roman Religion*, rev. ed., trans. Philip Krapp (Baltimore)

Dundes, A. (ed.) (1984), *Sacred Narrative: Readings in the History of Myth* (Berkeley)

Eadie, John W. (ed.) (1971), *The Conversion of Constantine* (New York)

Eden, P.T. (1964), 'Mezentius and the Etruscans in the *Aeneid*', *Proceedings of the Virgil Society* 4, pp.31–40

Edlund, I. (1981), 'The Archaeology of Rome and Latium in Virgil's *Aeneid*', *Vergilius* 27, pp.1–7

Edmunds, L. (2011), 'Epic and Myth', in *A Companion to Ancient Epic*, pp.31–44

Eliade, M. (1963), *Myth and Reality*, trans. W.R. Trask (New York)

Elliott, J. (2010), 'Ennius as Universal Historian: The Case of the Annales', *Historiae Mundi: Studies in Universal History*, ed. Peter Liddel (London), pp.148–61

Erskine, A. (2001), *Troy between Greece and Rome* (Oxford)

Evans, John Karl (1991), *War, Women and Children in Ancient Rome* (London)

Fabre-Serris, J. (ed.) (2015), *Women and War in Antiquity* (Baltimore)

Farrell, J. (2011), 'The Origins and Essence of Roman Epic', in *A Companion to Ancient Epic*, pp.417–28

Farrell, J. (2013), *Augustan Poetry and the Roman Republic* (Oxford)

Feeney, D.C. (1991), *The Gods in Epic: Poets and Critics of the Classical Tradition* (Oxford)

Feldherr, A. (ed.) (2009), *Cambridge Companion to the Roman Historians* (Cambridge)

Ferrill, A. (1997), *The Origins of War: From the Stone Age to Alexander the Great* (Boulder CO)

Fishwick, D. (1991), 'Ovid and Divus Augustus', *Classical Philology* 86, pp.36–41

Fletcher, K.F.B. (2008), 'Systematic Genealogies in Apollodorus' Bibliotheca and the Exclusion of Rome from Greek Myth', *Classical Antiquity* 27, pp.59–91

Flower, H.I. (ed.) (2004), *The Cambridge Companion to the Roman Republic* (Cambridge)

Foley, H. (2011), *A Companion to Ancient Epic* (Chichester)

Foley, H. (2011), 'Women in Ancient Epic', in Foley, *A Companion to Ancient Epic*, pp.105–18

Ford, M.C. (2004), *The Last King: Rome's Greatest Enemy* (New York)

Forsythe, G. (1999), *Livy and Early Rome* (Stuttgart)

Forsythe, G. (2005), *A Critical History of Early Rome: From Prehistory to the First Punic War*, Berkeley

Fox, M. (2011), 'The Myth of Rome', in Ken Dowden (ed.), *A Companion to Greek Mythology* (Chichester)

Frank, R. (1975), 'Augustus' Legislation on Marriage and Children', *California Studies in Classical Antiquity* 8, pp.41–52

Frank, T. (1927), 'Roman Historiography Before Caesar', *American Historical Review* 32, pp.232–40

Frier, Bruce W. (1979), '*Libri Annales Pontificum Maximorum*: The Origins of the Annalistic Tradition', *Papers & Monographs of the American Academy in Rome*, No. XXVII, Rome: American Academy, p.260

Gabba, E. (1981), 'True History and False History in Classical Antiquity', *Journal of Romans Studies* 61, pp.50–62

Gaisser, J. (1994), 'The Roman Odes at School: The Rise of the Imperial Horace', *The Classical World* 87 (5), pp.443–56

Galinsky, G.K. (1967), 'The Cipus Episode in Ovid's *Metamorphoses*', *Transactions and Proceedings of the American Philological Association* 98, pp.181–91

Gansiniec, Z. (1949), *Tarpeia: The Making of a Myth* (Wratislavia)

Garani, M. (2011), 'Revisiting Tarpeia's myth in Propertius (IV, 4)', *Leeds International Classical Studies*, https://www.academia.edu/1995576/Revisiting_Tarpeias_myth_in_Propertius_IV_4_

Gardner, Jane F. (1993), *Roman Myths: The Legendary Past* (Austin)

Garlan, Y. (1975), *War in the Ancient World* (London)

Garlick, B. (ed.) (1992), *Stereotypes of Women in Power* (New York)

Gartrell, A. (2015), 'Caesar's Castor – The Cult of the Dioscuri in Rome from the Mid-Republic to the Early Principate', Diss PhD, St Edmund Hall, Oxford

Gates, Charles (2013), 'Rome from its origins to the end of the Republic', *Ancient Cities: The Archaeology of Urban Life in the Ancient Near East and Egypt, Greece and Rome* (London), p.318

Gera, D.L. (1997), *Warrior Women: The Anonymous Tractatus De Mulieribus* (Leiden)

Gill, C. (ed.) (1993), *Lies and Fiction in the Ancient World* (Liverpool)

Girgis, S.F. (1991), 'Theban Legion', *The Coptic Encyclopedia*, Vol. 7 (London), p.9

Gjerstad, E., *Legends and Facts of Early Roman History* (Lund), pp.36–39

Glenn, J. (1971), 'Mezentius: *Contemptor Divum*', *Vergilius* 7, pp.7–8

Glenn, J. (1972), 'The Fall of Mezentius', *Vergilius* 18, pp.10–15

Goldberg, S.M. (2011), 'Early Republican Epic', in *A Companion to Ancient Epic*, pp.429–39

Gosselin, C.A. (1994), *Rape, Seduction and Love in Ovid's Metamorphoses* (Ann Arbor)

Graf, F. (1984), 'Women, War and Warlike Divinities', *ZPE* 55, pp.245–54

Grandazzi, Alexandre (1997), *The Foundation of Rome: Myth and History*, trans. Jane Marie Todd (Ithaca NY)

Grant, M. (1995), *Greek and Roman Historians: Information and Misinformation*

Grant de Pauw, L. (2000), *Battle Cries and Lullabies: Women in War from Prehistory to the Present* (Oklahoma)

Grebe, S. (2004), 'Augustus' Divine Authority and Vergil's "*Aeneid*"', *Vergilius* 50, pp.35–62

Griffith, J.G. (1968), 'Again the Shield of Achilles', *Proceedings of the Virgil Society* 7, pp.54–65

Grimal, P. (1951), 'Enée à Rome et le triomphe d'Octave', *REL* 53, pp.51–61

Grimal, P. (1975), 'Les "Odes romaines" d'Horace', *REL* 53, pp.135–56

Guy-Bray, Stephen (2001), 'Cowley's Latin Lovers: Nisus and Euryalus in the *Davideis*', *Classical and Modern Literature* 21, pp.25–42

Hall, Edith (2013), 'Pantomime: Visualising Myth in the Roman Empire', in *Performance in Greek and Roman Theatre*, ed. George Harrison (Leiden), pp.451–43

Hallett, J. (1971), 'Book IV: Propertius' *Recusatio* to Augustus and Augustan Ideals', Ph.D. diss., Harvard, pp.115–21

Halliday, W.R. (1924), 'Passing under the Yoke', *Folklore* 35, pp.93–95

Haniszewski, K. (2004), 'The *Origo Gentis Romanae* Origin of the Roman Race', Canisius College Translated Texts, Number 3 (Canisius College, Buffalo)

Hard, R. (1997), *Apollodorus: The Library of Greek Mythology*, Oxford

Hard, R. (2004), *The Routledge Handbook of Greek Mythology* (London)

Hardie, P.R. (2014), *The Last Trojan Hero: A Cultural History of Virgil's Aeneid* (London)

Hardwick, L. (1990), 'Ancient-Amazon Heroes: Outsiders or Women?', *Greece & Rome* 37, pp.14–36

Harris, S.L. (2003), *Classical Mythology: Images and Insights* (Boston)

Harris, W.V. (1979), *War and Imperialism in Republican Rome*

Harrison, S.J. (1988), 'Virgil as a Poet of War', *Proceedings of the Virgil Society* 19, pp.48–68

Harrison, S.J. (2005), 'Hercules and Augustus in Propertius 4.9', *PLLS* 12, pp.117–32

Hawes, G. (2014), *Rationalizing Myth in Antiquity* (Oxford)

Hawkes, C. (ed.) (1973), *Greeks, Celts and Romans: Studies in Venture and Resistance* (London)

Hejduk, J.D. (2011), 'Epic Rapes in the Fasti', Classical Philology 106, pp.20–31

Hemker, J. (1985), 'Rape and the Founding of Rome', *Helios* 12, pp.41–47

Herbert-Brown, G. (1994), *Ovid and the Fasti: An Historical Study* (Oxford)

Heslin, P. (2018), *Propertius, Greek Myth and Virgil: Rivalry, Allegory and Polemic* (Oxford)

Higbie, Carolyn (2007), 'Hellenistic Mythograpers', in *The Cambridge Companion to Greek Mythology* ed. Woodard (Cambridge)

Hogg, O.F. (1968), *Clubs to Cannon: Warfare and Weapons Before the Introduction of Gunpowder* (London)

Holloway, R.R. (1996), *The Archaeology of Early Rome and Latium*

Holmes, R. (2004), *Acts of War: The Behaviour of Men in Battle* (London)

Horsfall, N. (1987), '*Non Viribus Aequis*: Some Problems in Virgil's Battle-Scenes', *Greece & Rome* 34, pp.48–55

Humphries, Mark (2002), 'In Mommsen's Shade: Roman Historiography, Past and Present', *Classics Ireland* 9, pp.28–45

Indick, William (2004), 'Classical Heroes in Modern Movies: Mythological Patterns of the Superhero', *Journal of Media Psychology* 9 (3), pp.93–95

Jaeger, M. (1995), *Livy's Written Rome* (Ann Arbor)

James, S.L. (2012), *Companion to Women in the Ancient World* (Chichester)

Jameson, M. (1991), 'Sacrifice Before Battle', in V. Hanson (ed.), *Hoplites*, p.220

Janan, M., (1999), '"Beyond Good and Evil": Tarpeia and Philosophy in the Feminine', *The Classical World* 92, No. 5, Power, Politics, & Discourse in Augustan Elegy, pp.429–43

Janssen, L.F. (1981), 'Some Unexplored Aspects of devotio Deciana', *Mnemosyne*, pp.357–81

Jed, S. (1989), *Chaste Thinking: The Rape of Lucretia and the Birth of Humanism* (Bloomington)

Jestice, P.G. (2006), 'Greek Women and War in Antiquity', in Cook, *Women and War*, pp.256–58

Jones, D.E. (1997), *Women Warriors: A History* (Washington)

Jones, H.P. (1918), 'Usages of Ancient Warfare', *Edinburgh Review*, January 1918

Joplin, P.K. (1990), 'Ritual Work on Human Flesh: Livy's Lucretia and the Rape of the Body Politic', *Helios* 17, pp.51–70

Joshel, S.R. (1992), 'The Body Female and the Body Politic: Livy's Lucretia and Verginia', in Richlin, *Pornography*, pp.112–30

Keaveney, A. (1987), *Rome and the Unification of Italy* (Liverpool)

Keegan, J. (1993), *A History of Warfare* (London)

Keith, A. (2002), 'Ovid on Vergilian War Narrative', *Vergilius* 48, pp.105–22

Kenens, U. (2011), 'The Sources of Ps.-Apollodorus' Library: A Case Study', *Quaderni Urbinati di Cultura Classica* 97, p.129–46

Kenens, U. (2013), 'Text and Transmission of Ps.-Apollodorus' Bibliotheca: Avenues for Future Research', in *Writing Myth: Mythography in the Ancient World*, ed. S.M. Trzaskoma (Leuven), pp.95–114

Kern, P.B. (1999), *Ancient Siege Warfare* (London)

Kirk, G.S. (1973), *Myth: Its Meaning and Functions in Ancient and Other Cultures* (London)

Knapp, B.L., 'Women in Myth', *Helios* 33

Knapp, B.L. (1977), 'Virgil's *Aeneid*: Let us Sing of Arms and Women: Dido and Camilla', in Knapp, *Women in Myth* (New York)

Koortbojian, M. (2013), *The Divinization of Caesar and Augustus* (Cambridge)

Kraus, Christina Shuttleworth (1997), *Latin Historians* (Oxford)

Kraus, Christina Shuttleworth (ed.) (2010), *Ancient Historiography and its Contexts: Studies in Honour of A.J. Woodman* (Oxford)

Lada-Richards, Ismene (2006), 'Cum Femina Primum …': Venus, Vulcan, and the Politics of Male Mollitia in *Aeneid* 8', *Helios* 33

Laing, G.J. (1910), 'The Legend of the Trojan Settlement in Latium', *Classical Journal* 6, p.55

Laqueur, W. (1977), *Guerrilla Warfare: A Historical & Critical Study* (London)

Laroche, R.A. (1982), 'The Alban King-List in Dionysius I, 70–71: A Numerical Analysis', *Historia: Zeitschrift für Alte Geschichte* 31, pp.112–20

Lauriola, R. (2013), 'Teaching About the Rape of Lucretia', *Classical World* 106, pp.682–87

Lee, A.G. (1953), 'Ovid's Lucretia', *Greece and Rome* 22, pp.107–18

Lee, W.E. (2011), *Warfare and Culture in World History* (New York)

Leeming, D.A. (2001), 'Myth and Therapy', *Journal of Religion and Health* 40, pp.115–19

Leitao, D.D. (2014), 'Sexuality in Greek and Roman Military Contexts', in Hubbard, *Companion to Greek and Roman Sexualities*, pp.230–43

Levene, David S. (ed.) (2002), *Clio and the Poets: Augustan Poetry and the Traditions of Ancient Historiography* (Leiden)

Levithan, J. (2013), *Roman Siege Warfare* (Ann Arbor)

Lintott, Andrew (2010), *The Romans in the Age of Augustus* (Chichester)

Lissarrague, F. (2015), 'Women Arming Men: Armor and Jewelry', in J. Fabre-Serris (ed.), *Women and War in Antiquity*, pp.71–81

Litchfield, H.W. (1914), 'National Examples of *virtus* in Roman Literature', *HSCPh* 25, pp.1–71

Little, D.A. (1972), 'The Non-Augustanism of Ovid's "*Metamorphoses*"', *Mnemosyne* 25, pp.389–401

Little, D.A. (1976), *Ovid's Eulogy of Augustus, Metamorphoses 15.851–70*

Lloyd, R.B. (1957), '*Aeneid* III and the Aeneas Legend', *AJP* 78, pp.382–400

Louden, B. (2006), 'Aeneas in the Iliad: the One Just Man', 102nd Annual Meeting of CAMWS, Classical Association of the Middle West and South

Louden, B. (2011), 'The Gods in Epic, or the Divine Economy', in *A Companion to Ancient Epic*, pp.90–104

Luce, T.J. (1990), *Livy, Augustus and the Forum Augustum*

Lund, A.A. (2007), 'About interpretatio Romana in the "Germanic" of Tacitus', *Zeitschrift für Religions- und Geistesgeschichte* 59, pp.289–310

Lyne, R.O.A.M. (1983), 'Virgil and the Politics of War', *Classical Quarterly* 33, pp.193–203

Lynn, J.A. (2003), *Battle: A History of Combat from Ancient Greece to Modern America* (Boulder CO)

Lynch, E.W. (1971), 'The Blindness of Mezentius', *Arethusa* 4, pp.83–89

MacL. Currie, H. (1998), 'Virgil and the Military Tradition', *Proceedings of the Virgil Society* 23, pp.177, 192

Mader, G.J. (1987), 'Poetry and politics in Horace's first Roman Ode: A reconsideration', *AClass* 30, pp.11–30

Mader, G.J. (1989), 'Propertius 4.6.45–52: Poetry and Propaganda', *Wiener Studien* 102, pp.141–47

Makowski, John F. (1989), 'Nisus and Euryalus: A Platonic Relationship', *The Classical Journal* 85.1, pp.1–15

Man, J. (2017), *Searching for the Amazons: The Real Warrior Women of the Ancient World*

Marache R. (1956), 'Le mythe dans les Odes d'Horace', *Pallas* 4, pp.59–66

Mason, M.K., *Annotated bibliography of Women in Classical Mythology*, www.moyak.com/papers/women-classical-mythology.html

Mathes, M.M. (2000), *The Rape of Lucretia: Readings in Livy, Machiavelli and Rousseau* (University Park PA)

Mayor, A. (2014), *The Amazons: Lives and Legends of Warrior Women across the Ancient World* (Princeton)

Mazzoni, Cristina (2010), *She-Wolf: The Story of a Roman Icon* (Cambridge)

McClellan, A.M. (2019), *Abused Bodies in Roman Epic* (Cambridge).

McCune, B.C., 'Horace's Mythological Lexicon: Repeated Myths and Meaning in Odes 1–3', dissertation presented to the Graduate Faculty of the University of Virginia for the Degree of Doctor of Philosophy

McDonald, A.H. (1975), 'Theme and Style in Roman Historiography', *Journal of Roman Studies* 65, pp.1–10

McDonnell, M. (2006), *Roman Manliness: Virtus and the Roman Republic* (Cambridge)

McDougall, I. (1990), 'Livy and Etruscan Women', *Ancient History Bulletin* 4, pp.24–30

McIntyre, G. (ed.) (2019), *Uncovering Anna Perenna: A Focused Study of Roman Myth and Culture*

McNeill, W. (1986), 'Mythistory, or Truth, Myth, History, and Historians', *The American Historical Review* 91 (1), pp.1–10

Mehl, Andreas (2011), *Roman Historiography: An Introduction to its Basic Aspects and Development*, trans. Hans-Friedrich Mueller (Chichester)

Meletinsky, E.M. (2014), The Poetics of Myth *(London)*

Melichoff, V.A. (1914), *'The Role of Ovid in the History of the Cult of Emperors',* *ГЕРМЕС VII, pp.299–308 (in Russian)*

Mendelsohn, Daniel, '"Epic Fail?" Is the Aeneid a Celebration of Empire – or a Critique?', *New Yorker*, 15 October 2018, https://www.newyorker.com/magazine/2018/10/15/is-the-aeneid-a-celebration-of-empire-or-a-critique

Michalopoulos, D. (2016), *Homer's Odyssey beyond the myths* (Piraeus: Institute of Hellenic Maritime History)

Miles, G.B. (1997), *Livy: Reconstructing Early Rome* (New York)

Miles, G.B. (1997), 'The First Roman Marriage and the Theft of the Sabine Women', in *Livy: Reconstructing Early Rome*

Miller, Paul Allen (2013), 'Mythology and the Abject in Imperial Satire', in *Classical Myth and Psychoanalysis: Ancient and Modern Stories of the Self*, ed. Vanda Zajko (Oxford), pp.213–30

Milnor, K. (2009), 'Women in Roman Historiography', in Feldherr, *Cambridge Companion*, pp.276–87

Mitchell, R. (1991), 'The Violence of Virginity in the *Aeneid*', *Arethusa* 24, pp.219–38

Mommsen, T., *History of Rome* (London, 2014 repr.)

Montagu, J.D. (2000), *Battles of the Greek and Roman Worlds* (London)

Montagu, J.D. (2006), *Greek and Roman Warfare: Battles, Tactics and Trickery* (London)

Monti, R.C. (1981), *The Dido Episode and the Aeneid: Roman Social and Political Values in the Epic*

Moore, M.K. (1930), 'The Divine Mythology of Horace', *Transactions of the American Philological Society*, p.61

Moore, Nicole (2017), 'Virgil's *Aeneid*: Subversive Interpretation in the Commissioned Epic', *Conspectus Borealis* 2

Morwood, James (1991), 'Aeneas, Augustus, and the Theme of the City, *Greece & Rome* 38, pp.212–23.

Morwood, J. (1998), 'Virgil's Pious Man and Menenius Agrippa: A Note on "*Aeneid*" 1.148–53', Greece & Rome 45, pp.195–98

Moses, D. (1993), 'Livy's Lucretia and the Validity of Coerced Consent in Roman Law', in Laiou, *Consent and Coercion to Sex and Marriage in Ancient and Medieval Societies* (Dunbarton Oaks)

Moulton, Carroll (1973), 'Ovid as Anti-Augustan: Met. 15.843–79', *The Classical World* vol. 67, no. 1, pp.4–7

Murgatroyd, P. (2000), 'Plotting in Ovidian Rape Narratives', *Eranos* 98, pp.75–92

Murgatroyd, P. (2002), 'The Rape Attempts on Lotis and Vesta', *Classical Quarterly* 52, pp.622–24

Murgatroyd, P. (2005), *Mythical and Legendary Narrative in Ovid's Fasti* (Leiden)

Murray, W. (2012), *Hybrid Warfare: Fighting Complex Opponents from the Ancient World to the Present* (Cambridge)

Mustakallio, K. (1999), 'Legendary Women and Female Groups in Livy', in Setala, *Female Networks*, pp.53–64

Nagy, G. (2011), 'The Epic Hero', in *A Companion to Ancient Epic*, pp.71–89

Neel, Jaclyn (2017), *Early Rome: Myth and Society: A Sourcebook* (Hoboken NJ)

Newark, T. (1989), *Women Warlords: An Illustrated History of Female Warriors* (London)

Newby, Zahra (2012), 'The Aesthetics of Violence: Myth and Danger in Roman Domestic Landscapes', *Classical Antiquity* 31, pp.349–89.

Newlands, Carole Elizabeth (1995), *Playing with Time: Ovid and the Fasti* (Ithaca)

Newman, J.K. (1967), *Augustus and the New Poetry* (Brussels: Latomus)

Newman, J.K. (1997), *Augustan Propertius: The Recapitulation of a Genre* (Hildesheim)

Nguyen, N.L. (2007), 'Roman Rape: An Overview of Roman Rape Laws from the Republican Period to Justinian's Reign', *Michigan Journal of Gender and Law* 13, pp.75–112

Nisbet, R.G.M., 'Aeneas Imperator: Roman Generalship in an Epic Context', *Proceedings of the Virgil Society* 17, pp.50–61

Noonan, J.D. (1990), 'Livy 1.9.6. The Rape at the Consualia', *Classical World* 83, pp.493–501

Noonan, J.D. (2006), 'Mettius Fufetius in Livy', *Classical Antiquity* 25 (2), pp.327–49

Oakley, S.P. (1985), 'Single Combat and the Roman Republic', *Classical Quarterly* 35, pp.39–410

Oakley, S.P. (1993), 'The Roman Conquest of Italy', in J. Rich (ed.), *War and Society in the Ancient World*, pp.9–37

Oakley, S. P. (1997), *A Commentary on Livy Books VI–X*, Volume 1, Introduction and Book VI (Oxford)

Oakley, S.P. (1998), *A Commentary on Livy Books VI–X*, Volume 2, Books VII–VII (Oxford)

Ogden, D. (2013), *Dragons, Serpents, and Slayers in the Classical and Early Christian Worlds: A sourcebook* (Oxford)

Ogden, D. (2013), *Drakon: Dragon Myth and Serpent Cult in the Greek and Roman Worlds* (Oxford)

Ogilvie, R.M. (1960), *Livy: The Early History of Rome* (Harmonsdsworth)

Ogilvie, R.M. (1965), *A Commentary on Livy Books 1–5* (Oxford)

Ogilvie, R.M. (1974), *The Romans and their Gods in the Age of Augustus* (London)

Ogilvie, R.M. (1976), *Early Rome and the Etruscans* (Glasgow)

Ogilvie, R.M. (1980), *Roman Literature and Society* (Harmondsworth)

O'Neill, K. (1995), 'Propertius 4.4: Tarpeia and the Burden of Aetiology', *Hermathena* (158), pp.53–60.

O'Reilly, D.F. (1978), 'The Theban Legion of St Maurice', *Vigiliae Christianae* Vol. 32, No. 3

O'Reilly, D.F. (2011), *The Lost Legion Rediscovered* (Barnsley)

Otis, B. (1938), 'Ovid and the Augustans', *Transactions and Proceedings of the American Philological Association* 69, pp.188–229.

Otterbein, K.F. (2004), *How War Began* (College Station TX)

Pais, E. (1906), *Ancient Legends of Roman History* (London)

Parker, H.N. (2004), 'Why Were the Vestal Virgins?', *AJP* 125, pp.563–601

Payen, P. (2015), 'Women's Wars, Censored Wars?', in J. Fabre-Serris, (ed.), *Women and War in Antiquity*, pp.214–27

Peddie, J. (1994), *The Roman War Machine*, Gloucester

Peel, M. (ed.) (2004), *Rape as a Method of Torture*, London

Pelling, C.B.R. (2002), 'Making myth look like history: Plutarch's Theseus–Romulus', in *Plutarch and History* (London), pp.171–95

Pennington, R. (ed.) (2003), *Amazons to Fighter Pilots: A Biographical Dictionary of Military Women* (London)

Penwill, J.L. (2014), *Reading Aeneas's Shield*, https://classicsvic.files.wordpress.com/2014/01/penwillvol18.pdf

Pfuntner, Laura (2017), 'Death and Birth in the Urban Landscape: Strabo on Troy and Rome', *Classical Antiquity* 36.1, pp.33–51

Phillipides, S.N. (1983), 'Narrative Strategies and Ideology in Livy's "Rape of Lucretia"', *Helios* 10, pp.113–19

Phillips, E.D. (1953), 'Odysseus in Italy', *Journal of Hellenic Studies* 73, pp.53–67

Pintabone, D.T. (1998), *Women and the Unspeakable: Rape in Ovid's Metamorphoses* (Ann Arbor)

Platt, V. (2018), 'Double Vision: Epiphanies of the Dioscuri in Classical Antiquity', *Archiv für Religionsgeschichte* 20.1, pp.229–56

Pollini, J. (1990), 'Man or God: Divine Assimilation and Imitation in the Late Republic and Early Principate', in K.A. Raaflaub (ed.), *Between Republic and Empire: Interpretations of Augustus and His Principate* (Berkeley), pp.333–63

Pope, K. (1998), *The Trojan Origin Theme in Book 1 of Virgil's Aeneid*, http://ancientroadpublications.com/Studies/AncientLanguage/TrojanOrigins.pdf

Poulsen, B. (1991), 'The Dioscuri and ruler ideology', *SO* 66, pp.119–46

Powell, A. (ed.) (1992), *Roman Poetry and Propaganda in the Age of Augustus*, Bristol

Powers, D. (ed.) (2013), *Irregular Warfare in the Ancient World* (Chicago)

Putnam, Michael C.J. (1986), *Artifices of Eternity: Horace's Fourth Book of Odes* (Ithaca, NY: Cornell University Press)

Quinn, K. (1981), 'Poet and audience in the Augustan Age', *ANRW* 2.30.1, pp.75–180

Quint, David (1993), *Epic and Empire: Politics and Generic Form from Virgil to Milton* (Princeton)

Raaflaub, Kurt A. (1986), *Social Struggles in Archaic Rome: New Perspectives on the Conflict of the Orders* (Berkeley)

Raaflaub, Kurt A. (2011), 'Epic and History', in *A Companion to Ancient Epic*, pp.55–70

Rahner, H. (1971), *Greek Myths and Christian Mystery* (Biblo & Tannen Publishers)

Ramsby, T. (2010), 'Juxtaposing Dido and Camilla in the *Aeneid*', *The Classical Outlook* 88, pp.13–17

Richlin, A. (1992), 'Reading Ovid's Rapes', in A. Richlin (ed.), *Pornography and Representation in Greece and Rome* (Oxford), pp.158–79

Ridgway, D. (ed.) (1979), *Italy Before the Romans* (Edinburgh)

Robinson, V. (ed.) (1943), *Morals In Wartime* (New York)

Rodgers, W. (2004), 'Exemplarity in Roman Culture: The Case of Horaius Cocles and Cloelia', *CPh* 99, pp.1–56

Rodríguez Mayorgas, Ana (2010), 'Romulus, Aeneas and the Cultural Memory of the Roman Republic', *Athenaeum* 98 (1), pp.89–109

Roller, Matthew (2009), 'The Exemplary Past in Roman Historiography and Culture', in Andrew Feldherr (ed.), *The Cambridge Companion to the Roman Historians* (Cambridge), pp.214–30

Ross, D.O. (1975), *Backgrounds to Augustan Poetry: Gallus, Elegy and Rome* (Cambridge)

Rothman, J. (2014), 'The Real Amazons', *The New Yorker*, 17 October 2014

Rothwell, K.S. Jr (1996), 'Propertius on the site of Rome', *Latomus* 55 (4), pp.829–54

Rousseau, P. (2015), 'War, Speech and the Bow are Not Women's Business', in J. Fabre-Serris (ed.), *Women and War in Antiquity*, pp.16–33

Rudd, N. (1986), 'The Idea of Empire in the *Aeneid*', in *Virgil in a Cultural Tradition*, pp.25–42

Rutledge, H. (1964), 'Propertius' "Tarpeia": The Poem Itself', *The Classical Journal* 60 (2), pp.68–73

Rutter, J.B. (2004), 'Troy VII and the Historicity of the Trojan War', http:// www.dartmouth.edu/~prehistory/aegean/?page_id=630#L27Top

Saddington, D.B. (1999), 'Roman soldiers, local gods and *interpretatio Romana* in Roman Germany', *Acta Classica* 42, pp.155–69

Saggs, H.W.F. (1989), *Civilisation Before Greece and Rome* (London)

Salmon, E.T. (1953), 'Rome and the Latins', *Phoenix* 7, pp.93–104, 123–55

Salmon, E.T. (1967), *Samnium and the Samnites* (Cambridge)

Salmon, E.T. (1969), *Roman Colonization under the Republic* (London)

Salmon, E.T. (1982), *The Making of Roman Italy* (London)

Salmonson, J.A. (1991), *The Encyclopedia of Amazons* (London)

Sanders H.A. (1903), *The Myth about Tarpeia in Roman Historical Sources and Institutions*, Volume 1 of Studies: Humanistic series (University of Michigan), pp.1–47

Santirocco, M. (1995), 'Horace and Augustan ideology', *Arethusa* 28.2–3, pp.225–43

Schenker, D. (1992), 'Poetic Voices in Horace's Roman Odes', *The Classical Journal* 88 (2), pp.147–66

Schultze, C.E. (1995), 'Dionysius of Halicarnassus and Roman Chronology', *Cambridge Classical Journal* 41, pp.192–214

Scott, K. (1930), 'Emperor Worship in Ovid', *Transactions of the American Philological Society* 61, pp.43–69

Scullard, H.H. (1981), *Festivals and Ceremonies of the Roman Republic* (London)

Seager, R. (1980), '"Neu sinas Medos equitare inultos": Horace, the Parthians and Augustan foreign policy', *Athenaeum* 58, pp.103–18

Seager, R. (1993), 'Horace and Augustus: Poetry and Policy', in N. Rudd (ed.) *Horace 2000: A Celebration* (Ann Arbor), pp.41–63

Segal, C. (1969), *'Myth and Philosophy in the Metamorphoses: Ovid's Augustanism and the Augustan Conclusion of Book XV'*, *The American Journal of Philology* 90 (3), pp.257–92

Segal, R. (2015), *Myth: A Very Short Introduction (Oxford)*

Shapiro, H.A. (1983), 'Amazons, Thracians and Scythians', *GRBS* 24, pp.105–14

Sharrock, A. (2015), 'Warrior Women in Roman Epic', in J. Fabre-Serris (ed.), *Women and War in Antiquity*, pp.157–78

Siefert, R. (1992), 'Rape in Wars: Analytical Approaches', *Minerva – Quarterly Report on Women and the Military* 11, pp.17–22

Slayman, Andrew (2007), 'Fact or Legend? Debate Over the Origins of Rome – Were Romulus and Remus Historical Figures?', *Archaeology* 60.4, pp.22–27

Small, J.P. (1976), 'The Death of Lucretia', *American Journal of Archaeology* 80, pp.349–60

Smethurst, S.E. (1950), 'Women in Livy's "History"', *Greece and Rome* 19, pp.80–87

Smith, Christopher (2007), 'The Religion of Archaic Rome', in *A Companion to Roman Religion* (Oxford)

Smith, R., 'The Rape of the Sabine Women: Present at an Empire's Corrupted Birth', *New York Times*, 21 February 2007

Sobol, D. (1973), *The Amazons of Greek Mythology* (Cranbury NJ)

Solmsen, F. (1962), 'Tibullus as an Augustan Poet', *Hermes* 90, pp.295–325

Spaulding, O.A. (1933), 'The Ancient Military Writers', *CJ* 28, pp.657–69

Stahl, H.P. (1985), *Propertius: 'Love' and 'War': Individual and State under Augustus* (Berkeley)

Starr, C. (1955), 'Virgil's Acceptance of Octavian', *AJP* 76, pp.34–46

Starr, C. (1969), 'Horace and Augustus', *The American Journal of Philology* 90 (1), pp.58–64

Stehle, E. (1989), *Venus, Cybele and the Sabine Women: The Roman Construction of Female Sexuality in Scafuro*, pp.43–64

Stirrup, B.E. (1977), 'Techniques of Rape: Variety and Art in Ovid's Metamorphoses', *Greece and Rome* 24, pp.170–84

Sullivan, J.P. (1976), *Propertius: A Critical Introduction* (Cambridge)

Sullivan, J.P. (1984), 'Propertius Book IV: Themes and Structures', *Illinois Classical Studies* 9 (1), pp.30–34

Suzuki, M. (1989), *Metamorphoses of Helen: Authority, Difference, and the Epic* (Ithaca)

Syme, R. (1978), *History in Ovid* (Oxford)

Syndikus, Hans Peter (2010), 'The Roman Odes', in Gregson Davis (ed.), *A Companion to Horace* (Chichester), pp.193–209

Tacaks, S. (2008), *Vestal Virgins, Sibyls, and Matrons* (Austin TX)

Tennant, P.M.W. (1988), 'The Lupercalia and the Romulus and Remus Legend', *Acta Classica* 31, pp.81–93

Thom, S. (2012), 'Myth as Historic Benchmark in Horace Odes 3:1–6', *Akroterion* 51

Thom, S., 'Lyric Double Talk in Horace's Roman Odes', *Akroterion* 43, file:///C:/Users/Paul/Downloads/183-335-1-PB%20(1).pdf

Tracy, S. (1987), 'Laocoon's Guilt', *The American Journal of Philology* 108 (3), pp.451–54

Usher, Stephen (1970), *The Historians of Greece and Rome* (New York)

Van Berchem, Denis (1956), *The Martyrdom of the Theban Legion* (Basel)

Vikman, E. (2005), 'Ancient Origins: Sexual Violence in Warfare, Part I', *Anthropology & Medicine* 12 (1), pp.21–31

Vivante, B. (2006), *Daughters of Gaia: Women in the Ancient Mediterranean World* (Westport CT)

Walcot, P. (1991), 'On Widows and their Reputation in Antiquity', *SO* 66, pp.5–26

Walker, Henry J. (2015), *The Twin Horse Gods: The Dioskouroi in Mythologies of the Ancient World* (London)

Walker, S. (1981), *The Image of Augustus* (London)

Walsh, P.G. (1961), *Livy: His Historical Aims and Methods* (Cambridge)

Walters, J. (1997), 'Invading the Roman Body', in J.P. Hallet (ed.), *Roman Sexualities* (Princeton), pp.29–43

Warde Fowler, W. (1913), 'Passing Under the Yoke', *Classical Review* 27, pp.48–51

Warnock, J.D. (1921), 'The Parable of Menenius Agrippa', *The Classical Weekly* 14 (17), pp.130–33

Wasinski, V.M. (2004), 'Women, War and Rape: The Hidden Casualties of Conflict', diss., University of Leeds

Weiden Boyd, B. (1992), 'Virgil's Camilla and the Traditions of Catalogue and Ecphrasis', *AJP* 113, pp.213–34

Weiss, Peter (2003), 'The Vision of Constantine', trans. A.R. Birley, in *Journal of Roman Archaeology* 16, pp.237–59

Welch, T. (2012), 'Perspectives On and Of Livy's Tarpeia', *Journal on Gender Studies in Antiquity*

Welch, T. (2016), *Tarpeia: Workings of a Roman Myth* (Ohio State University Press)

Welch, T.S. (2005), *The Elegiac Cityscape. Propertius and the Meaning of Roman Monuments* (Columbus OH)

Wellesley, K. (1969), 'Propertius' Tarpeia Poem (IV,4)', *Acta Classica*, pp.93–103

West, D.A. (1976), '*Cernere erat* – the Shield of Achilles', *Proceedings of the Virgil Society* 15

West, G.S. (1975), 'Women in Virgil's *Aeneid*', diss. UCLA

West, G.S. (1979), 'Vergil's Helpful Sisters: Anna and Juturna in the *Aeneid*', *Vergilius* 25, pp.10–19

West, G.S. (1985), 'Chloreus and Camilla', *Vergilius* 31, pp.23–25

Wheelwright, J. (1989), *Amazons and Military Maids* (London)

White, P. (1993), *Promised verse: Poets in the society of Augustan Rome* (Cambridge MA)

Wilhelm, H. (1987), 'Venus, Diana, Dido and Camilla in the *Aeneid*', *Vergilius* 33, pp.225–26

Williams, Gordon (1996), 'Virgilian Studies', *The Classical Journal* 92, pp.185–89

Williams, R.D. (1978), 'Virgil and Rome', *Proceedings of the Virgil Society* 17, pp.1–9

Williams, R.D. (1981), 'The Shield of Achilles', *Vergilius* 27, pp.8–11

Winterbottom, M. (1993), 'Aeneas and the Idea of Troy', *Proceedings of the Virgil Society* 21, pp.17–34

Wiseman, T.P. (1979), *Clio's Cosmetics* (Leicester)

Wiseman, T.P. (1983), 'The Wife and Children of Romulus', *Classical Quarterly* 33, pp.445–52

Wiseman, T.P. (1987), 'The Credibility of the Roman Annalists', in *Roman Studies: Literary and Historical* (Liverpool), pp.293–96

Wiseman, T.P. (1993), 'Lying Historians – Seven Types of Mendacity', in Gill, *Lies and Fiction in the Ancient World*

Wiseman, T.P. (1993), 'The She-wolf Mirror: an Interpretation', *PBSR* 61, pp.1–6

Wiseman, T.P. (1995), *Remus: A Roman Myth* (Cambridge)

Wiseman, T.P. (1996), 'What do we Know about Early Rome?', *Journal of Roman Archaeology* 9, pp.310–15

Wiseman, T.P. (1997), 'The She-wolf Mirror (Again)', *Ostraka* 6, pp.441–43

Wiseman, T.P. (1998), *Roman Drama and Roman History* (Exeter)

Wiseman, T.P. (1998), 'Roman Republic, Year One', *Greece & Rome* 45, pp.19–26

Wiseman, T.P. (2004), *The Myths of Rome* (Exeter)

Witke, C. (1983), *Horace's Roman Odes: a critical examination* (Leiden)

Wood, M. (1985), *In Search of the Trojan War* (London)

Woodard, R.D. (ed.) (2007), The Cambridge Companion to Greek Mythology (Cambridge)

Woodard, R.D. (2013), *Myth, Ritual, and the Warrior in Roman and Indo-European Antiquity* (Cambridge)

Woodman, A.J. (1989), 'Virgil the Historian: *Aeneid* 8.626–662 and Livy', in J. Diggle (ed.), *Studies in Latin literature and its tradition: in honour of C.O.Brink* (Cambridge Philological Society, Cambridge), pp.132–45

Woods, David (1994), 'The Origin of the Legend of Maurice and the Theban Legion', *Journal of Ecclesiastical History* 45, pp.385–95

Worsfold, T.C. (1934), *The History of the Vestal Virgins of Rome* (London)

Zaidman, L.B. (2015), 'Women and War: From the Theban Cycle to Greek Tragedy', in J. Fabre-Serris (ed.), *Women and War in Antiquity*, pp.82–99

Zanker, P. (1988), *The Power of Images in the Age of Augustus* (Ann Arbor)

Index

Romulus and Remus, xiii, xvii, 10, 42,
    78–9, 84–6
    Foundation Myth, 76ff, 83ff, 86

Sabines, xiv, 5, 29, 32, 91, 93–4, 95, 106,
    116, 148, 154, 161
Sabine women, xiv–xv, 9, 29, 35, 50, 69,
    91–5, 98, 105–106, 115–16, 148, 156,
    171
Shield of Aeneas, 69–70, 76
Sibyl of Cumae, the, 65, 67, 120, 134,
    136, 150, 158
Siena, xiii, 79
Sinon, xii, 134, 136
Social media, ancient, 6
Statius, *Thebaid*, 15, 25, 49, 123, 125–8
Strabo, 42, 79–80

Tabula Pontificum, 6
Tacitus, *Germania*, 2, 33, 46–8
Tarpeia, 94, 105–106, 108–109, 115–16,
    119, 146–8, 150–1, 161, 165, 167
Theban Legion Massacre, xvi, 174–6, 182
Trajan's Column, xx
Troy, xii, xix, 7–8, 10, 18, 38, 40–3, 45–6,
    49, 52–65, 76–7, 79, 81, 92, 103, 111,
    121, 132, 134, 136, 139, 141, 146–7,
    151, 154–7, 160–2, 167, 171, 181,
    184–5
    flight from, xii, 41, 157
    sacking of, xii, 55, 155–7

Tullia, xvi, 98, 172–3
Turnus, 16, 18–19, 34, 40, 49, 52, 67–8,
    70–6, 120, 122, 132–3, 158–60, 172
    death of, xiii

Verginia, xv, 34, 92, 102–104, 116, 120,
    126
Vica Pota, 27
Victoria, xx, 27, 88
Virgil, xii–xiii, xvi, xviii–xx, 8–9, 16,
    18–19, 32, 35, 40–1, 43–4, 46, 49–51,
    55, 57–65, 67–9, 72–4, 76–8, 80,
    118–19, 121, 131–4, 137, 139, 143, 152,
    154, 156, 160, 169, 172, 181, 186–8,
    200, 202 n.1
    and Augustus, 43–4
    reading the Aeneid, xvi
Virtus, 17–18, 26–7, 30, 33, 48, 126, 131,
    141, 197, 201

War, and religion, 31
    and Rome, 28ff, 49–51, 86–7, 181
    just (*iura belli*), 31–3
    protocols and ritual, 14–15, 31–3, 87
Women in Greek war myth, 38
Women in Roman war myth, 39, 104–105,
    108–10, 115–16, 118ff, 204 n.6

Xenophobia, 33